Slavery's Reach

FRANK LESLIE'S ILLUSTRATED NEWSPAPER

No. 89—Vol. IV.]   NEW YORK, SATURDAY, JUNE 27, 1857.   [Price 6 Cents.

Slavery's Reach

Southern Slaveholders in the North Star State

CHRISTOPHER P. LEHMAN

MINNESOTA
HISTORICAL
SOCIETY PRESS

mnhspress.org

The Minnesota Historical Society Press is a member of the Association of University Presses.

Manufactured in the United States of America

10 9 8 7 6 5 4 3 2 1

♾ The paper used in this publication meets the minimum requirements of the American National Standard for Information Sciences—Permanence for Printed Library Materials, ANSI Z39.48–1984.

International Standard Book Number
ISBN: 978-1-68134-135-4 (paper)
ISBN: 978-1-68134-136-1 (e-book)

Library of Congress Cataloging-in-Publication Data
Names: Lehman, Christopher P., author.
Title: Slavery's reach : Southern slaveholders in the North Star State / Christopher Lehman.
Other titles: Southern slaveholders in the North Star State
Description: Saint Paul : Minnesota Historical Society Press, 2019. | Includes bibliographical references and index. | Summary: "From the 1840s through the end of the Civil War, leading Minnesotans invited slaveholders and their wealth into the free territory and free state of Minnesota, enriching the area's communities and residents. Dozens of southern slaveholders and people raised in slaveholding families purchased land and backed Minnesota businesses. Slaveholders' wealth was invested in some of the state's most significant institutions and provided a financial foundation for several towns and counties. And the money generated by Minnesota investments flowed both ways, supporting some of the South's largest plantations. Christopher Lehman has brought to light this hidden history of northern complicity in building slaveholder wealth"— Provided by publisher.
Identifiers: LCCN 2019020093 | ISBN 9781681341354 (paperback) | ISBN 9781681341361 (ebook)
Subjects: LCSH: Slavery—Minnesota—History—19th century. | Slavery—Minnesota—Economic aspects. | Investments—Moral and ethical aspects—Minnesota. | Slaveholders—Minnesota—History—19th century. | Slaveholders—Southern States—History—19th century. | Slaves—Minnesota—History. | Businesspeople—Minnesota—History—19th century. | Slaveholders—Minnesota—Economic conditions. | Minnesota—Economic conditions—19th century.
Classification: LCC E445.M57 L44 2019 | DDC 306.3/6209776—dc23
LC record available at https://lccn.loc.gov/2019020093

Contents

Slavery's Reach

Hidden in Plain Sight

Many communities throughout the southern United States are graced with visually stunning architectural artifacts of the nation's era of legal slavery. These Greek Revival mansions with columned facades once were home to some of the country's wealthiest slaveholders. Robert Caruthers, who held one hundred enslaved people, established his domicile in Lebanon, Tennessee. The palatial home of William Aiken, who held seven times the number of slaves as Caruthers, stands in Charleston, South Carolina. Fountain F. Beattie's house, where he resided with his two dozen slaves, is in Greenville, South Carolina. Samuel Boyd—owner of a half dozen plantations throughout the South— lived in Natchez, Mississippi, where his mansion still stands.

These homes have special historical importance because they are rare surviving structures connecting slavery to Minnesota. The slaveholders who lived in these mansions spent tens of thousands of dollars—profits made from slave labor—on real estate in the northwestern territory and state.

The connections between Minnesota and slavery went beyond those made by distant, wealthy enslavers. A slaveholding financier provided much of the capital behind the fur trade in southern and central Minnesota. Military officers, federal appointees, commuting businessmen, small farmers, banks and insurance companies, hotelkeepers, and land speculators all brought connections to slaveholders' wealth into Minnesota Territory. Some brought slaves, too.

Minnesota existed as a territory and a state during only the last sixteen of the nation's 246 years of legal slavery, and it now has even fewer buildings that reflect its involvement in slavery than the South does. The hotels

William Aiken home, Charleston, SC, 1963. *Library of Congress, Prints & Photographs Division*

where slaves stayed with slaveholders burned down or were demolished over a century ago, and the summer homes that enslavers built met similar fates. The buildings have not survived to bear witness to the tremendous impact of wealth from slave labor on Minnesota's development in those sixteen years. And the choices of Minnesotans in remembering this history have done even more to minimize its significance.

✦

From the establishment of Minnesota as a territory in 1849 to the passage of the Thirteenth Amendment to the Constitution in 1865, slaveholders invested in land and businesses in Minnesota. Many of them traveled from their southern homes to make the transactions in person, but others arranged for Minnesotans with power of attorney to facilitate the purchases. The investors' practices spanned the gamut of human possession, represented by yeomen who owned a single enslaved person, elite planters who kept hundreds of people captive, reluctant heirs who manumitted slaves whenever possible, and enthusiastic masters who acquired as many people as possible.

Rear view of Aiken home showing service building and stable on right, slave quarters on left, 1963. *Library of Congress, Prints & Photographs Division*

It is not surprising that southerners who were prosperous enough to invest or vacation in Minnesota relied on slaveholding wealth. This is not, however, the point. The recruiting of investors by Minnesota's political leaders, the eagerness of new communities to attract those investments, the participation of financial institutions, the catering to rich tourists— all were part of the web of connections tying northern development to southern slavery. Indeed, wealth pouring into Minnesota from the northeastern United States was also made in banking and industries that grew because of the labor of enslaved people. Minnesotans and other northerners have forgotten their states' complicity in the slaveholding economy, just as some southerners have denied that the Civil War was fought over slavery.

A reader might question the relative level of slaveholder investment in Minnesota land and businesses. Did it comprise one percent or ten percent or 40 percent of all investment in the state? While it is not possible to calculate this figure, it is abundantly clear that people in Minnesota invited, encouraged, and welcomed any investments and expenditures from slaveholders—and broke their own laws in order to facilitate such income. Investments made by slaveholders were crucial to Minnesota's development at times and in specific areas of the state. This book does not argue that slaveholder wealth was the defining element in the growth of the new territory. Instead it uncovers the ties and demonstrates how Minnesotans allowed illegal slaveholding in their communities and benefited from it. Minnesota was not a distant land, far from the turmoil of 1850s US politics. It was the front lines of the prewar battle over slavery. In tracing the people, financial institutions, and political entities that brought slaves and slaveholding wealth into the territory and state, this book demonstrates slavery's reach.

◆

In the 1850s, non-slaveholding Minnesotans knew that southern slaveholders and the people they enslaved were in their midst. Some locals created businesses catering to southern travelers in the tourist-friendly communities along the Mississippi River, which connected the Northwest to the South. The presence of the slaves required some legal compromises by the locals. Minnesota was a free territory and a free state by law from 1849 to 1865, but it did not criminally charge any southerners who arrived with slaves. Southern dollars from slave plantations helped Minnesota's businesses, communities, and institutions to develop, and Minnesotans disregarded federal law in order to keep the money flowing. As they actively downplayed their role in supporting slavery, they encouraged slaveholders to do likewise. They permitted hotel guests to refer to their slaves as "servants," and local newspapers also called them "servants" when documenting the arrivals. The state also officially honored some masters by naming places for them on lands they had so recently taken from Dakota and Ojibwe people.

Minnesota's hunger for cash in the early 1850s is hard to exaggerate. The greatest source of money was the federal payments made in specie to Dakota and Ojibwe people, to satisfy treaty obligations. "One would suppose by promises about town," the St. Paul–based *Minnesota Pioneer* noted on August 8, 1850, "that the Indian payment would square every debt in Minnesota, but the 'debt of Nature.' Every reply to a dun is, 'after the payment.'" Dakota leaders were enticed and forced to sign the Treaty of Traverse des Sioux and Treaty of Mendota in 1851, turning over their homelands. Even before they were ratified, a spectacular land boom began in southern Minnesota. Land purchases in hard currency or notes drawn on reputable banks allowed speculators to pay off debts and build on other plots. When new dollars were paid to suppliers and tradesmen, they could likewise buy and build and sell, setting off a multiplier effect.[1]

The lands taken from Dakota people in 1851 were a huge attraction to investors because the potential profits were spectacular. In 1854 Henry McKenty, a prominent real estate dealer in St. Paul, bought several thousand acres of farmland near Stillwater for $1.25 an acre; he sold it the following year for $5 an acre. In 1855 McKenty offered a new acquaintance an interest rate of 3.5 percent per month—42 percent per year. The loan was made. McKenty purchased land in the Cottage Grove area at $1.25 an acre and sold it the following year for $2.50 an acre, clearing a 58 percent return.[2]

Minnesotans generally did not acknowledge their participation in the slave trade beyond their welcoming of tourists into hotels. Locals had no idea how many enslaved people a southern investor held unless the investor shared that information. They had no access to the Census Bureau's Slave Schedules, which listed enslavers by name in southern states every ten years, nor could they see southern probate court records of the slaves inherited by the investors. Perhaps because they did not know the specifics, Minnesotans may have failed to see themselves as participants in American slavery.

The presence of slaveholding federal officers in Minnesota led some Minnesotans to consider slavery as something brought in by outsiders but not supported by locals. Military officials brought slaves to Fort Snelling and other military posts, as did administrators appointed by Democratic presidents during the territorial years. The Democratic Party dominated the federal government from 1853 to 1861, and the proslavery political views of territorial officers of that party often clashed with locals who either opposed slavery or simply did not want the institution in Minnesota.

Because no one was arguing that Minnesota should be a slave state, the settler-colonists who took up the land might have assumed that the practice did not affect Minnesota itself. Locals across the political spectrum agreed that Minnesota's land and climate were not conducive to plantation slavery, and even southerners did not want to bring masses of slaves to the state. Throughout the 1850s only the most strident abolitionists in Minnesota complained about hotels quartering slaveholders and their "servants" for months at a time. The guests always went home to the South in the fall, and the northern cities they visited benefited each year from tourism dollars. Meanwhile, Minnesota's political leaders engaged in business transactions with slaveholders while decrying the South's legal slavery. For the most part, Minnesotans saw only the slaveholders and their money. They did not witness the sale, labor, or whipping of slaves, and slavery consequently remained abstract for them. Moreover, the dozens of African American residents of antebellum Minnesota found limited options for employment beyond domestic service, thus performing some of the same labor as their enslaved southern counterparts.

Similarly, most of the enslaved people belonging to Minnesota's masters never laid eyes on the state that their bondage helped to build. A small minority of the slaves stayed with their captors in Minnesota for days or weeks at a time in hotels before returning to the South to further fund Minnesota's growth. Even fewer stayed permanently in Minnesota when their masters moved to the state.

Regardless of the ignorance of Minnesotans, they were complicit in some of the worst cruelties of southern slavery by conducting business with the slaveholders inflicting the cruelties. Slaves walked woefully onto auction blocks in states all over the South so that their sellers would have money to buy land in Minnesota. Family members bade anguished farewells to each other so their sellers could start new lives with plenty of money and without slaves when leaving the South permanently for Minnesota. Minnesotans were enriched by money that came from such transactions. Moreover, they provided for their families and built local communities with that income, thus inextricably linking slave sales to the foundations of local economies throughout Minnesota.

After the United States legally abolished slavery in 1865, scholars of Minnesota's history followed the examples of state leaders and minimized slavery's role in the state's development. They wrote of slavery as a political issue of little direct consequence beyond the timing of Minnesota's admission as a state. Historians portrayed slavery as merely a series of isolated incidents instead of a system of violence and theft in which Minnesotans participated. They focused on only the most famous enslaved men who had resided in the area before statehood. James Thompson, the only slave bought and sold on land within the future Minnesota's borders, received his emancipation and stayed on as a free person for decades, witnessing the formation of Minnesota Territory and Minnesota statehood firsthand. Dred Scott, whose lawsuit reached the US Supreme Court and determined the course of slavery nationwide for the remainder of the practice's legal existence, left the Northwest before Minnesota Territory was organized and died four months after Minnesota became a state. His wife, Harriet, had resided there with him in bondage.

As time further distanced Minnesota from its past involvement in slavery, scholars chose not to delve into this story. Instead they found new individual stories that enhanced the state's post-1865 narrative depicting it as fundamentally antislavery. Published in 1915, the two-volume *History of Stearns County, Minnesota*, by St. Cloud resident William B. Mitchell, recounts the activism of the state's most celebrated antislavery activist, journalist Jane Grey Swisshelm. Eliza Winston, an enslaved woman brought from Mississippi by her vacationing owners, successfully sued for her freedom in Minnesota in 1860, and Theodore C. Blegen's *Minnesota: A History of the State* notes that Minnesotans in general agreed on Winston's legal right to liberation. The narratives of Thompson and Winston included happy endings, and the writers fashioned Swisshelm as a stereotypical northern protagonist crusading against the few immoral slaveholders in central Minnesota.

The story of slavery in Minnesota, however, is much more complex than this. The narrative involves hundreds of enslaved people across the South, people whose labor generated tens of thousands of dollars that their captors directed to establishments in Minnesota. Investors left behind a paper trail that connected their money to their human chattel in the South and to their purchases of real estate in the Northwest. Slave schedules, probate court documents, and wills listed the slaves, and deed books in the offices of Minnesota's county recorders documented the land sales. Scholars of Minnesota history have overlooked the state's role in exploiting the slaves that never set foot on state soil, and they have failed to identify money from slave labor as an important foundation of Minnesota's early development. This book uses the paper trail that ties slaveholders to Minnesotans to tell a more complex story of Minnesota's longtime dependence on capital from the unseen unfree, and it shows how those papers also comprise part of Minnesota's founding documents.

Slavery's Reach builds on two decades of scholarship about slavery's importance to states outside of the South. In the twenty-first century, historians have increasingly written about the involvement of free states and slave states in each other's economies. David Brion Davis's *Challenging the Boundaries of Slavery* looks at how northern businesses such as textile manufacturers needed cotton and other raw materials that slaves cultivated in the South. Because of this dependence, northerners assured their southern slaveholding suppliers that abolitionists were lunatic radicals. *Complicity: How the North Promoted, Prolonged, and Profited from Slavery*, by Anne Farrow, Joel Lang, and Jenifer Frank, further probes the North's business ties to slave states and focuses on the concessions that free states gave to slave states to maintain those ties. Minnesotans similarly permitted slavery to encroach in their state in order to continue to attract wealthy slaveholders to buy land within Minnesota's borders.

By examining Minnesota, *Slavery's Reach* adds to recent secondary literature that explores multiple aspects of northern slavery. The books *Ten Hills Farm: The Forgotten History of Slavery in the North*, by C. S. Manegold, and *The Dawn of Detroit: A Chronicle of Slavery and Freedom in the City of the Straits*, by Tiya Miles, look at geographically specific northern communities that benefited from slavery. Marc Howard Ross's *Slavery in the North: Forgetting History and Recovering Memory* argues that because the North outlawed slavery decades before the South did, public memory of slavery concentrates largely on the years in which southern states alone were slave states. Ross's work reminds readers of the North's long involvement in the practice from the colonial era to the early nineteenth century. And just as Craig Steven Wilder's *Ebony and Ivy: Slavery, Race, and the Troubled History of America's Universities* examines the funding of Ivy League institutions through sales of enslaved people, *Slavery's Reach* explores how a loan from a slaveholder brought the fledgling University of Minnesota out of financial insolvency.

Minnesotans' transactions with slaveholders extended the North's involvement in slavery to the eve of the Civil War in 1861. As a result, the state's history with slavery corresponds to the topics of the above-noted books and others. The US Supreme Court made Minnesota a slave territory from March 1857 to May 1858, but Minnesota's much longer period as a free state has created significant chronological distance from that time and earlier, more proslavery territorial days. On the other hand, in recent years historians have revisited the state's long-neglected sympathies to slavery. Rhoda R. Gilman's article "Territorial Imperative: How Minnesota

Became the 32nd State," William D. Green's book *A Peculiar Imbalance: The Fall and Rise of Racial Equality in Early Minnesota*, and Mary Lethert Wingerd's *North Country: The Making of Minnesota* note that the federal government's extension of slavery to territories divided Minnesota's Democrats and Republicans to the point of their holding separate constitutional conventions in 1857.

The first five chapters of *Slavery's Reach* illustrate the economic and social diversity among slaveholding investors in Minnesota. Chapter One discusses the influence of enslaver Pierre Chouteau of Missouri, his slaveholding partners in the American Fur Company, and the company's employees in Minnesota. Agents like Henry Sibley and Henry Rice became powerful local leaders through their work for Chouteau, and Chouteau owned a considerable amount of land in Minnesota. Chapter Two describes the work of slaveholders who were appointed to territorial offices by Democratic presidents, exacerbating Minnesota's reliance on capital from slave labor. Chapter Three discusses southern slaveholders who chose to leave the South and reside permanently in Minnesota. Chapters Four and Five focus on slaveholders who stayed temporarily—the elite vacationers and commuting entrepreneurs.

The next three chapters closely examine relationships between slaveholders and Minnesotans. Chapter Six looks at the business ties that Rice cultivated with slaveholders after entering Congress in 1853. Chapter Seven concerns another former agent of Chouteau—Sylvanus Lowry—and the network of enslavers he recruited to fund his development of central Minnesota. Chapter Eight describes Minnesota's ties to some of the South's most powerful supporters and enablers of slavery: banks giving credit to plantations and insurance companies providing policies on enslaved people.

The rest of the book shows the decline of slaveholding investment in Minnesota. Chapter Nine tells the story of slaveholder-friendly hotels and the vulnerable state of their industry after Minnesota became a free state in 1858. Chapter Ten discusses how the Civil War caused Minnesota and the South to become estranged from one another and how that estrangement essentially brought active business between them to a halt. The book's conclusion looks at the legacy in Minnesota of money from slavery.

In concentrating on slaveholder wealth and Minnesotans' complicity, it might be easy to lose sight of the impact of these transactions on enslaved men, women, and children. When people were sold to fund purchases of real estate, families and communities were torn apart. Slaves who accompanied masters on trips to and from Minnesota experienced not only disrupted lives but also the cruelness of returning to a slave state after temporary residence in a free territory. The growth of Minnesota in its first sixteen years is linked closely to the pain endured by these slaves, and this book identifies and describes those connections.

CHAPTER ONE

Fur Traders

In St. Louis, Missouri, in the 1850s, a small number of enslaved people lived no differently than other unfree laborers throughout the United States. They catered to the whims of the people who held them in slavery. They reserved the best of what they produced for their captors. They neglected their own families in order to care for all of the members of their owners' families. In the meantime, the possibility of their removal from their communities loomed constantly. They could be permanently sold away from their families.

This select group of slaves belonged to three people who invested all over Minnesota—a territory hundreds of miles away to the northwest. These investors were among the elite class of St. Louis. They controlled the fur trade, making money from the sale of goods to Dakota families and furs to eastern buyers, and they purchased real estate. With the wealth they reaped from these enterprises in the Northwest, they could invest in more property or more goods for the trade—or they could acquire more enslaved people. St. Louis was a major market for domestic slave sales, so customers had many captives from which to choose. Although the slaves that these three men bought had never set foot in Minnesota, they were affected by their new masters' actions there.

◆

The St. Louis–based investors were not the first people to bring slavery into the area that would become the Minnesota Territory. For decades officers and government officials held enslaved people at Fort Snelling. The US Army named the facility in 1825 after Colonel Josiah Snelling,

who oversaw the fort's construction in the early 1820s, and Snelling himself went on to be a slaveholder in 1827. Enslaved people remained a presence at the fort for decades afterward as new officers from the South
typically brought one or two unfree laborers with them when beginning
their deployment—and other officers at the fort purchased slaves, either
from each other or, with the help of the quartermaster, from the St. Louis
market. Before the late 1820s, fewer than one out of ten officers at the fort
participated in slavery, but the transfer of officers from the First Infantry
Regiment in the slave state of Louisiana to Fort Snelling in 1828 escalated
the proportion of slaveholders to over 80 percent of the fort's officers in
the 1830s. Moreover, these thirty to forty slaveholding officers received
an allowance from the federal government to pay for servants, and many
preferred to purchase a person and pocket the allowance.[1]

The only Minnesota-based slaves to ever free themselves had to use a
slave state's court to do so, and both of them had belonged to officers
at Fort Snelling. An enslaved woman named Rachel successfully sued
her owner for emancipation in Missouri after her transfer from Fort Snelling to St. Louis in 1837, and a slave named Courtney also won her freedom through court after suffering the same relocation. In both cases the
St. Louis circuit court cited the Northwest Ordinance and the Missouri
Compromise as the legal bases for freedom, and the court ruled that the
holding of enslaved people did not function as a necessary part of the
appointments of the officers who owned Rachel and Courtney.[2]

After the 1830s, civilians joined the officers in developing Minnesota
Territory through slave labor. By 1842 four men from Missouri—three of
them slaveholders—had taken over the American Fur Company, which
oversaw and supplied trading posts in the Northwest. The foursome collectively owned and operated Pierre Chouteau, Jr. & Company, which
paid local residents to manage the posts. Henry H. Sibley oversaw the
Sioux (Dakota) Outfit from the town of Mendota. Henry M. Rice managed the Chippewa (Ojibwe) Outfit from St. Peter and oversaw Sylvanus B. Lowry's facilitation of the Winnebago (Ho-Chunk) Outfit in Long
Prairie. Norman W. Kittson supervised trading posts at multiple locations, including Big Stone Lake and Lac qui Parle. These locals, working
for a salary plus a share of the profits, supervised the work of employees
spread out throughout the area, from Pembina in the northwest to Traverse des Sioux in the south. Over the next two decades, the slaveholding Missourians sent money and goods upriver to the employees, and the

Minnesotans in turn sent furs and proceeds from sales of both fur and land to the employers.[3]

The Minnesotans stood to gain more than just southern payment for their employment. They participated in and manipulated treaty payments, ensuring that they would be paid for the enormous credit they had extended to Indigenous hunters in anticipation of such payments. When the lands became available for purchase, they bought claims near their posts (often sited on important waterways and trails), established and promoted communities, and then became political leaders of those communities. They later used their power to expand their political influence, and some of them became officials of Minnesota at large. Some of the political victors worked for the slaveholders while ascending in power, thus tying Chouteau & Company inextricably to the history of Minnesota's territorial years.

At the center of the business was Jean-Pierre Chouteau Jr. (known as Pierre), one of the most powerful men of the northwestern United States and a lifelong St. Louis resident. He was born in 1789, the year the US Constitution was ratified. St. Louis belonged not to the United States but to Spain at the time. His paternal grandmother, Marie-Thérèse Chouteau, was a slaveholder who had children with the founder of the city, and one of the offspring was Pierre Chouteau Sr. As the years passed, the Chouteau family, whose wealth came from the fur trade, essentially developed into a dynasty in St. Louis, and each generation passed its hold of the city on to the next. When the United States bought the city as part of the Louisiana Purchase in 1803, during Pierre Chouteau Jr.'s fourteenth year, the Chouteaus became a powerful American family. They had a monopoly on trade with the Osage people—widely resident in what are now Missouri, Kansas, Arkansas, and north Oklahoma—that they maintained under US rule. Concerned that the United States might abolish slavery in Louisiana Territory, the family joined with others to argue against abolition. The Chouteaus tasked their slaves with labor in their homes and such businesses as American Fur Company warehouses, the family mill, and the family distillery. Some of them worked closer to the Mississippi, laboring as stevedores. As the 1820s ended, Pierre Sr. held fourteen slaves; the junior Pierre kept eighteen. Pierre Jr. also occasionally profited from slavery by arranging for some of his slaves to be sold in New Orleans.[4]

In 1827 two of Pierre Jr.'s enslaved people petitioned for the right to sue him for their emancipation—Francois La Grange on March 27 and a woman named Theotiste on July 25. Pierre Jr. and his business partners had collectively purchased La Grange in 1815, in a private transaction, but Chouteau alone had bought Theotiste in the 1820s, at a public auction. La Grange and Theotiste had lived in the free state of Illinois before their forced relocation, with their previous owners, to the slave state of Missouri, and both argued that their time as residents of Illinois emancipated them from slavery.[5]

The Circuit Court of St. Louis County agreed to let the slaves sue for their freedom. La Grange and Theotiste had strong legal cases, because the federal law known as the Northwest Ordinance of 1787 stipulated that the US Northwest Territory, situated next to the Great Lakes, prohibited slavery. That territory consisted of the future states of Illinois, Indiana, Michigan, Ohio, Wisconsin, and part of Minnesota. The Chouteau slaves lost their cases, but over the next decade that same circuit court freed other enslaved people in Missouri, including Rachel and Courtney (noted above), on the basis of that law. Those decisions showed Chouteau that slaveholders were vulnerable to losing any slaves kept in the Northwest Territory.

The rulings did not discourage Pierre Jr. from seeking opportunities to make money in the Northwest. The American Fur Company owned trading posts all over the region, and the profits from the fur sales made John Jacob Astor, the company's owner, a wealthy man. In the 1830s, with some partners, Chouteau bought the American Fur Company's Western Department, becoming the dominant force in the Missouri River trade, the main focus of his efforts, for decades. In 1842 the firm Pierre Chouteau, Jr. & Company—consisting of Chouteau and his business partners John F. A. Sanford, John B. Sarpy, and Joseph Sire—took over ownership of the American Fur Company's posts in the Northwest. The office of Chouteau & Company in St. Louis was a large storehouse, from which goods were sent to the posts. At the posts, according to one employee, "Skins and furs are received in exchange and are sold throughout the world, especially in Russia. In every district there is an agent, employed at a fixed salary ($2,000) and paid in addition certain profits on sales. He has charge of several posts. He orders supplies from the company." Agents paid annual interest on the capital that was advanced to them, the insurance coverage for goods, and the shipping costs.[6]

For the next twenty-five years, until the end of slavery, money from the slaveholders of Chouteau & Company funded economic development in the Northwest. Pierre Jr. held six slaves in 1840, fifteen in 1850, and five in 1860. Sarpy held four slaves in 1850, and Sanford claimed at least one slave before his death in 1857. Whenever agents paid Chouteau & Company, the partners could use their shares of the income to pay for the care of their slaves. In turn, the agents could spend the salaries received from the enslavers to help build the communities where their trading posts stood. Both parties, of course, profited from the labor of Dakota and Ojibwe families who trapped and processed furs.[7]

John Berald Sarpy had a strong pedigree of slaveholding in St. Louis. His maternal grandfather—Silvestre Labbadie Sr., who had married into the Chouteau family—initiated his family's participation in the city's slave trade in the late eighteenth century. In 1817, at age eighteen, Sarpy started working for Chouteau & Company, and he stayed with the firm for the next four decades. When he was in his twenties, Sarpy married into a slaveholding family; the father of his first wife, Adele Cabanne, held at least one slave in St. Louis. Because of Sarpy's connections to slavehold-ers and the wealth from their slaves, he became rich without having to leave St. Louis. In 1850 his holdings in real estate totaled $30,000—about a million dollars in current value.[8]

His life as an enslaver had its occasional setbacks. In the late 1830s, his slave Andrew petitioned the Third Circuit Court in St. Louis for his "right to freedom." Decades earlier Andrew's grandmother had lived in Kentucky, but her owner had taken her in the late 1790s to the Northwest, where slavery was prohibited by the Northwest Ordinance of 1787. Andrew argued that his grandmother's residence in that region legally freed her, and thus himself, from slavery. He successfully asked the court to allow him to sue as a poor person and to receive a court-appointed lawyer to handle the case. Sarpy, therefore, became the defendant in the freedom suit that Andrew brought on his own behalf; another owner held Andrew's grand-mother. Andrew won his suit and his freedom in 1837.[9]

No other enslaved person sued Sarpy for liberation, and his slave community remained stable for years afterward. The memoirs of Sarpy's youngest child, Adele, born in 1842, provide a picture of family life from the slaveholder's perspective. Of her childhood she remembered that "in those days, all well-to-do people possessed numberless slaves, and we had our share."[10]

She knew of slaves only as people who lived to serve and to do so hap-pily. Her father's captives catered well to all of her needs throughout her childhood: they "considered it their duty to humor the child of the family, and as a consequence I grew up scarcely knowing what it was to have a dissenting voice where my wishes were concerned." Also, the Sarpy household had a tradition for every New Year's Day, which the slaves anticipated "with great joy," as Adele put it. On the morning of January 1, "as they bade 'Master' a happy New Year, each one received a piece of money, which was accompanied by kind words from us all and renewed good cheer on their parts to serve us more joyfully than ever."[11]

Their services occasionally consisted of nursing, but Adele considered those services as merely an extension of their love for the family. She reminisced, "Our slaves were fond of us all and, in sickness, never wearied caring for us." Their nursing practices were less medical than comforting, as Adele recalled them. She said, "I remember old Uncle Frank taking me on his knee and smoking in my ears long and untiringly when I had earache, and then in the fumes of the smoke trying to soothe me into sleep."[12]

The Sarpy family believed that they offered benevolent management of their slaves. Adele bragged that "one pleasure that was allowed to our slaves . . . was a free indulgence of their musical talent. We had in our household four men who played on different instruments and formed a sort of band." They had Sarpy's permission to perform at various engagements for pay, but, if they forgot to obtain a pass from him before departing the household, the police detained them overnight and notified the master for retrieval in the morning. While Sarpy did not refrain from physically punishing any of his slaves, Adele saw nobility in his acceptance of full responsibility for distributing it. "My father allowed his servants to be chastised by none but himself," she stated, "and then never when he was in anger." The slaves provided constancy for the Sarpy family while the patriarch went on business trips for Chouteau & Company. He often had to travel to American Fur Company's trading posts in the Northwest, and his absences from home often lasted three months at a time. According to Adele, he frequently took "trips to Council Bluffs and the Yellowstone" for "dealings . . . with the Indians."[13]

John Sanford married Pierre Chouteau Jr.'s daughter Emilie and enjoyed a long employment as a partner in his father-in-law's company. He had a relationship with another slaveholding family through his sister Irene's marriage to John Emerson; she inherited her husband's enslaved people upon his death. When Irene's slave Dred Scott sued for his freedom, Sanford took on the role of defendant in the lawsuit that went to the US

Supreme Court. (A misspelling by a clerk of the court has forever recorded his name as "Sandford.") He did not spend as much time in St. Louis as in New York City, where another branch of the company existed, but his employment by a slaveholder allowed him to receive income from three regions—the South, the North, and the Northwest.

Joseph Sire also acquired wealth from slavery through marriage, and his marriages made him an extended member of each of his business partners' families. He married Sarpy's first cousin Virginia Labbadie 1827, but she died unexpectedly in 1828 at age twenty. He lived with her parents until 1836, when he started work at Chouteau & Company. Years later, in 1852, Sire married Rebecca Chouteau, widow of Pierre Chouteau Jr.'s cousin Augustus, but she herself passed away two years later. By then, however, Sire was a full partner in the business.[14]

◆

In 1848 Northwest residents Henry Sibley, Henry Rice, and Sylvanus Lowry established the Northern Outfit, supported by Chouteau & Company, which owned half of the enterprise. Chouteau's posts for the company in Minnesota were subsequently reorganized as the Northern Outfit and consisted of Sibley's Sioux Outfit and Rice's and Lowry's Winnebago and Chippewa Outfits. Sibley's annual salary was $500, but Rice and Lowry each received $750. Sibley, however, had seniority at the company, having served as an agent in the Northwest since 1834. His management of the Sioux posts over the subsequent fifteen years made him the "virtual Governor of Minnesota," as one St. Paul newspaper later put it. He had unlimited influence over the region because of the proliferation of posts there, and the capital advanced to him by his slaveholding employers made possible his ascension in power. Meanwhile, through the Winnebago and Chippewa Outfits, Rice and Lowry managed the Ho-Chunk and Ojibwe trade. Customarily all three partners of the Northern Outfit bought property in Minnesota but held it in trust for Chouteau.[15]

The partners in Chouteau & Company ran the American Fur Company as absentee employers, monitoring the cold northwestern posts from their warm offices in St. Louis. Although Pierre Chouteau Jr. and the agents conducted business by letter, the employer invited Sibley and Rice to meet with him at his home. Sibley had first traveled to St. Louis in 1841, when he experienced a rare opportunity to witness southern slavery firsthand. Upon arrival via the Mississippi, he likely was met by Chouteau's enslaved

Henry Hastings Sibley,
about 1860. Oil on
canvas by John Bligh.

coachman, who whisked him off to the Chouteau estate. Chouteau's home,
a mansion on the southeastern corner of Seventh Street and Market Street,
included an adjacent garden along Seventh Street. Once inside the house,
the visitor probably enjoyed services provided by his host's other slaves.[16]

Rice visited Chouteau in St. Louis years later, in August 1849, but he
was already intimately acquainted with slavery by then. He had married
Matilda Whitall, daughter of Virginia slaveholder Gilbert Whitall, five
months earlier. The Whitall family resided in Richmond, Virginia, where
slaveholders at massive tobacco plantations hired out their human property
to work in tobacco factories, ironworks, and other city-based businesses.
In her move from Richmond to St. Paul, Matilda lost the accessible and
skilled slave labor of her hometown.[17]

For Chouteau & Company, the establishment of Minnesota Territory on
March 3, 1849, meant business as usual. Sibley, Rice, and Lowry remained
at their posts, although Sibley took on additional duties when he was
elected territorial delegate. In June Sibley addressed the territory's residents, bragging that he had kept an antislavery provision out of the legislation that established the territory:

Sibley's limestone house, built in 1835 at Mendota, has been preserved as a historic site.

An effort was made, in Committee [on Territories], to append the Wilmot Proviso to the territorial bill, but this I resisted, as I determined, so far as it was in my power, not to allow it to be clogged by a provision wholly superfluous, as the introduction of slavery was prohibited on the east of the Mississippi by the ordinance of 1787, and on the west of that river by the act of 1819 establishing the Missouri line [the Missouri Compromise]. The proposition was therefore voted down before the bill was reported to the House, but was brought in as an amendment by the minority of the Committee and was only kept from being adopted, and producing consequently a fierce and angry discussion, which would have resulted in the loss of the bill, by my moving and refusing to withdraw the previous question, which cut off all amendments.

Sibley thus managed to finesse both sides of the issue of slavery in Minnesota—a situation necessitated jointly by the territory's legal "free" status and his employment by a slaveholder as well as his political status as a Democrat. His rationale for opposing the proviso rested on the legal precedents prohibiting slavery in the Northwest, but his remarks allowed him to go on record as opposing an antislavery bill.[18]

Sibley's point about federal antislavery laws was correct but also misleading. The Northwest Ordinance of 1787 and the Missouri Compromise indeed rendered slavery illegal in Minnesota, but the delegate's employment by Chouteau & Company showed that those laws did not prevent slaveholders like his business associates from using funds from their unfree laborers to develop Minnesota and occasionally use the slaves themselves. After all, the company purchased American Fur's trading posts two decades after passage of the Compromise, and southern soldiers still kept enslaved people in the territory's forts into the 1850s. Minnesota's status as a new federal territory ultimately left President Zachary Taylor responsible for the enforcement of the antislavery measures. However, he himself had brought slaves to Minnesota as a military officer commanding Fort Snelling, and his lax enforcement of the ordinance and compromise allowed other southerners to do the same.[19]

John Sanford wrote to Sibley about business matters concerning Chouteau & Company. He included a letter of introduction from himself for a visitor to the Northwest. In the letter, Sanford admitted of himself, "J. F. A. Sanford was owner of Dred Scott when the latter brought the famous suit of 'Scott vs. Sanford,' commonly known as the Dred Scott case. Sanford was connected with the Fur Company and in 1830–1840 operated chiefly on the Upper Missouri."[20]

The working relationship among Lowry, Rice, and Sibley collapsed in late 1849 amid allegations of Rice's self-dealing but not before Chouteau & Company made more direct efforts to stabilize its northwestern interests. Joseph Sire traveled from St. Louis to Minnesota to try to settle the matter in person—one of the few times a company partner traveled northwest on company business. Soon thereafter Lowry and Rice left the American Fur Company. Rice acknowledged in a letter two days later, "I have disposed of all of my interest in all of the outfits." Chouteau and Sibley announced the dissolution of the partnership on October 12, 1849. "The liquidation of the amounts properly due by said business or co-partnership, as well as the general adjustment of all matters appertaining thereto, will be attended to by said H. H. Sibley."[21]

Chouteau reorganized American Fur by replacing the Northern Outfit with the Minnesota Outfit, managed by Charles W. Borup, and the St. Paul

Outfit, managed by William H. Forbes. The reconfiguring came at a time of declining business in the fur trade, and Chouteau & Company began to wind down its fur operations in the early 1850s. Sibley constantly received correspondence from agents in Minnesota about poor sales. His employee in Pembina, Norman W. Kittson, sent him a letter of "unfortunate news" about trading posts. Kittson concluded, "I have I believe sufficiently tired your patience with unpleasant news."[22]

Sibley capitalized on his federal office by reaching out to his congressional colleagues, and his new contacts included southern slaveholders. In a letter to Senator Henry S. Foote of Mississippi, Sibley tried to make the Northwest as attractive as possible, and doing so meant exaggerating the region's virtues and minimizing its legal prohibition of slavery. He wrote of Minnesota as "a land where nature has lavished her choicest gifts, where sickness has no dwelling-place." And he made a vow that hinted at defending slavery, promising to all those entering the territory that "their persons and property are fully protected by the broad shield of law." Foote was an important ally for Minnesota regarding southern approval, because he shared Sibley's cautious approach to extending slavery into territories. As the delegate drafted his letter, Foote called for more than a dozen of his fellow senators—from the North and the South—to form a committee to develop a compromise on the issue of territorial slavery.[23]

The majority of Minnesotans opposed making slavery legal in their territory. Some wanted the practice abolished nationwide, but most opponents simply did not want the economic competition that slavery threatened. Minnesota's government officials did not want wealthy slaveholders to replace them as the territory's political leaders, and working-class laborers did not want competition with slave labor to cause their wages to decline. Sibley's ties to Chouteau & Company made him a target of Minnesotans who disliked his northwestern reach, and his former coworker Rice challenged him for the delegate seat in 1850. A newspaper in Mississippi commented, "The political test in Minnesota is opposition to or advocacy of the American Fur Company! A very interesting question in a freezing latitude. Were we a Minnesotian, we should go in for the Fur—decidedly!" Neither man, however, spoke publicly about slavery itself. To them, the practice had no relevance among Minnesotans, and slaveholding had not gained traction with them ever since the establishment of Minnesota Territory. Also, Rice and Sibley were Democrats, and their colleagues in the party, especially those living in the South, were content with slavery's existence.[24]

In 1851 Sibley was a major force in negotiating the treaties that stripped the Dakota people of their land and, through trickery, garnered $210,000 to pay debts that fur traders claimed against Dakota hunters. It is not clear exactly how much Sibley himself received—his biographer estimates something less than $14,000—but, as Chouteau's agent, he took receipt of the $181,000 paid to Chouteau & Company. As the fur trade became the Indian trade, other traders continued to make money by supplying goods due to Dakota and Ojibwe nations under treaties. Sibley and Chouteau turned to real estate and townsite speculation. Chouteau was Sibley's silent partner and major client through 1859.[25]

As a Democrat in Washington and as an agent for enslavers, Sibley refused to jeopardize the slaveholders' power in the US Senate. Southern senators worried that too many settlers in Minnesota would lead to the territory's entry into the Union as a free state. A new free state threatened to upset the North-South balance in the Senate, and a northern advantage with more free states meant more antislavery representation in Congress. After much struggle, Sibley was able to persuade Congress to ratify the 1851 treaties, but he had to appease his southern colleagues by canceling his plan to negotiate with the Ojibwe to surrender more of their land for settler-colonists. As a result, Minnesota's population would remain too low for a bid for statehood—at least for the time being.[26]

To help build the territory, Sibley—while receiving a salary from a slaveholder—supported the effort by the territorial government to establish a university. In 1851 he secured a land grant for the institution. The next year the school's board of regents chose him to lead a committee to select and locate land for the university, and the board's report for 1854 included correspondence received by Sibley at his post in Mendota.[27]

As Sibley's tenure in Congress wound down, he made an unsuccessful bid for territorial governor. Because of his continued employment by enslavers, he maintained steady income after leaving public service in 1853. Sometime in the mid-1850s, he compiled a list of year-by-year amounts of money in the accounts he oversaw for Chouteau & Company. Concerning American Fur, the accounts were for the "West Outfit" in 1845, the "St. Peter's Outfit" from 1846 to 1848, and the Sioux Outfit from 1849 to 1854. The list also included the account labeled "H. H. Sibley," which stood at $4,660.50 as of 1854—Sibley's first full year outside of public life. In 1856 the company paid "less half to H. H. Sibley $16,018.20" from that year's sales of properties.[28]

During this time Sibley oversaw a significant range of land in Minnesota Territory, some of it connected to Pierre Chouteau Jr. and his associates. As late as March and June 1855, the slaveholders wrote letters from St. Louis in the French language to Sibley about business matters. Around 1857 Sibley compiled a list of lots and blocks owned by himself, Chouteau, or both of them jointly in the cities of Hastings and Mendota. Their joint property "Sibley's Addition to Mendota" also appeared on the list. Meanwhile, Sibley's adopted hometown of Mendota became incorporated, and it served as the seat of Dakota County from 1854 to 1857.[29]

Other political figures in Minnesota with ties to Chouteau emerged after Sibley became territorial delegate in 1849. In late 1851 current and former agents ran for the territorial legislature, and three of them won elections to two-year terms: Lowry, Kittson, and Martin McLeod, who remained with Chouteau & Company while serving in office. In addition, Minnesota's legislature held its 1853 assembly in a facility in St. Paul that the slaveholder owned—the Chouteau Building. Aside from the sessions of 1852 and 1853, McLeod served in the assembly of 1851 and Kittson in 1854.[30]

After eleven years with American Fur, Kittson moved to St. Paul in 1854 and began to sever his ties to Chouteau & Company. He had overseen trading posts at Big Stone Lake and Lac qui Parle, and as late as February 1854 he sent Sibley a list of "articles required for Kittson's Outfit." On the other hand, his service in the territorial legislature required him to spend more time in St. Paul. He and a business partner bought Sibley's St. Paul Outfit, and in 1855 Sibley closed the Sioux Outfit. Thus, Kittson was no longer a fur trader for Chouteau when he became St. Paul's mayor three years later.[31]

Charles Borup remained in Chouteau's employment into the mid-1850s while participating in major businesses in Minnesota Territory. By 1852 he claimed land in Ramsey County and Winona County, and he was one of the proprietors of Sauk Rapids in 1854. In 1853 he helped to incorporate the St. Paul Mutual Insurance Company, and among his fellow incorporators was Governor Alexander Ramsey.[32]

As of early 1855, Chouteau, Borup, Sanford, and Sibley were among the "partners, acting and trading under the name of the 'St. Anthony Outfit.'" By this time the posts in Minnesota were real estate agencies instead of trading posts, but the company's employees there entertained ideas of expanding Chouteau's business interests in Minnesota beyond fur and

Dr. Charles William
Wulff Borup, 1856. Oil
on canvas by C. Merck.

land. When Governor Isaac Stevens of Washington Territory surveyed the West for possible railroad development, he stopped in Minnesota. He wrote, "To Mr. Sibley and Mr. Culbertson, partners in the American Fur Company, in charge of the posts on the Mississippi and Missouri, am I especially indebted, the former both in Washington City and at his residence on the St. Peters [the Minnesota River], devoted much time and attention to the survey and rendered us very valuable assistance." Borup served as the St. Paul–based agent of Chouteau, Harrison & Valle—a business of rolling mills and iron mining headquartered in St. Louis.[33]

Borup then left Chouteau's companies to strike out on his own. On August 31, 1855, he and Chouteau & Company severed all of their business ties, which meant divesting himself of all of his land purchases for the firm in St. Paul. The company dissolved the Minnesota Outfit and the Sioux Outfit and assumed all control of the real estate. His work for the Missourians had allowed him to establish himself in Minnesota Territory, and he remained in the Northwest for years after leaving their firm.[34]

The St. Louis enslavers soon found someone else to handle their business affairs in the territory. On September 1, 1855, Chouteau & Company announced that John S. Prince had become the company's agent in Minnesota. The company also said that its agreement with Sibley concerning the Northern Outfit had expired and that Sibley would be the company's agent for the Sioux Outfit in Minnesota. Prince moved to St. Paul in 1854 to work for Chouteau after having served the company in several states since 1840. While handling the company's interests in his new location, he also took advantage of new business opportunities independent of Chouteau. He helped start the St. Paul Fire and Marine Insurance Company. As of April 1857, Chouteau & Company owned a sawmill in St. Paul called the Rotary Mill, and Prince managed it for the slaveholder well into the 1860s. In 1858 Prince was president of the Minnesota State Mutual Fire and Insurance Company.[35]

The relocation of Kittson and Prince to major cities in the 1850s reflected political and demographic trends. Most of the American-born newcomers to Minnesota Territory by then were northerners who opposed slavery. Republicans predominated in rural Minnesota. Democrats, who approved the extension of slavery into territories, ruled major commercial areas like St. Anthony (predecessor of Minneapolis), St. Paul, and Stillwater. Prince teamed with Pierre Chouteau Jr.'s son-in-law Sanford and others on

St. Paul Fire and Marine Insurance Company, St. Paul, 1872. In 2007 the company became the Travelers Companies, one of the largest insurance companies in the United States.

February 26, 1856, to incorporate the St. Anthony Falls Water Company—an enterprise outside of Chouteau & Company. On the other hand, the relocations did not mean complete disinterest in rural areas. In April 1856 Prince was one of five men who platted a village named for him in Benton County—Princeton.[36]

In the 1850s and 1860s, Pierre Chouteau Jr. owned real estate in several locations throughout Minnesota, many of them having come from his management of American Fur. Most of his land was in the cities of Hastings and St. Paul. His former employee Norman Kittson had facilitated the acquisition of the majority of the property in St. Paul, and that portion was named Kittson's Addition. Just outside the city lay Chouteau's 160 acres by White Bear Lake and additional property by Pig's Eye Lake. In southern Minnesota he owned more than one hundred lots in St. Anthony, twenty-five lots in Belle Plaine, and land in Washington County and at Traverse des Sioux. He also invested considerably in central Minnesota, possessing almost 150 lots in Sauk Rapids and two lots in lower St. Cloud. In the meantime, he remained a slaveholder, keeping captive at least five slaves in St. Louis.[37]

◆

The year 1857 marked two decades since Sanford's slave Dred Scott sailed up the Mississippi River with an earlier master from Missouri to Fort Snelling in Minnesota. Scott lived at the fort for only three years, but while there he met and married an enslaved woman named Harriet Robinson. They were sent together down the Mississippi to St. Louis, where they resided for the next seventeen years. However, Dred never forgot his legal free status upriver. He sued in 1854 for his emancipation on the basis of having lived in a free territory, and the US Supreme Court finally decided his case in March 1857. Scott had legal precedent on his side: Rachel and Courtney had won their emancipation lawsuits after having resided in Minnesota.

Scott was no match for slaveholder politics, though, and he lost his case. The Supreme Court, whose justices consisted in part of enslavers, sided with Sanford in *Dred Scott v. Sandford*; the verdict overturned the Missouri Compromise and permitted slavery's existence in all US territories—including Minnesota. Chief Justice Roger Taney ruled that African Americans, enslaved or free, were excluded from the Constitution's definition of "citizen." Therefore, Scott had no legal rights and, by extension, no

Dred and Harriett Scott, from *Frank Leslie's Illustrated Newspaper*, June 27, 1857

right to bring an emancipation lawsuit in the first place. The decision crushed any further opportunities for enslaved people who had traveled through free states and territories to obtain their freedom through the courts. Moreover, the case's outcome marked the federal government's blessing on the encroachment of slaveholders like Sanford and Chouteau into Minnesota's economy. Sanford himself, who had openly bragged about his ownership of the plaintiff just a few years earlier, was too ill to revel in his judicial victory, and he passed away later that year. The decision galvanized northerners who were content to ignore slavery as long as it was confined to southern states, and it encouraged southern slaveholders to push for more rights.

With Sanford's death, Pierre Chouteau Jr. became the sole surviving partner of Chouteau & Company. (Sarpy had died a few weeks before Sanford's passing, and Sire had succumbed three years earlier.) From 1857 until the company was dissolved in 1864, Chouteau and his heirs held total control of all of the land that his company owned in Minnesota. Meanwhile, two of his employees (current and former) held public offices in the territory. Rice served as Minnesota Territory's congressional delegate in Washington, DC, and Lowry ruled central Minnesota as the president of St. Cloud's town council—a position akin to mayor.

Pierre Chouteau Jr.'s slavery-tainted financial reach extended throughout Minnesota before and during its territorial period. His firm's transition from fur to real estate and the resignations of some of his agents diminished that reach. However, voters elected supporters of slavery to the White House during Minnesota's territorial years, and presidents had the power to appoint governors, lieutenant governors, and other federal officials to the territory. Some presidential appointees were slaveholders, and their presence in Minnesota complemented Chouteau's influence from the South.

CHAPTER TWO

Presidential Appointees

With the establishment of Minnesota Territory in 1849, the president of the United States gained the responsibility—and opportunity—to appoint new federal officers for positions ranging from land officer and receiver of public moneys to the two highest territorial executive offices: territorial governor and the second-in-command territorial secretary. The appointees served for no longer than the duration of a presidential term, and they often did not last for the entire four years. Nevertheless, if a proslavery president chose slaveholding appointees, they—like military officers—could bring one or two slaves to Minnesota with them without fear of legal repercussions. With slaveholders serving in the highest offices of the territory, it was inevitable that additional slaveholders would bring their human chattel into Minnesota.

From 1853 to 1861, the Democratic Party, which supported the extension of slavery to territories across the country, controlled the White House, and appointments by Franklin Pierce in 1853 and James Buchanan in 1857 produced legislative, executive, and judicial reinforcement for proslavery Minnesotans. The slaves of the appointees had to sacrifice their ties to family and community for four years. Some enslaved people had to suffer even longer estrangements, because their enslavers chose to stay in the Northwest after their terms expired.

A posting to Minnesota Territory was not a choice appointment for a politician at the height of his career. Instead Minnesota was a place where a young federal official could develop skills at the dawn of his career—or where an elder statesman, in his twilight, could rest on his laurels. President Pierce appointed a slaveholder to an urban area with a free

African American community. President Buchanan sent slaveholders to less-populated areas with strong proslavery support and no free African American communities. Buchanan thus astutely generated grassroots Democratic, proslavery support with his appointees, better positioning them to lead Minnesota Democrats and rise in the party.

◆

Franklin Pierce, a Democrat from New Hampshire, was a compromise candidate, uniting northern and southern Democrats in the 1852 election. He did not hold slaves, but he announced his stance on the issue in his inaugural address on March 4, 1853: "I believe that involuntary servitude, as it exists in different States of this Confederacy, is recognized by the Constitution." As a result, he asserted, "The constituted authorities of this Republic are bound to regard the rights of the South in this respect as they would view any other legal and constitutional right, and . . . the laws to enforce them should be respected and obeyed, not with a reluctance encouraged by abstract opinions as to their propriety in a different state of society, but cheerfully and according to the decisions of the tribunal to which their exposition belongs." He vowed to do his part in upholding the rights of the South, and, as far as he was concerned, his declaration definitively settled the matter of slavery. "I fervently hope that the question is at rest, and that no sectional or ambitious or fanatical excitement may again threaten the durability of our institutions or obscure the light of our prosperity." His appointment of a slaveholder to the free territory of Minnesota exemplified his determination for the North and the South to work together without slavery impeding progress. This was easier said than done.

For four years, an enslaver who was a minor but rising figure in the Democratic Party served as second-in-command of the executive branch of Minnesota Territory. Joseph Travis Rosser served as the territorial secretary from 1853 to 1857, and he became the acting governor on at least two occasions in 1854. Born the son of a slaveholding grocer around 1820 in Virginia, he established himself politically and professionally in that state. He earned his law degree from the University of Virginia in 1841 and then set up a law practice in Petersburg. He joined the Petersburg Democratic Association in 1843, and President James Polk appointed him in 1845 to the position of customs collector for that city. Rosser's term terminated with the end of Polk's presidency in 1849, and he became a schoolmaster. However, he remained politically active and was elected a delegate to the 1852 Democratic National Convention, where he cast a vote for Franklin Pierce as the party's presidential nominee.[1]

By the time Pierce won the presidency that fall, Rosser was a husband, father, and slaveholder. In June 1843, in Petersburg, he had married Mary Armistead, one of two daughters of a respected brigadier general who had fought in the War of 1812. Rosser's marriage raised his social status. He was the son of a yeoman who held one slave, but the bride's parents owned nineteen people. As of 1850, Rosser owned a forty-year-old woman, a thirty-year-old woman, and a thirteen-year-old girl. The slaves were valuable assets for the Rossers, for all three were of childbearing age and therefore old enough to reproduce an enslaved labor force for him for years to come.[2]

On March 31, 1853, Pierce named Rosser to the position of secretary of Minnesota Territory—perhaps as a reward for voting for his presidential nomination. Four days later, the Senate confirmed the nomination. Rosser left his family and slaves behind and arrived in Minnesota alone on June 22. Two months later, Rosser joined the community of land speculators: he bought a portion of land on the northern side of College Avenue in St. Paul. Despite his sudden uprooting from a slave state to a free territory, he adjusted well to his new surroundings and his new position. "The people of that place appear to be well pleased with him," reported the *Richmond (VA) Daily Dispatch*. T. M. Newson, editor of the *St. Paul Daily Times*, later recalled that Rosser was "tall, slender, well-dressed . . . genial, pleasant," and "chivalrous." He was, however, also "a lover of slavery and a hater of abolitionists."[3]

Although Rosser's new job still involved managing money and documenting activities, he had more governmental powers and duties in Minnesota than in Virginia. As secretary of the territory, he immediately assumed the gubernatorial office in the event of Governor Willis Gorman's incapacity to serve. Day to day, however, Rosser merely recorded the legislature's new laws and the governor's official actions. He was also treasurer of the building fund, which concerned the capitol and the prison.[4]

According to accounts from Rosser's acquaintances, he brought opulence to his new position. Approximating the domestic slavery he had practiced in Petersburg, he hired multiple washerwomen and tailors to manage his wardrobe in St. Paul. He also kept a horse and a piano at his new home. In one room he displayed a copy of an oil painting of Italian noblewoman Beatrice Cenci. His predecessor in office, Alexander Wilkin, had acquired the painting in the Italian city of Florence, and, when Rosser admired the painting, Wilkin graciously gave it to him.[5]

Rosser's most influential acts took place within the first two years of his term. He entered office as territorial leaders searched for ways to make Minnesota grow. On February 1, 1854, Governor Gorman and Rosser were among a group of seven men purchasing five hundred acres on the Minnesota River—70 percent of the land of Rock Bend, the settlement that they renamed St. Peter. They and three other men formed the St. Peter Company and invested in the area's growth. In Dakota County, Rosser was among the original proprietors of West St. Paul. He also became a legal pioneer, founding one of St. Paul's first law practices, and he placed his law office in the secretary's room at the Minnesota Capitol.[6]

The secretary revealed a thin skin and hot temper whenever publicly criticized. He had never before taken on a high-profile government position, and he answered violently to his critics. In 1854 an African American man went to work as a janitor in the capitol. The secretary was largely accustomed to enslaved African Americans, and he treated the free janitor so poorly that the editor of a local newspaper chastised Rosser in print. The editor claimed that the secretary had acted in an "arrogant Southern manner," and he declared that "no gentleman would be guilty of the act imputed to him." In response, Rosser threatened to whip the editor.[7]

Nevertheless, the secretary's eye for details in documents proved beneficial for the territory. On March 4, 1854, the Minnesota legislature approved the creation of a railroad, and three months later Congress passed a bill authorizing this. That summer, Rosser went with Gorman and two others to Washington, DC, to raise money for railroad construction. While there, Rosser learned that two different versions of the law had reached Minnesota. He caught and disclosed the fraudulent parts.[8]

Gorman occasionally traveled out of the territory while in office as governor. At those times an enslaver became the head of Minnesota's executive branch, for Rosser assumed the role of acting governor for the duration of each of Gorman's absences. As early as April 18, 1854, Rosser served in that capacity, signing a contract to arrange the transportation of goods for Dakota people living on their new reservation on the Minnesota River. At the time Gorman was accompanying the Dakota leader Little Crow and Henry Sibley on a trip to meet with President Pierce in Washington.[9]

Rosser's responsibility for the territory's building fund gave him an important role in the preservation of Minnesota's history. The Minnesota Historical Society was incorporated shortly after the territory's establishment in 1849, but as of 1855 its members were dissatisfied with their physical location. They wanted to move from a room above the post office to the capitol. Rosser granted their request, giving the society a room on the first floor in the east wing of the capitol. His approval showed that he valued the society's work as an important part of Minnesota's government.[10]

On the other hand, Rosser's work in Minnesota did not overshadow his reputation as a slaveholder, and his ownership of people made him a political target as federal restrictions of slavery in territories loosened in the 1850s. In 1854 President Pierce signed the Kansas-Nebraska Act, which meant that the Missouri Compromise's prohibition of slavery in northern territories no longer applied to Kansas and Nebraska. One year later in Chatfield, Minnesota, territorial delegate Henry Rice gave a stump speech opposing both that law and the federal officers who were overseeing his own territory. He lamented the appointees made to Minnesota by "imbecile Pierce," and he complained about Rosser's ties to slavery. He reminded the audience that Rosser's wife resided in Virginia instead of Minnesota, and he claimed to have told the crowd that "Mr. Rosser could not live out of a slave state with his family." However, other accounts alleged sharper comments. One newspaper cited him as saying, "Mrs. Rosser is so fine a lady that she could not live in Minnesota, because she could not have a dozen slaves to wait upon her." According to another source, he said that Rosser's wife "had to go back to Virginia where she could be waited on by slaves."[11]

From January to March 1856, the legislature held its usual annual sixty-day session, but the working relationship between the legislators and Rosser rapidly deteriorated. Money—not slavery—was the primary issue. As secretary, Rosser was responsible each year for requesting an amount of money from the federal government to pay the territory's legislators for the following year's session. As of February 1856, the two-month session was halfway completed, but the legislature was underpaid. On February 4, the Minnesota Council—later renamed the Minnesota Senate—passed Joseph Rolette Jr.'s motion for a resolution blaming "a violation of duty on the part of the Secretary alone" for the lack of funds to pay mileage or per diem to legislators. The resolution also assigned a group of three to "wait upon the Secretary of the Territory and inquire the cause of the delay . . . and report his answer to the Council." Twenty thousand dollars had been appropriated for the session. The resolution also said that Rosser was "in gross violation of duty" for not estimating additional expenses for the current session or expenses for the next session.[12]

Rosser took personal offense at the resolution, and the next day he responded by letter to the council's president. "It would seem that my explanations to the members of your body have not been satisfactory, in relation to the funds for defraying the expenses thereof," he observed. He explained that the previous year, just one day before Congress approved the $20,000 appropriation, the Minnesota legislature had voted to nearly double its size from twenty-seven to fifty-three members. When Rosser and Congress acted, they had no way of knowing that the Minnesota legislature would double its membership. He said that he was not "gifted with the power of fore-knowledge," nor was he "a medium of the spirits." He complained, "Your honorable body have seen cause to pronounce judgment upon me, in your resolution, before you have heard me, and without the least particle of evidence." He declared, "I now demand the proof. . . . If you shall fail to show that I am responsible, or to amend the injury attempted to be done me, the judgment of the country is invoked upon such wanton attacks of private and public character."[13]

On February 12, Rolette, a member of the three-person committee investigating the matter, took the floor of the council to condemn the secretary's letter as self-serving and manipulative. Rolette called the letter "a willful perversion of facts, for the purpose of creating sympathy as unnecessary as unmerited." He claimed that the council was not passing judgment upon Rosser himself but merely seeking accountability for the money due to legislators the previous month. After all, said Rolette, "it was, beyond a doubt, the duty of the Secretary to be prepared with funds to meet those demands." Rolette complained that "the semi-official charge thus openly made against the Council deserves, in the opinion of your Committee, an unqualified rebuke." Thus, he introduced the resolution: "That the Secretary of the Territory, by his letter to the Council, has offered to the Committee appointed by the Council an act of discourtesy uncalled for and highly improper." The council passed the resolution. Unfortunately for Rosser, his reputation was sullied, and his political foes would talk about his perceived ineptitude for years to come.[14]

The other body of territorial legislature—the Minnesota House of Representatives—offered Rosser a salve of sorts. On March 1, the house thanked Rosser "for the kindness and courtesy with which he [had] treated the members of the House during the present session, and his readiness to respond to their wants when in his power." The gesture came on the last day of the 1856 legislative session, and it showed that the house as a collective did not share the council's opinion about the secretary's job performance. Rosser still had one more legislative session to endure as secretary before the end of his term the following spring, and the house's gratitude signaled its willingness to work cordially with him again.[15]

On the other hand, Rosser was ready to leave his position. He had the confidence of only one of the territory's two legislative bodies, and in Virginia his wife, Mary, suffered failing health. On April 26, Rosser wrote to President Pierce, requesting a leave of absence. However, the secretary had to serve as acting governor at least one last time the following month. Gorman was in Washington, DC, where he witnessed South Carolina senator Preston Brooks strike his Massachusetts colleague Charles Sumner with a cane on the floor of the Senate.[16]

In July Rosser left Minnesota and arrived at a hotel in Washington, DC. At the time, many of his detractors were happy to see him go. According to one account, they took up a collection to pay his travel expenses. Rosser was back in a slaveholding city and close to his wife and daughters. Mary's illness was terminal, and he was in Virginia when his wife died in January 1857.[17]

Mary's passing resulted in an unexpected uprooting for the family household in Virginia—including the slaves. Rosser's mother-in-law, Elizabeth Armistead, took his children into her home in Fauquier County, Virginia, where she held at least one dozen enslaved people. Meanwhile, Rosser returned to Minnesota to resume his position. The 1857 census for the territory did not list African Americans in his household. He either passed them along to his children at Armistead's home, sold his slaves before his return to Minnesota, or brought them with him without documenting their names in the census.[18]

◆

In James Buchanan's presidential inaugural address of March 4, 1857, he echoed his predecessor's sentiment that the slavery issue was resolved—at least concerning its presence in federal territories like Minnesota. He claimed, "The whole Territorial question being thus settled upon the principle of popular sovereignty—a principle as ancient as free government itself—everything of a practical nature has been decided." Thus, Buchanan suggested that the Kansas-Nebraska Act applied to Minnesota, because it—as a territory—was part of the "whole Territorial question." He further argued that only an individual state could choose its legal status concerning slavery, and he blamed the public discussion of slavery, not the institution itself, for sectional strife. "Throughout the whole progress of this agitation, which has scarcely known any intermission for more than twenty years, whilst it has been productive of no positive good to any human being it has been the prolific source of great evils to the master, to the slave, and to the whole country," Buchanan complained. "It has alienated and estranged the people of the sister States from each other, and has even seriously endangered the very existence of the Union. Nor has the danger yet entirely ceased."

The only advice Buchanan gave to the American people was to let time heal the wounds of division. "Time is a great corrective," he observed. "Political subjects which but a few years ago excited and exasperated the public mind have passed away and are now nearly forgotten." Buchanan did acknowledge, "This question of domestic slavery is of far graver importance than any mere political question, because should the agitation continue it may eventually endanger the personal safety of a large portion of our countrymen where the institution exists." On the other hand, he believed that if people would only stop discussing slavery, the issue would become less relevant to the nation over time. Buchanan proposed, "Let every Union-loving man, therefore, exert his best influence to suppress this agitation, which since the recent legislation of Congress is without any legitimate object."

By the start of 1857, Rosser was back in St. Paul and desperate to remain in power. He confided to Sibley, "I have just determined to ask from Mr. Buchanan a reappointment," and he asked the former delegate to write a recommendation letter for him. Rosser confidently predicted, "I am satisfied that I can obtain the autographs or the marks of 11/12 of the members of our assembly." On the other hand, he admitted that he was writing "in haste" and that he wanted the legislature to approve a new term for him within the first week of its new session. "To succeed would be a triumph for us," he noted. But he did not receive a new appointment and consequently had to leave office. A man named J. J. McCullough served as acting secretary in Rosser's absence before Buchanan's new appointee arrived in St. Paul.[19]

On March 6, 1857, the Minnesota legislature was in the penultimate day of its legislative session when the federal government legalized slavery in the territory. The Supreme Court ruled in *Dred Scott v. Sandford* that the practice was legal in all federal territories. The verdict intensified the debate over slavery among Minnesotans. In May Rosser and local abolitionist Morton Smith Wilkinson were discussing "Southern rights," according to a Virginia-based newspaper, but the discussion escalated into an argument and then a fistfight. Rosser won the fight, and the paper heralded his victory with the headline "Defending the South."[20]

The former territorial secretary took yet another shot at regaining political power that August. Minnesota's Democratic Convention met, and Rosser was one of seven candidates running to be the party's nominee for congressional delegate. He received the most votes, even besting incumbent Henry M. Rice, but had to compete in a runoff with the runner-up, William Kingsbury. On the second ballot, Rosser lost to Kingsbury. After this crushing defeat by his own party, only months after having been the second most powerful Democrat in the territory, he retreated to Virginia.[21]

President Buchanan replaced not only Rosser but also all of the territory's land agents and registers, and he chose enslavers for some of the positions. Some of his appointees were Democrats who had helped him with the 1856 election. At least one appointee, George Clitherall, was related to a powerful, pro-Buchanan Democrat.

◆

George Bush Bergwin Clitherall was born in 1814 to former planters in North Carolina. His father died in 1829, and his widowed mother took the family to the town of New Bern. In 1836 he married Sallie Ann Forbes, whose father held sixteen slaves in 1830, and during their marriage Clitherall and his wife held eight enslaved people. In 1837 the couple moved to Greene County, Alabama, and he opened a store and employed his younger brother Alexander Baron Clitherall as a clerk. In the 1840s the elder Clitherall brother became the assistant secretary of the Alabama legislature while rising in the business world.[22]

Alexander became a judge and a delegate to the 1856 Democratic National Convention, and he spoke favorably for Buchanan in Pickens County, Alabama, in 1856. He was asked to run for office, but he refused. "I am willing to remain a private in the ranks of the Democratic Party— to fight its battles, rejoice over its victories, lament its defeats," he wrote in January 1857. "But its offices I do not seek. Those I leave to others who deserve them better, or want them more than I do." Thus, a way was made for George Clitherall to take advantage of his brother's declination.[23]

The 1840 census shows that George Clitherall owned four male and four female slaves in Greene County, Alabama. His holdings were almost evenly divided by age. For two of the age groups (ten to twenty-three and thirty-six to fifty-four), he possessed one male and one female. One woman and two men comprised his young adult slaves (ages twenty-four to thirty-five). The only enslaved person ten years old or younger at Clitherall's household was a girl. The young adults, at their peak of physical health, were considered the most valuable, because of their fitness or potential fitness for labor. The child would eventually grow into adulthood. Until then the girl could serve as a playmate for his young daughter, Elizabeth.[24]

By 1850 Clitherall relocated his family to the town of Mobile in Mobile County, Alabama. He still enslaved African Americans: three males (aged eight, six, and four) and three females (aged thirty-five, nineteen, and ten) performed unfree labor for him there. The shift toward a female-headed slave community reflected that Elizabeth was now a teenager and that the slaves had to serve two young women but only one man.[25]

Clitherall was one of three enslavers appointed by President James Buchanan to a federal position in Minnesota Territory in the spring of

Main Street, Clitherall, Minnesota, about 1910

1857. On March 6 that year—two days after Buchanan's inauguration—the US Supreme Court legalized slavery in all territories including Minnesota. The new administration had a vested interest in the verdict, since Vice President John Breckinridge was a southern slaveholder who owned land in Minnesota Territory. The legalization of slavery there created potential for more southerners to invest in the Northwest, now that they could travel with their slaves. Buchanan's appointments to the territory seemed to encourage such transactions. He chose a slaveholder from South Carolina to head the land office in Stillwater and one from Virginia for receiver of public moneys in Sauk Rapids. The president sent Clitherall to Otter Tail County to serve as its register of public lands. Clitherall purchased land in the county, and Lake Clitherall there was named for him.[26]

At some point between the 1850 census and the 1857 appointment, Clitherall had moved from Mobile to Minnesota. Buchanan's statement when appointing him identified him as "George B. Clitherall of Minnesota." In contrast, the president referred to the two other slaveholding appointees according to their respective southern states. When Buchanan reappointed all three to their positions upon Minnesota's transition to statehood in 1858, he still referred only to Clitherall as a Minnesotan.[27]

In the Minnesota census of 1860, Clitherall and his wife, Sallie Ann, are listed as North Carolina–born, and their daughter, Elizabeth, as born in Alabama. Books written since then have speculated that a "servant" in the household, John Battle, was an African American whom the Clitheralls had brought from Alabama, but the census does not designate his color as "B" for "black" or "M" for "mulatto." Scholarship also notes Clitherall's service as a volunteer in the Home Guard, which was a military group in Alabama that supported the Confederate States of America without officially becoming a part of the Confederate army.[28]

Buchanan's appointee from Virginia had a long tenure in the Democratic Party, and the appointment brought experienced southern Democratic leadership to the Northwest. Samuel Lewis Hays was semiretired from a long career in politics in Gilmer County, Virginia, when he relocated to Minnesota at the president's request. Hays had served in Virginia's House of Delegates sporadically between the 1830s and 1850s, and he held a single term in the US House of Representatives from 1841 to 1843. Meanwhile, his holdings of African Americans grew from one in 1830 to eleven in 1850. His political comeback began when the governor of Virginia named him an elector for the 1856 presidential election. Hays belonged to the Democratic Party, and he cast his vote for the party's candidate, James Buchanan. After Buchanan's inauguration the following March, the new president rewarded Hays with an appointment to the office of receiver of public moneys—federal tax collector—for Sauk Rapids, Minnesota.[29]

On November 16, 1856, a judge in Virginia ordered Hays to pay a debt he owed to a bank. The local sheriff levied the court's judgment on Hays's enslaved people, sold the slaves, and paid the debt. Thus, Hays and his sons John and Calhoun relocated to Sauk Rapids without any enslaved people in the spring of 1857. They resided at a hotel in town, where they also set up business offices. John started a law practice to work on disputes in the land office, and the local newspaper *Frontiersman* praised him as a "competent lawyer and able to give satisfaction to those who may desire his services." The *St. Paul Daily Pioneer* called the patriarch "a good specimen of a Virginian."[30]

The elder Hays left for Virginia in October 1857 and returned to central Minnesota by early 1858 with his wife, his niece, and two slaves that belonged to his son Peregrine in Calhoun County, Virginia. The junior Hays owned a slave family consisting of father Stephen, mother Chloe, sons Charles, Napoleon Bonaparte ("Bone"), and Albert, and daughter Ellen. Peregrine, like Chloe, was born in 1819, and he was old enough to be the father of Chloe's children—all of whom were marked "M" for "mulatto" in censuses. Bone even wrote of his owner many years later, "A man by the name of Hays raised me." Peregrine's father took Chloe and Ellen with him to Minnesota, thus severing them from their family.[31]

Hays occasionally delivered proslavery lectures, and his oratory revealed a limit to the public's tolerance for slavery in Minnesota. In March 1858 he cited biblical passages to argue that African Americans were too inferior to rise above enslavement. A writer for the pro-Democrat Sauk Rapids newspaper *Frontiersman* had looked forward to hearing a leader of the party speak but "beg[ged] to dissent" from Hays's remarks about African Americans. The writer took no issue with Hays's holding of local slaves but took offense, as did other central Minnesotans, at public proclamations of the institution's rightness.[32]

Meanwhile, Hays was part of a community of slaveholders who invested in local real estate. In the summer of 1856, five slaveholders from Tennessee purchased lots in northern St. Cloud, but only one lived full-time in town when summer ended. In April 1858 Hays bought land in Stearns County and purchased more in July in Benton County, bordering Stearns to the north. His establishment of residential roots in Minnesota significantly diminished Chloe's and Ellen's chances of ever reuniting with their family.[33]

Buchanan's third appointee, Charles G. Wagner from South Carolina, had headed a group of South Carolinians dedicated to helping the Democratic Party win the US presidency. He held two slaves in 1850. That same year his father, Effingham, an owner of the Lexington Plantation in Charleston, held eighty slaves. In 1857 Effingham sold forty of his slaves to one buyer for $44,000. That same year, the junior Wagner led the land office in Stillwater, Minnesota, where he integrated himself into the Stillwater community, holding the rank of brigadier general in the Stillwater Guard.[34]

◆

In May 1858 Minnesota entered the union as a free state, but the new illegality of slavery did not alter Samuel Hays's holding of Chloe and Ellen. The new state did not offer any official mechanism for freeing any slaves within its borders. Hays did not provide documentation for his slaves, and the absence of papers left Chloe and Ellen vulnerable. Any slave in a free state could be captured and returned to the owner because of the Fugitive Slave Act of 1850. Moreover, Hays put the onus of freedom on his slaves. According to local antislavery journalist Jane Grey Swisshelm, he claimed that Chloe and Ellen were free to leave him but that they chose to stay with him. The rest of their family remained in Virginia, and the best chance for reunification with them was to stay with Hays until the end of his presidential appointment.[35]

In 1858 Hays completed construction of a gristmill in Stearns County, his most significant contribution to central Minnesota. The facility lay in the two-year-old community of Sauk Rapids "at or near mouth of Sauk River," according to a deed for the business. By the following year, the Sauk City Mills was in operation and won instant acclaim. The *Sauk Rapids Frontiersman* called the business "a substantial service to the people of our town and county" and credited it for the addition of three new buildings to Sauk Rapids. Before Sauk City Mills, according to the newspaper, "no effort was made to cause improvements to be made there," but Hays's enterprise fueled the growth of Sauk Rapids's business community.[36]

As he established more permanence in Minnesota and sought local customers, Hays substituted patriotic themes for his divisive proslavery rhetoric. He distanced himself from fellow slaveholders who preached secession and instead promoted himself as loyal to the country. In a speech he delivered at a hotel in St. Cloud, calling for national and local unity, he asked, "When I hear men talk of dividing the Union which is cemented by the blood of our forefathers, what can be more ignoble? Ought we not to cultivate a feeling of brotherly kindness?" He then noted his new state's diversity, saying, "Minnesota has representations from all parts of the United States, and in fact from all parts of the world." To him, the state's strength lay in its varied populace, and he wanted the people to focus on their commonalities instead of the differences—especially differences about slavery. He pleaded, "Ought we not then to cement those bonds which bind us together?"[37]

◆

Minnesota's transition to free statehood did not completely rid its government of ties to slavery. With Minnesota no longer a federal territory, the White House no longer had the power to appoint governors and lieutenant governors. The people currently in those positions resigned, and an election took place that spring to fill the seats. One of Chouteau's men—Henry Sibley—won the gubernatorial race. Sibley, in fact, was still on Chouteau's payroll when inaugurated; he continued to manage some of the real estate that the slaveholder owned in Minnesota. Thus, ironically, the leader of a free state received money from a slaveholder while enforcing his state's prohibition of slavery.[38]

Sibley followed Hays's example by passively mentioning the slavery debate in his public rhetoric. He talked about national unity and suggested that officials stop agitating the South about their enslaving of African Americans, but he did not specifically mention slavery when doing so. "Minnesota enters the Union as the thirty-second state," he said in his inaugural address. "She extends a friendly hand to all her sisters, north and south, and gives them the assurance that she joins their ranks not to provoke sectional discord or to engender strife—not to enlist in a crusade against such of them as differ with her in the character of their domestic institutions—but to promote harmony and good will, and to lend her aid, on all occasions, in maintaining the integrity of the Union."[39]

Statehood ironically marked the apex of the rise in power of slavery's supporters in Minnesota since the Pierce administration. In only five years, the proslavery element in Minnesota's government ascended from an enslaver one heartbeat away from governorship to a governor employed by a slaveholder. Also, statehood only removed appointed territorial governors and lieutenant governors, but other appointees, like Hays, were not affected by the transition and stayed in the positions. Together the appointees and elected officials served the needs of a constantly increasing population, and some Minnesotans were as invested as the officials in preserving slavery because of their own ties to the practice.

Migrants

With the exceptions of the states of California, Texas, and Iowa, all of the United States to the west of the Mississippi River consisted of federal territories as of 1854. That year President Franklin Pierce signed the Kansas-Nebraska Act, allowing the residents of the new territories Kansas and Nebraska to determine whether to become free states or slave states. The new law nullified the Missouri Compromise, and it created the possibility of new slave states from northern territories—including Minnesota. On the other hand, for southerners who were considering moving west in the 1850s, severe difficulties came with relocation to almost all territories. Washington Territory, Oregon Territory, and Utah Territory lay more than one thousand miles away from the nearest slave states. Meanwhile, residents of Kansas inflicted deadly violence upon one another while deciding their territory's fate as a slave state, and New Mexico Territory had a climate too hot and soil too dry for farming.

In contrast, Minnesota was an ideal territory for southerners. Like Kansas and Nebraska, Minnesota did not have New Mexico's extreme heat, nor was it as distant from the South. And just as the Missouri River gave southerners access to Kansas and Nebraska, the Mississippi River extended from Minnesota down to the slave state of Louisiana. On the other hand, Minnesota had political stability because of its organization as a free territory, which contrasted with the popular sovereignty at the root of the organization of Kansas and Nebraska. As a result, the question of slavery did not divide Minnesotans as badly it did the residents of "Bleeding Kansas." Federal officials and military officers from the South brought their slaves to Minnesota, but civilians without enslaved people in the territory comprised the majority of the population. The southern civilians who moved to the territory with slaves followed the lead of the federal appointees in bringing no more than two or three unfree laborers with them; therefore, they did not attempt to establish plantation slavery in the Northwest.

Throughout the 1850s, southerners left behind either some or all of their slaves to permanently relocate to Minnesota. Urban areas like St. Anthony and St. Paul attracted people from southern cities who sought new opportunities. Generally, they had inherited slaves rather than purchasing their own, and they established businesses that did not rely on slave labor. In contrast, rural areas like Shakopee and Belle Plaine in Scott County drew slaveholders who were willing to sell off their large holdings of captives before leaving the South, and they redefined themselves as yeoman farmers in Minnesota. Whether in the cities or in the country, these migrants came from families enriched by slave labor, and they used those riches to start their new lives in the Northwest.

The taking of land in Minnesota Territory from the Dakota provided the impetus for mass migration from across the Mississippi River. "The conclusion of the Sioux Treaty last summer decided large numbers of citizens in their determination to make Minnesota their future home," said a Tennessee-based newspaper in May 1853. Pierre Chouteau Jr.'s hometown of St. Louis was the nearest major southern city along the Mississippi River, and the city's residents were most likely among the enslavers to arrive first for settlement. St. Louis businessmen had long supplied Chouteau's trade networks, and they were accustomed to seeking northern business opportunities. Chouteau's employee Henry Sibley had played a major role in convincing the Indigenous leaders of the territory to sign the treaty, and his success showed slaveholders that someone in Minnesota wanted them to come to the Northwest to stay.[1]

For the new arrivals, the demographics of the Northwest no longer had relevance. Whether Indigenous people, French Canadians, or people with combined ethnicities lived in Minnesota, they would not have it to themselves anymore. A writer from Maryland noted in 1852 that some settlers in Minnesota believed that the Dakota were having second thoughts about the treaty. The writer advised that the Indigenous people let the matter drop. "The white man has set his eye and heart upon their soil, and will have it—honestly if he may—but he will have it." This is the heart of settler-colonialism: rather than establishing domination over those who were in place, as colonial powers did on other continents, the newcomers in the United States took the land from its original inhabitants.[2]

The life of a southern transplant in Minnesota was one of regional solitude and isolation. Settlers were cut off from new information about their homeland for weeks at a time, and the winter months delayed the arrival of southern news even longer. In 1852, "From the 10th to the 20th of November, no southern mail had arrived, and the editor does not look for one under a week or ten days longer," said a Tennessee-based newspaper of its migrants in the Northwest. As the Mississippi River began its annual freeze over the next few weeks, the ice blocked access by boat from the South to Minnesota. No vessel could bring newspapers from southern communities, nor could visitors from the South travel via river to Minnesota to bring information from home. After the freeze, the mail traveled upriver on a wagon trail that was passable only after muddy ground froze.[3]

Still the migrants traveled northwest, and one of the earliest of the former slaveholders arrived in 1852. Upon reaching his destination, St. Anthony, Minnesota, Jackson Lansing Ray sent information to the people he had left behind in Tuskegee, Alabama. "We are indebted to our friend J. L. Ray, formerly of [Tuskegee] but now of Saint Anthony, Minnesota, for interesting documents about that far-off region, for which he will please accept our thanks," said the *Tuskegee Republican*. Ray had been a modest slaveholder in Tuskegee, where he was the proprietor of a livery stable. In 1850 he enslaved four people: two men aged forty-five, a woman aged twenty, and a two-year-old girl. When Ray prepared to leave Alabama, the state did not allow manumission except by permission of the state legislature. He likely sold his slaves before relocating to Minnesota, where he became a farmer; the 1857 territorial census did not list African Americans in his household. Ray died within a decade of his arrival, but his widow and children continued farming in Minnesota, residing in the town of Richfield.[4]

Willis A. Gorman, President Pierce's appointee as Minnesota's territorial governor, left the territory briefly sometime between May 1853 and the fall of 1854 to visit his son, who was studying at the US Naval Academy at Annapolis, Maryland. While there, the governor encountered two young men: William Sprigg Hall and Harwood Iglehart. Gorman struck up a conversation with them, and they talked at length about the "far West, and particularly of Minnesota," he later recalled.[5]

Willis A. Gorman,
Minnesota's second
territorial governor,
1865

Gorman was an appropriate promoter of Minnesota to slaveholders.
As a southerner, born and raised in Kentucky, he was exposed to slavery.
As a Democrat, he supported the rights of slaveholders to take slaves to
territories. By leaving Minnesota temporarily for Maryland, he showed
that he trusted a slaveholder—Territorial Secretary Joseph Travis Rosser—
to govern the territory in his absence. Moreover, with a Democratic president choosing Gorman to run the territory, the governor could tell southerners with credibility that they would prosper in Minnesota.

Indeed, Gorman convinced Hall and Iglehart, and by October 1854
they left their homes in Anne Arundel County, Maryland, traveled west,
and set up a law office in St. Paul. Both men, only in their twenties, were
well on their way to establishing themselves professionally in the city. Hall
and Iglehart also entered the field of real estate, owning property jointly
and individually in Ramsey County. They shared possession of a housing
addition, and they also joined with Iglehart's cousin Charles Mackubin in
the purchase of another series of blocks in St. Paul.[6]

In St. Paul, Hall and Iglehart found a free African American community, which both resembled and differed from the free community of Anne Arundel County. In both locations free people constituted the majority of African Americans. In 1850 Anne Arundel County's 25,000 free African Americans barely outnumbered the 21,000 enslaved people there. In contrast, only thirty African Americans resided in Ramsey County—all in St. Paul—that year, and all of them were legally free. Half of them were free by virtue of birth in a free state, and the other half had become free by setting foot in the territory. Also, Minnesota's community of free African Americans was less stable than that of Maryland. As a slave state, Maryland only recognized African Americans as free through manumission and "free papers"—official documents. Minnesota's status as a free territory meant that slaves did not need free papers for liberation, and some African Americans in Ramsey County were, in fact, fugitive slaves.[7]

The free status of African Americans in Minnesota became much less secure after 1850. That year the Fugitive Slave Act became federal law, and it required any enslaved fugitives throughout the country to be returned to their southern enslavers. As a result, the absence of a legal process for emancipating slaves in Minnesota left enslaved fugitives vulnerable, without any means to acquire free papers there. They therefore could not build a strong legal case for emancipation, and estranged enslavers could easily claim them and return them to the South in enslavement. In general, if African Americans in Minnesota lacked free papers, served soldiers at forts, or accompanied presidential appointees, they were likely slaves.

Minnesota's African American population fared even worse for fourteen months in the late 1850s. Before March 1857, any enslaved people traveling with slaveholders for a temporary stay in Minnesota were legally free while in the territory; upon crossing back into the South, they returned to enslavement. But in its *Dred Scott* decision that spring, the US Supreme Court removed free status from all who had escaped slavery and lived in US territories. After Minnesota became a free state in May 1858, residents who had escaped slavery returned to their pre–*Dred Scott* precarious freedom under the Fugitive Slave Act. The new state's constitution prohibited slavery but did not stipulate how to emancipate the enslaved Minnesotans who became legally free upon statehood, nor did it specifically declare free all southern slaves entering Minnesota from May 1858 onward. Bounty hunters could thus kidnap people and return them to slavery.

William Hall owed his legal career to the income that resulted from owning enslaved people. He had been a child when his father died, and his mother managed the slaves and other assets that he had inherited. After he left home to study law at St. John's College in Maryland, his mother periodically sent him money generated by the labor of his slaves to cover tuition and other expenses. At age twenty he successfully petitioned for an increase in his allowance from the slaves' interest, because taxes took away a significant portion of each payment. In his statement to the Anne Arundel County Orphans' Court, he complained in the third person that "the interest on his monied property and the hire of his negroes . . . is entirely inadequate for his yearly support and to enable him to prosecute the study of the law, about which he is now engaged."[8]

Hall's acquaintance Harwood Iglehart came from a large family headed by a slaveholding patriarch. The Iglehart household was wealthy, owning $150,000 in real estate in 1850, and with wealth came educational opportunities. Iglehart also attended St. John's College in Maryland but then

William Sprigg Hall,
about 1858

graduated from Harvard University at age twenty-four in 1852. Like his father and siblings, Iglehart practiced slavery upon entering adulthood, but he owned just one African American—a woman in her thirties named Rosetta Johnson. She remained his property while he lived in St. Paul, but she lived at his father's household in Annapolis.[9]

The Halls and Igleharts lived near the slaveholding Mackubins in Annapolis, and Harwood Iglehart's mother and Charles Mackubin's mother were sisters. Mackubin's father owned at least eleven African Americans in Anne Arundel County, but Charles himself did not hold enslaved people as an adult. Upon reaching adulthood, his six siblings followed their father's example by remaining in Maryland and acquiring slaves. Mackubin, in contrast, left the slave state and lived in free states and territories for the rest of his life. He spent his early adult years in Massachusetts and then Illinois before coming to Minnesota. His marriage in Massachusetts to a woman named Ellen Marietta Fay meant that he would not gain any new slaves through wedlock.[10]

By June 1854 Mackubin relocated to St. Paul and achieved success in the world of finance. He started a bank with a New Yorker named

Charles Mackubin,
about 1840

E. S. Edgerton, and they set up a business office in the Winslow House. The enterprise earned a positive reputation until Edgerton broke from him and operated the bank alone in 1858. The people of the city respected Mackubin. One resident later recalled him as having "a fine face, indicating good blood," constantly wearing gold spectacles, and being "quiet" and an "able business gentleman."[11]

Mackubin's family respected his abstinence from slavery, and they did not impose any enslaved people on him. In 1853 Mackubin's father died, and his will passed all of his slaves to Mackubin's mother, Elizabeth. Five years later Elizabeth died. She left some silver and two paintings to Mackubin, but her six other children inherited her slaves.[12]

By 1856 Hall was acquainted with both Iglehart and Mackubin, and that summer they jointly bought a 160-acre tract north and east of downtown St. Paul, overlooking Lake Phalen. They added their personal stamp to the area by naming the neighborhood's streets after the flowers of their southern homeland: Ivy, Hyacinth, Orange, Hawthorn, Maryland, Rose, Geranium, Jessamine, and Magnolia.[13]

At the time the Democratic Party ran Minnesota Territory, and the affiliation of the Maryland migrants with the party led to some political perks. In 1856 Governor Gorman appointed Hall superintendent of Minnesota schools, thus placing a slaveholder in charge of a free territory's public education. In the next year St. Paul's Mercantile Library Association formed, and Iglehart was one of its first officers. Hall won election to the territorial senate at the end of the year, and he served in the 1857–58 session.[14]

Hall and Iglehart rose to political prominence during a brief era when slavery was legal in Minnesota Territory. The Supreme Court's *Dred Scott* decision in March 1857 legalized the practice in all territories, thus allowing Hall, Iglehart, and others to keep African Americans enslaved in Minnesota if they chose to do so. Over the next fourteen months, an influx of slaveholders traveled northwest for vacations, and some southerners settled permanently in Minnesota with their slaves. Locals did not take advantage of slavery's legality by purchasing and holding African Americans in the territory, but some of them now had masters and slaves for neighbors.

The three Marylanders defied political odds by winning more appointments and elections as the 1850s ended. In 1859 people from the town of Faribault chose Hall as part of a group that selected the location for

Minnesota's asylum for deaf and mute people. In October he won a second term in what had become the state senate, and Mackubin won his first term. They achieved two of the few electoral victories for Democrats in Minnesota that year. Republicans won most of the other local offices as well as the statewide offices of governor and lieutenant governor. In the free state of Minnesota, the ties of the three to the South and their slavery-generated wealth did not jeopardize their support from Minnesotans.[15]

◆

Brothers Benjamin and Zachariah Jodon were physicians born to a non-slaveholding family in the first decade of the nineteenth century in Frederick County, Maryland. By 1840 their mother Susan led a household of three women, and Zachariah headed his own household, which included a free African American man listed in the 1840 census as a boarder. Within the subsequent decade all of the Jodons moved to western Virginia, and in 1850 they shared a house in Lewis County. Zachariah, who was unmarried, led the household, and the other residents were his eighty-year-old mother, his children, his younger sister Adeline, his younger brother Benjamin, and Benjamin's wife and children.[16]

As of 1850 no free African Americans resided with the Jodons, but Benjamin held four valuable enslaved people: a woman in her twenties, a six-year-old boy, and two girls, ages four and one. If the woman birthed all three children, her fertility and prolific reproduction meant possible additional slaves for Benjamin. Also, the children had potential to grow into healthy and fertile adult slaves. At the time a slaveholder could sell an enslaved woman and her children as a collective unit for thousands of dollars.[17]

Slave ownership set the Jodons apart from most of their neighbors in Lewis County. Western Virginia's rocky soil and mountainous terrain discouraged most of its residents from holding slaves as agricultural workers, and that portion of the state depended on slavery much less than did eastern Virginia. Most slaves in western Virginia were domestic, and Benjamin's ownership of a young woman and three young children suggests that he did not require a strong and numerous unfree workforce at home.[18]

Susan died in 1853, and by 1857 the rest of the family had left Virginia and moved to Minnesota. Zachariah and Benjamin split up, each setting up a medical practice in a new community. The separation allowed Zachariah to sever his connections to Benjamin's involvement in slavery.

Zachariah and his new wife, Sarah, settled in Little Falls, where the couple built a Greek Revival house. At St. Anthony, Benjamin headed a household consisting of his nuclear family, his sister, and at least one African American from Maryland.[19]

Benjamin may have held a slave at his home in St. Paul. According to the 1857 territorial census, a six-year-old "mulatto" child from Maryland named Samuel Gram resided in Benjamin's household. That year the US Supreme Court's *Dred Scott* decision legalized slavery in Minnesota Territory, and the decision was seven months old when the territorial census was taken in October 1857. The census provided no space for slaveholders to list their enslaved people separately, as the federal census's slave schedules did. As a result, the decision to document the presence of slaves rested with the slaveholder, and any master choosing to record a slave by name in the territorial census could provide just a first name or both first name and surname for their human property. Benjamin chose the latter for Samuel.[20]

◆

John Nicols served in the legislatures of two states in two regions during the nineteenth century. In the 1830s he spent three terms as a representative and a senator in Annapolis, Maryland, and three decades later he served two terms in the Minnesota senate. Born in 1812, he spent his childhood and early adulthood in Caroline County, Maryland. After serving in the Mexican War, he moved to Pittsburgh and worked for merchant Peter Berkey. His employer moved to St. Paul in 1853, and Nicols followed suit for the sake of health two years later. He spent the remaining eighteen years of his life there, and during his first four years he was an enslaver.[21]

Nicols had no ties to Minnesota during the years he lived in Maryland, but he did have an important but reluctant financial connection to Maryland during his first years in Minnesota. In 1830 Nicols's father held eight enslaved people, but he died the following year. Nicols's mother had also passed away, in 1830, leaving only him to inherit the slaves, but he committed himself to manumitting each one as he or she reached adulthood. He arrived in Minnesota as an enslaver in 1855 but returned to Maryland twice to free all of his remaining slaves by 1859.[22]

Immediately upon reaching Minnesota, Nicols integrated himself into the St. Paul community. He and his former employer purchased a hardware store and renamed it Nicols & Berkey. He also worked as an insurance

John Nicols, about 1865

agent, covering customers' merchandise in transit. Before the end of the year, Nicols purchased a life membership in the Minnesota Historical Society.[23]

Nicols, like Iglehart, was an absentee slaveholder, but he made provision for the manumission of his enslaved people in Maryland after settling in Minnesota. On March 12, 1857, he decreed the freeing of his two remaining slaves, and the Caroline County Circuit Court acknowledged and recorded his statements in their land office. He first called for the liberation of a woman named Margaret Downs as of New Year's Day, 1858. She was thirty-one years old, five foot three, and she had "molatto" skin and a "mark" on her right wrist, according to the court. On January 1, 1858, the court followed Nicols's wishes, noting that "John Nicols of Saint Paul of Ramsey County Territory of Minnisota [sic] . . . did manumit and set free a certain negro woman named Margaret." A man named James Fountain identified the enslaved woman as Margaret Downs at the court, and twelve years later, according to the 1870 census, she still lived as a free woman under that name in Maryland.[24]

Nicols's second manumission ended his family's ownership of a family through three generations. Years earlier his father, Henry Nicols, had freed an enslaved woman named Mintah; the junior Nicols freed the rest of her family. While living in Pittsburgh in 1854, he requested the liberation of Mintah's forty-seven-year-old daughter, Charlotte Deverix. Three years later, he stipulated from Minnesota that Deverix's son—"one negro man called Alexander . . . present calling himself Alexander Ross"—was to be freed in January 1859. He was twenty-six years old, was five foot eight, and had a "chesnutt complexion" and "one scar on the right hand caused by the cut of a knife." At the time a man named Edgar Plummer sheltered Ross while Nicols lived in the Northwest. After manumission, Ross lived in Maryland with his family.[25]

◆

As land register George Clitherall bought land in Scott County in the mid-1850s, enslavers from all over the South moved there, not only to invest but also to permanently reside. They came from both the Upper South in Virginia and the Deep South in Louisiana. Earlier migrants had just platted new towns like Belle Plaine and Shakopee in the early 1850s, but they had barely populated their communities before the southerners arrived. In the late 1850s the slaveholders brought their wallets and their entire families. Slaves may or may not have accompanied them, but in either case their labor helped to make possible some of Scott County's development. The 1860 census did not list African Americans there.

Many of Scott County's migrants from Virginia had lived in the city of Petersburg, a center of the tobacco industry. Petersburg's enslaved people were not just plantation laborers; many of the city's enslaved people received training as skilled laborers and were hired out to businesses. Because Scott County was an agricultural area not suited for growing tobacco, and the small farmers had scant use for the slaves' specialized skills, it is likely that slaveholders leaving Petersburg placed some if not all of their human chattel up for sale, perhaps to be marched in chains to markets deeper in the South.[26]

Two prominent families from Petersburg left the city for good but sought different things in the Northwest because of their generational differences. Thirty-year-old Joel Alexander Pace and his wife, Mary, arrived in Scott

County by March 1857, and Pace set up a business partnership with local judge S. Albright. Mary's father, Henry Spain, moved there to take up farming. The Northwest allowed Pace to provide for his young family in ways that did not directly involve slavery; it presented Spain with a chance to retire from life as a large-scale planter.[27]

Spain arranged to sell his slaves before moving to Minnesota. The advertisement announcing the sale demonstrated the impersonal nature of the practice of slavery: it grouped the enslaved people according to age and gender, ignoring any of the relationships among them. Also, the advertisement did not identify any of the human merchandise by name. In July 1855 a Virginia newspaper announced the upcoming sale:

32 SLAVES FOR SALE.—On Thursday, the 9th of August, 1855, at Prince George Courthouse, that being Court day, by virtue of two Deeds of Trust from Henry M. Spain, duly recorded in the County Court of Prince George, for certain purposes therein specified, we shall sell to the highest bidder, for cash, Slaves as follows, to wit:

5 MEN from 20 to 35 years old,

4 LADS from 12 to 16,

10 WOMEN and 13 CHILDREN.[28]

Months later, in the fall of 1855, Spain also put up his land for sale. Another newspaper notice announced that he would sell his 425-acre plantation in Petersburg on November 10, retaining use of the property for himself and his family until January 1, 1856. By the time he moved to Minnesota with his family, he had given up the lush lifestyle of an elite planter. However, Spain did not completely abandon the culture of his home region. In Minnesota he grew tobacco and sweet potatoes, which the Belle Plaine newspaper called "Southern Staples."[29]

Pace, who was the son of slaveholders James and Ann Leigh Pace in Virginia, invested heavily in the town of Belle Plaine. After James passed away in 1848, Ann inherited his slaves and kept them until her death in 1858. After moving to Minnesota, presumably using his inherited wealth, Pace purchased $4,500 in land in Scott County between August 1857 and March 1858. In September 1858, he bought ninety-eight lots from local judge and town founder A. G. Chatfield for more than $12,000. He also helped expand the Democratic Party's hold on Minnesota; he was appointed teller of the county's Democratic convention.[30]

As Pace established himself in Minnesota, his extended family followed
him to the Northwest. His uncle Francis Pace, who was born around 1791,
worked as a merchant in Petersburg. Throughout Francis's life in Petersburg, he engaged in slavery. He held more than one dozen of his own
enslaved people and hired a slave named Mack from another enslaver in
1853. By the late 1850s he joined his nephew in Belle Plaine and purchased
one lot there in 1859. He was nearly seventy years old at the time and
relinquished his possessions to move to Scott County.[31]

Francis arrived in Scott County at a terrible time in its development,
and in 1860 he resided in his nephew's household and had no personal
estate of his own. (One's personal estate is made up of all of one's mov-
able property—at this time including enslaved people.) The nationwide
Panic of 1857 had hit Minnesota particularly hard. During the boom years
of 1855–57, land prices rose so quickly that speculators bought with funds
borrowed at exorbitant interest rates and still came out ahead. But with
the crash, immigration slowed, banks failed, and credit disappeared. Land
values plummeted, leaving original residents like A. G. Chatfield poorer
than when they arrived in Minnesota. The community of Belle Plaine
struggled to survive, and the influx of southerners could not reverse its
decline in fortune. Destitution throughout the town in 1859 and 1860
reduced almost all of its residents to tatters and impoverishment.[32]

For the Paces and Spains, arriving in Belle Plaine after 1857 provided
at least one advantage. They were able to purchase real estate at lower
prices than before the panic. (Chatfield himself was able to use the income
from these land sales to rebuild his personal estate.) The southerners'
sales of slaves before leaving Petersburg gave them a financial cushion to
carry them through Belle Plaine's turmoil. In addition, Pace further insulated his family from poverty by selling $3,100 of his Scott County land
between 1858 and 1859. As of 1860 Joel Alexander Pace still boasted a real
estate value of $14,000 and a personal estate of $1,000.[33]

As Belle Plaine's troubles mounted, Pace quartered some of his family
in St. Paul. His residence there was next door to the home of former territorial secretary Joseph Travis Rosser. The secretary himself was a slaveholder and originally from the same county in Virginia as Pace, and their
families may have known each other. When Rosser married into a prominent slaveholding family in 1843, he ascended to the same class of slaveholders as the Pace and Spain families. In St. Paul, Pace kept an African
American woman from Virginia named Mary Johnston, who may have

been one of his mother's slaves. She was twenty-six years old in 1857 and closely matched the age of Ann Pace's eighteen-year-old female slave listed in 1850. By 1860, however, Pace no longer held a residence in St. Paul, and he focused his energies on Belle Plaine. That spring he went fishing, and the local newspaper said, "Many thanks to J. Alex. Pace, esq. For a nice mess of wall-eyed pike."[34]

◆

As the Paces and Spains settled in Belle Plaine, southerners settling in nearby Shakopee brought generations of slavery's history with them. That history included participation in the transatlantic slave trade. At the dawn of the nineteenth century, an eight-year-old African boy disembarked from the slave ship *Success* to a new world in East Baton Rouge Parish, Louisiana. After months of writhing in the vomit and waste of his fellow captives in the vessel, he stood in iron restraints on dry land. He heard the auctioneer speaking quickly, and then a man took him away from the auction and brought him to a plantation. The boy became a slave at that moment, and the captor who called himself the boy's master was George Garig.[35]

George's son Philip was only two months old when the dark-skinned boy arrived on the plantation in July 1806. The young slave was the first purchase by the Garig family in little Philip's lifetime but far from the last, and Philip eventually grew into adulthood and acquired his own human chattel in East Baton Rouge. As of 1850 he held sixteen enslaved people of his own, and he lived comfortably as a farmer with a real estate value of $7,000. He was, therefore, a successful competitor in a crowded market in East Baton Rouge. The parish had few manufacturing jobs, and its residents consequently engaged in agricultural pursuits to make their living. Slaves, however, brought in wealth for their owners in ways beyond laboring for them; the masters could raise significant capital by mortgaging their human property. Most of the parish's farmers owned land worth less than $1,000. Garig was not the wealthiest planter in East Baton Rouge, but he ranked among the local elite.[36]

Anyone looking for other opportunities for wealth besides farming and slavery had to leave East Baton Rouge, and in the mid-1850s Garig and his family abandoned the parish and resettled permanently in the Northwest. They chose Scott County as their new home. Another of Garig's sons, George M. Garig, had traveled there and purchased land years earlier.

Before departing Louisiana for good, Garig sold his plantation and slaves. A newspaper advertisement noted, "The attention of persons desiring negroes and lands is directed to the advertisement elsewhere of Phil. Garig, Esq. His place is handsomely situated, and his fruit trees are of the best species." In an additional notice from Garig himself, he announced, "I will sell at public auction, in the town of Baton Rouge at the Court House door on the 14th day of February next at 11 o'clock A.M., a likely lot of CREOLE SLAVES, as follows—Five women, two men, and five children. Also, one tract of land containing 320 arpents. . . . Also, an undivided tract of land . . . containing 640 acres." He then established the terms of the sale: "The slaves and land, one-third cash, the balance in one and two years from day of sale, with good endorsed notes, and a mortgage retained until final payment. Persons desirous to purchase in block, the slaves or land, can see me at my Amite plantation previous to the day of sale."[37]

Garig and his family reunited with George in Scott County later that year. Father and son lived next door to each other, and both took up farming. The elder Garig likely farmed without the assistance of any captive African Americans. The low value of his personal estate in 1860 in Minnesota—only four hundred dollars—suggests that he indeed sold his sixteen slaves before relocating.[38]

When George Garig resided without his family in Scott County in the early 1850s, he initiated his family's longtime business relationship with another southern family in the county—the Spencers. Originally from Spencer County, Kentucky, where they held slaves, the Spencers migrated at mid-century to the free state of Indiana and then to Minnesota Territory. In 1852 Henry H. Spencer had barely turned thirty when he arrived at the town of Shakopee, and his younger relative Spier Spencer joined him there one year later. Henry built a store at the town but then moved it to land he owned southwest of Shakopee. He named the township Louisville in honor of his birth state. Meanwhile, Spier bought a considerable portion of real estate in Shakopee, and one person who sold land to him was George M. Garig.[39]

Spier also made money from the Garigs. Between 1855 and 1860, he sold $7,300 in Shakopee land to members of the Garig family. The influx of money allowed him to survive the Panic of 1857, and he stayed in Shakopee. Three years later his real estate was valued at $10,000, and he had a personal estate of $500. The Garigs owned a greater portion of the town than Spier did, and the family remained there for generations.

Through the actions of Spier and the Garigs the growth of Shakopee's economy was thus inextricably linked to wealth earned from slavery.[40]

Louisville did not thrive like Shakopee, but Henry Spencer also survived the Panic of 1857. Clitherall paid him at least two thousand dollars for lots, and proceeds from the sales gave Henry financial stability—and kept Louisville reliant on money from slaveholders. Henry tried to attract more people and business to Louisville. He built a gristmill in 1856, but the following year he began selling his real estate holdings in an indiscriminate manner. In 1859 he sold his store and had Louisville itself vacated soon afterward. He did not help matters by holding proslavery politics in a free state; he opposed abolition and supported the gradual emancipation of slaves. He could still boast of $2,750 in real estate holdings and a personal estate of $1,000 in 1860—not as much wealth as Spier but a respectable post-panic amount of money.[41]

Of the approximately 130,000 people who moved to Minnesota between 1850 and 1860, more than two thousand were southerners. They comprised a small portion of the migrants, but they bought significant amounts of real estate and therefore became an influential demographic toward the development of the communities in which they invested. These southerners gave up their lives as planters to make the journey. Others, however, had no interest in residing full time in the Northwest; rather, they traveled to Minnesota with the intent of merely visiting for a short while to conduct business. Then they returned to the warmth of the South and the wealth of slavery. These elite planters of the South had the means to make the largest investments and to travel the most often to and from their plantations, and they added to Minnesota's economy without having to leave slavery behind.[42]

CHAPTER FOUR

Elite Planters

When an enslaver owning at least fifty slaves invested in land in Minnesota, his transaction barely made an impact on most of his human chattel. The laborers were accustomed to an owner's absences for business trips and social gatherings, and a journey to the Northwest for real estate simply meant another reason for the master to temporarily leave the plantation. Owners of massive plantations generally employed overseers, who supervised the labor of the enslaved workers whether the slaveholder was present or not. An owner's departure did not disturb the work on the plantation. A slaveholder typically brought no more than three enslaved people with him on a prolonged trip, and their absence meant little to the work of the dozens of laborers who remained. The slaves continued to plow fields and plant seeds without missing a beat. They never saw the acres, blocks, and lots in Minnesota that their labor allowed their master to purchase.

Slaveholders owning more than one plantation or major enterprise saw even less of their slaves—and made more money from their work. These enslavers spent most of their time at the plantations where they lived and left their other plantations in the hands of overseers. Planters also contracted with other slaveholders' slaves for temporary labor on projects outside of the plantations. In North Carolina a company rented enslaved people for weeks at a time for the construction of roads, and these rental periods divided slave communities—sometimes permanently, if slaves died during their time away from the plantations.

Real estate in Minnesota was among the numerous fruits of slave labor acquired by wealthy owners, and federal statutes that relaxed antislavery

policies in northwestern territories gave southerners even greater incentive to expand beyond the South. For elite planters—those with real estate
or personal estates (or both) worth more than ten thousand dollars—land
investment in Minnesota was not worth significantly altering their way of
life. They had no interest in scaling back their slaveholding in the South
or in trying to create a plantation economy in the Northwest; their southern plantations remained their major sources of income. Land investment
in Minnesota generated a smaller additional amount and diversified their
financial interests. They rarely attempted to launch businesses on their
property in Minnesota.

On the other hand, the deals made by elite planters dramatically altered
some Minnesota communities and their residents. The influx of money
from the planters allowed locals to develop their communities, and the
departures of the buyers after their transactions meant that the elites would
not interfere with how the enriched Minnesotans spent the money. As a
result, Minnesotans began to encourage southerners to visit the territory
and invest in it, and local land agents were among those who reached out
most intensely to them. By promising that the elites would be welcome,
Minnesotans compromised on the issue of slavery.

◆

By 1852 some people of middle- and upper-class means had constructed
buildings in Minnesota that revealed, in part, the tastes of the wealthy.
The St. Paul–based *Democrat* newspaper, as quoted in the *New Orleans
Daily Delta*, presented the boastful, colonizing perspective of the burgeon-
ing community. The paper noted that in just four years, "brick church
edifices, school-houses, store-houses, private mansions, and comfortable
cottages have taken the place of the log huts and the lodge of the savage."
The Mississippi River flowed south from Minnesota to the slaveholding states of Arkansas, Kentucky, Louisiana, Mississippi, Missouri, and
Tennessee, and advancements in riverboats encouraged travel upstream.
Hotels built along the Mississippi River catered to southern vacationers.
Some wealthy southerners, interested in longer visits, built cottages for
seasonal vacations. A southern newspaper remarked about one, a lakeside
house: "Already has one gentleman from St. Louis erected a tasteful cottage
upon one of these aqueous mirrors, which he has furnished with a library,
and where he can indulge in the sport of angling, hunting grounds, or
chasing the deer."[1]

Visitors from St. Louis made up a significant number of the southern tourists to Minnesota during the early years of the territory. Missouri
was the closest slaveholding state to Minnesota, and St. Louis was Missouri's largest river city. A Tennessee-based newspaper noted in May 1853
that "citizens of St. Louis . . . spent the season at St. Paul in the summers
of 1851–52." Indeed, of the 171 steamboats coming to St. Paul in 1852,
twenty-two were from St. Louis. The other vessels came directly from
points of departure outside of the South: 131 from Galena, Illinois, thirteen from the Minnesota River, three from the St. Croix, and one from
Lake Pepin.[2]

Minnesotans spared few expenses in catering to their southern guests,
who could evidently pay for them. A writer for a Missouri-based newspaper noted the comforts provided for visitors and the going rates. "Livery
stables, fine horses and carriages are plenty and at moderate prices by the
day, week, or month," said the writer. On travel and lodging: "The cost of
coming here from St. Louis on a fine steamboat and omnibus is $10.50;
the hotel prices $3 per week for board, and everything else in proportion."
Among the southern visitors, it was said: "There are several Virginia gentlemen who spend their summers here and return home in the fall and
have done so for the past two seasons. Every thing is presented for their
reception and comfort."[3]

An enslaver from Missouri invested in Stillwater, Minnesota, and
groomed it for future masters. Levi Churchill, who held a slave in St. Louis
and was originally from Vermont, started a business partnership with
Socrates Nelson, who had similarly left New England for St. Louis in
the early 1840s. In 1844 Nelson moved to Minnesota, settled along the
St. Croix River, and established a store bearing the names of both partners in what would become the town of Stillwater. Nelson acquired furs
and sent them down the Mississippi River for Churchill to sell in St. Louis.
With money from those sales, Churchill then bought merchandise and
sent it upriver for Nelson to sell in Minnesota. Within months of the organization of Minnesota Territory in 1849, the partners billed themselves in
the local press as "Dealers in Fancy and Staple Dry Goods, Groceries and
Provisions, Hardware, Stoves, Nails, Crockery, Glass, Tin-ware, Hats, Caps,
Boots and Shoes, Clothing, Blank and School Books, [and] Stationery."
Three years later they also sold books.[4]

Much of the income generated by Churchill and Nelson came from
beyond their store. As early as 1845, they jointly invested in real estate,

and years later they were two of the incorporators of the village of Bay-
town in Washington County. In 1851 the two helped start the St. Croix
Boom Company, which organized and weighed all logs going down the
St. Croix River, and they converted logs into lumber. In the following year,
Churchill and Nelson built a sawmill that lay three miles to the north of
Stillwater.[5]

Nelson ascended socially and politically in Minnesota while engaging
in pursuits apart from Churchill, and the income from his partnership
with a slaveholder contributed to his ability to engage in those activities.
He helped to start an Odd Fellows lodge along the St. Croix River in 1849.
In the early 1850s he served as one of the first regents of the fledgling
University of Minnesota. He established the town of Greenfield in Wash-
ington County in 1858. That same year he won election to a term in the
Minnesota senate, where he served during the 1859–60 session.[6]

No other Missourians made as deep an impact on Stillwater as Churchill
and Nelson did, but other residents of St. Louis claimed their parts of the
northwestern city. Between 1854 and 1857, the commission business firm
Tillman, Rozier, & Company operated in St. Louis, and during that time
the firm's four partners purchased land in Stillwater. Senior partners

Main Street looking southeast, Stillwater, July 1865

Charles Tillman and Ferdinand Rozier Jr. held the most slaves—Tillman, five, and Rozier, three. Tillman owned $40,000 in real estate and had a personal estate of $25,000, and Rozier had $10,000 in land and $5,000 in personal effects. William Fullager, the third slaveholding partner, possessed one person, and partner Amadee Berthold lived with his slaveholding father Pelagie.[7]

As the Missourians held on to their real estate holdings in Stillwater, other slaveholders from beyond St. Louis gravitated toward the city's land and lumber. During the tourism season following the *Dred Scott* decision on March 5, 1857, masters from all over the South bought lots in Stillwater, and they were wealthy in various ways. Lester Markham of Georgia purchased $120 in land, which comprised part of his $8,000 in real estate years later; he also owned a $5,000 personal estate. John Henry of the Upper South state of Delaware had real estate worth nearly seven times his personal estate value—$75,000 and $11,000. In contrast, Thomas R. Smith and Levi Joy of the Middle South state of Tennessee, who co-invested $600 in property in Stillwater, each had five times their real estate values in their personal estates. Smith had $3,300 in real estate and $16,000 for a personal estate, and Joy held $10,000 in real estate and $50,000 in his personal estate.[8]

Among the enslavers in Stillwater that summer, Lewis Hyman of Virginia invested the most money in land in Washington County. He spent $5,000 on real estate there, thus giving him a total value of $32,000 in real estate holdings nationwide. His personal estate was only $6,000, which consisted in part of the two slaves he kept. On the other hand, the land in Minnesota helped him with his business of importing watches and jewelry. After having returned from Stillwater in the summer of 1857, Hyman claimed that some of the merchandise at his store in Virginia had been acquired in the Northwest.[9]

Although Hyman held a small number of enslaved people, he experienced a great amount of trouble with them. He had hired another owner's slave in 1856, but that slave successfully fled from him. The fugitive, named Henry Lewis, had received four days leave from Hyman to ostensibly see his sister on her deathbed, but instead he boarded a boat, paid the cook fifty dollars to hide him in a stateroom, and sailed to the free state of New York to reunite with his wife and child. Hyman tried in vain to retrieve him, placing a notice in the local newspaper: "30 DOLLARS REWARD—Ran away from the subscriber, on the 7th inst., a negro man named HENRY. He is about 38 years old, of a dark brown color, medium size and height. The said negro was hired by me from Martha Allen. I will pay the above reward of $30 for his apprehension and confinement in any jail in the State of Virginia, so that I get him again." The fugitive was almost twice the age of most runaway slaves who reached New York, who tended to be in their twenties, but his escape by boat was a common means of transportation toward liberation.[10]

Several of Stillwater's slaveholders in the 1850s were not originally from the South and, thus, were new to the institution. Both Churchill and Smith had left New England for southern states. Hyman had left England for Virginia, and Tillman had departed from France to relocate permanently in Missouri. Having moved to the South, they were accustomed to traveling to a different region of the country and making a living in new surroundings. In their cases, however, the investors were content to return to the South from Minnesota Territory and manage their holdings from a distance.[11]

In the spring and summer of 1857, some enslaved people in St. Louis traveled to Minnesota without their masters. These slaveholders hired out their male captives to captains of riverboats carrying freight, and the slaves labored to keep the vessels clean and running while sailing up the Mississippi. Before *Dred Scott*, slaves rarely worked as crew members of riverboats sailing north of St. Louis. Any destination north of Missouri placed the slaves in free states and territories, and slaveholders ran the risk of permanently losing their slaves to legal freedom. After *Dred Scott*, Minnesota's new legal status as a slave territory sharply decreased that risk, and slaves from St. Louis reported to work on vessels bound for points northwest.[12]

◆

The cities of St. Paul, Minnesota, and Natchez, Mississippi, shared more than their location on the Mississippi. The two cities also provided similar types of labor for both enslaved and free African Americans. St. Paul was an urban area in a free territory, and, without agricultural employment, slaves and free African Americans were likely to perform the same kind of labor—domestic service for European Americans. Natchez was in a slave state, and its government rigidly enforced its slavery laws. However, slaves by the river conducted the same tasks as the few free African Americans in town. Lumber companies hired both the free and the unfree to load, unload, and navigate lumber rafts and flatboats along the Mississippi by themselves. For the slaves, this labor provided a change from the toil of growing cotton and granted them independence from violent overseers.[13]

In the early 1850s, neither enslavers nor Minnesotans discussed slavery in the context of travel to the Northwest. The territory's free population was small, but it significantly outnumbered the slaves kept by residents there. About three-fourths of Minnesota's forty African Americans were born in free states and were thus legally free from birth. The majority of Minnesota's slaveholders were southern military officials stationed at the territorial forts. In at least one instance, a slave at the fort was recorded in the 1850 census as a free person but in a receipt from the US Army as a slave. The bans on slavery in the Northwest Ordinance and the Missouri Compromise applied more to civilians than to the military.[14]

When President Pierce signed the Kansas-Nebraska Bill in May 1854, Minnesota's residents and southern visitors took notice. Some people interpreted the new law's popular sovereignty as applying also to Minnesota, and proslavery locals relished the possibility of slavery in the territory. "This glorious institution will shortly pervade our beauteous territory," said a resident to a tourist in St. Paul that year. "Slave-grown corn will wave upon our hillsides, and the melodies of the happy nigger will re-echo through the vales of Minnesota!" Hotel guests favored slavery, and one observer considered support for slavery "almost universal in the Northwest."[15]

A newspaper editor in Natchez, Mississippi, boasted about the lavish hotels in St. Paul. A traveler had sent the editor copies of St. Paul newspapers and a dinner bill listing "mock turtle soups, pickerel and bass, turkeys and oysters, plum puddings, ices, creams and pastries." Marveling at the city's population growth, the editor mused that "flourishing cities and busy villages and social comforts have sprung up as if the land had been touched by an enchanter's wand." The writer also noted a financial motive for the influx, saying that "very large investments have been made too, of late, in real estate and property in the territory by citizens of the states, and among them by some of our own."[16]

Land agent Henry McKenty of St. Paul was not originally from the South, but he astutely and quickly learned how to enrich himself in the Northwest through patronage from that region. He promoted his land agency in newspapers near the head and mouth of the Mississippi River in the spring of 1854—one in St. Paul and another in Natchez. That fall he spread the word in other parts of the South, advertising in newspapers in Louisiana and Virginia. Meanwhile, notices for another agency in Minnesota—Tracy & Farnham—appeared in periodicals in Maryland and North Carolina.[17]

To an extent, the advertisements worked. In November a newspaper in St. Paul cited the Kansas-Nebraska Act's passage as significantly responsible for the visits by numerous southerners to Minnesota. Although Minnesotans did not express desire for their territory to become a slave state, they welcomed the money that slaveholders paid them. The *St. Paul Minnesotian* published a letter that a Louisiana resident wrote to a friend in Minnesota. "The Minnesota fever rages high here," the southerner wrote, "and we shall send a delegation to St. Paul next spring to take observation." The Louisianan asked the Minnesotan to make a "small" investment of four thousand dollars. "You will choose upon Denegre & Pettipane, New Orleans, for the money." Additional agencies emerged in Minnesota, and one of them—Dayton & Packard—cited slaveholder Pierre Chouteau Jr.'s company Chouteau, Harrison & Valle as a reference.[18]

Even more southerners visited Minnesota in 1855. Five steamboats from St. Louis arrived in St. Paul on April 27 alone, and more than three hundred passengers disembarked. One of the vessels, the *Ben Bolt*, was owned and operated by enslaver Thomas Woolverton. McKenty had predicted before that tourism season that twenty families would move from Natchez to Minnesota. F. A. W. Davis, a small slaveholder from Natchez, bought $10,500 of land in St. Anthony and St. Paul for his children in 1854 and made a second trip to the territory in 1855, but he returned to Mississippi after making his purchase.[19]

Another slaveholder with ties to Natchez, Henry Sanford Dawson, left a more significant mark on Minnesota. By 1854 Dawson owned land there, and he visited the territory on multiple occasions over the next few years. On the other hand, he remained committed to his plantation in the South and the management of his slaves. He was at least a second-generation enslaver. His father, Samuel J. Dawson, was an elite planter in Virginia, and he moved the family to Natchez in the late 1820s. The elder Dawson announced his relocation in a local newspaper, saying that he would arrive "with between 50 and 60 Virginia Negroes of both sexes, all very likely—among the lot, there are some first rate Copers and Blacksmiths, and one excellent Seamstress: all of which can be sold as low as any negroes in market of the same description." When the patriarch died in 1837, Henry Dawson served as the estate's administrator and carried on the family's slaveholding tradition in Louisiana.[20]

After leaving Natchez, Dawson moved to Vicksburg, Mississippi, to purchase real estate and establish himself separately from his father's legacy. He and J. J. Chewning were business partners in Vicksburg until 1833. Both men were among the commissioners of the Commercial and Railroad Bank of Vicksburg. Dawson was also an agent and director of the Bank of Vicksburg. The sale of his Vicksburg property was announced in the fall of 1840; he had reportedly owed money on it. Another land sale was announced in 1842, and delinquent taxes from Dawson were the reason. He had not paid off a promissory note of three thousand dollars to the Atchafalaya Railroad and Banking Company in Louisiana, but the bank dissolved and could not legally recover the money from him.[21]

Dawson practiced a different kind of cruelty than Davis toward slaves. By repeatedly traveling to and from the Northwest with some of his slaves, he subjected them to experiencing and then having to leave a society that outlawed slavery. During the weeks that Dawson's slaves set foot in Minnesota, they were actually free. Although the Kansas-Nebraska Act clouded the issue, the tourism season of 1857 was the only time that federal law clearly protected slavery in Minnesota Territory. On the other hand, Minnesota had no substantial communities of free African Americans to help servants of tourists leave their masters and adjust to independence. In addition, the one or two slaves accompanying slaveholders usually constituted a small portion of the enslaved people owned by the traveler. When Dawson took a slave with him in 1860, sixty-four other slaves— presumably their families, certainly their community—stayed behind in Madison Parish, Louisiana, where they suffered the field work of growing corn or cotton. Whenever Dawson departed the free Northwest in the fall, the enslaved people who accompanied him declined freedom in a strange land for the violent, oppressive, but familiar drudgery of slavery with their families and community.[22]

◆

Elsewhere in Madison Parish lay the Elcho Plantation, but its owner, a judge named Samuel S. Boyd, resided across the river and downriver in Natchez. He traveled to Minnesota to invest in land in 1855, adding to his collection of properties throughout the United States. Boyd's business partner was Rice C. Ballard, who also hailed from Natchez. The two subsequently acquired and ran more than six plantations with a total of five hundred slaves in Arkansas, Louisiana, and Mississippi. The slaves grew 2,500 bales of cotton per year, grossing $100,000.[23]

A slave broker in Louisiana named C. M. Rutherford facilitated many transactions for Boyd and Ballard. He arranged for the sale of twenty-three slaves to the partners' Magnolia Plantation in December 1853. The agent bragged that "you may think them high, but they are low for the market. I am satisfied you cannot buy the same negroes here within $2,000 of the same money." Boyd approved the deal and bought the sixteen men and seven women for a total of $27,500. In the following month Boyd and Rutherford separated two "large stout women" from a group of ten recently purchased. "Boyd and myself thought it best for me to sell them and buy two other younger [slaves]," Rutherford reported to Ballard. "I think I will be able to get the average price for the two—$900 each." Concerning the Boyd-Ballard plantation Out Post, Rutherford announced, "I need the boy Jim from Out Post. I think I will get $1,250 or $1,300 for him."[24]

Boyd did not come from colonial-era plantation money but rather was a self-made elite planter. He was not even a native southerner; he had been born in Maine in 1807. At the age of sixteen, he was orphaned; his older brother took on responsibilities for caring for the younger siblings, and Boyd left Maine for Natchez, eventually started a legal practice there, and purchased the first of hundreds of slaves.[25]

In some ways Boyd was a typical member of Natchez's planter elite. He wed his bride in 1838 at his home plantation, Arlington. By 1850 he and his family resided there with seventy slaves. His personal library held eight thousand volumes of literature in a dozen languages.[26]

Boyd had a complicated history with African Americans. In the 1840s he served as one of two lawyers for a free African American woman who successfully sued to live and work in Natchez. On the other hand, the judge was one of the cruelest and most violent slaveholders known to own real estate in Minnesota. He whipped his slave Maria to the point of drawing blood. Also, he bought and sold slaves without considering their family relationships, and his own sexual activity with slaves provided context for some of the transactions. He fathered at least two children with his slave Virginia, but he sent them away to Texas in order to keep his wife from suspecting his paternity.[27]

On at least one occasion, however, Boyd's wife learned about his sexual indiscretions. One of his sons was a slave named James Boyd. The judge engaged often in sexual intercourse with James's mother, and the frequency of their encounters enraged Mrs. Boyd. She successfully pressured him to transfer the female slave to another plantation—upriver in Vicksburg. Meanwhile, James remained at Arlington and was favored among the slaves because of his status as the master's son; his fellow slaves even waited on him.[28]

Women were not the only enslaved people seeking refuge from Boyd. In 1856 a male slave named Frank Kelly fled Boyd's plantation in Natchez. He managed to travel thirty miles to the south before his capture in Wilkinson County, Mississippi. It fell to a Mississippi-based newspaper north of Natchez—the *Vicksburg Daily Whig*—to notify readers that Kelly was detained at the Wilkinson County Jail. The notice read, "FRANK KELLY— Says he belongs to S. S. Boyd of Natchez."[29]

As with F. A. W. Davis, Boyd did not live on his northwestern land but rather reserved it for his family—in his case, for his siblings. His younger brothers Edward and Walter and Edward's wife and children departed from Maine to relocate to Boyd's property in Ramsey County, in the town of Little Canada, and by 1857 all of them resided together in the same household on that land. Boyd's generosity provided a foundation on which his brothers could develop themselves professionally in the Northwest. Edward started a medical practice, becoming one of the few doctors of Minnesota's territorial period. Walter took up farming, and he also served as the first postmaster of Minnesota Territory as of 1856.[30]

The land in Minnesota was different from most of the judge's other real estate properties, because slavery was absent there. However, Little Canada was not the only location in which Boyd refrained from slavery. In Mississippi he also owned "wild lands," as a local newspaper put it, in Warren, Washington, and Yazoo Counties.[31]

◆

Among the elite planters of longest standing in the South to own land in Minnesota were the Mendenhalls of Guilford County, North Carolina. When North Carolina was one of the original thirteen English colonies, England's Earl of Granville deeded land there to a member of the Mendenhall family. The family stayed on that land, building a large and lucrative plantation. A gristmill, a sawmill, a blacksmith operation, a carpenter shop, and a massive farm comprised the plantation. Slaves did not work there before the 1820s. The Mendenhalls were a family of Quakers, and slavery ran counter to the religious community's values.[32]

By the 1820s, lawyer George C. Mendenhall headed the family plantation. In 1824 he became a slaveholder by marriage, and he tasked his new slaves with labor on the plantation. His first wife, Eliza Dunn, who was not a Quaker, had inherited slaves from her first husband upon his death, and she still owned them when she wed Mendenhall in 1824. After barely one year of marriage, Eliza died during childbirth. George suddenly had not only a newborn child to raise alone but also his late wife's slaves to manage without her.[33]

Mendenhall was legally bound to retain ownership in North Carolina, because the state prohibited anyone from freeing slaves within its borders. The slaves, however, were not valuable in Guilford County. The local staple crops were grains rather than cotton, and most of the area's residents were non-slaveholding yeomen who did not need a force of bonded laborers. Mendenhall put his slaves to work on the family farm, training them with specific skills. He profited from the sales of the products his slaves cultivated or manufactured, and, when he did not have enough work for them, he hired them out to others as artisans. He also owned at least nine slaves in Pope County, Arkansas. He sold one of his enslaved women there and annually hired out each of her eight children to a different renter.[34]

On the other hand, he demonstrated his Quaker roots by taking measures to decrease his holdings of enslaved people. He bought land in the free state of Ohio and brought slaves there in order to legally manumit them and for them to resettle as freedpeople. He made at least four such trips and freed fifty of his eighty slaves. Some critics claimed that he waited too long to liberate them. They accused him of only freeing his laborers after having maximized his exploitation of them. An editor in South Carolina opined, "Modern philanthropy teaches some men to work their negroes down and, after acquiring a fortune by their labor, turn them off to grase, like an old horse, at the expense of others. George C. Mendenhall is one of this class, we believe." He was alienated not only from his fellow Quakers but also from abolitionists from outside the community.[35]

Also, even slaves of relatively reluctant enslavers were impatient for their freedom and seized it for themselves. George's nephew Richard

Junius "R. J." Mendenhall worked on the family plantation briefly as a teenager, and his failed attempt with his cousin to recover one of George's fugitive slaves demonstrated how valuable African American unfree laborers were to the plantation. The two boys traveled six hundred miles, crossing through the states of Virginia and Ohio, chasing the runaway. They entered Indiana before giving up the pursuit.[36]

George Mendenhall purchased land in central Minnesota in the mid-1850s. His nephew R. J. by then had relocated to the territory and arranged the transactions. George bought real estate in Wright County in November 1856, and two years later he acquired one lot in Stearns County. These properties were likely investments for him and his family and not prospective settlements for any of the slaves he had yet to liberate. He did not free any of his slaves in Minnesota, nor did he give any of his properties there to them. Rather, ownership of land in the Northwest allowed the southerner to geographically diversify his real estate holdings.[37]

◆

Some of the elite southerners who traveled northwest to invest in Minnesota were yeoman slaveholders. They had increased their income principally through other means besides slave labor, but their small participation in the practice still tied their investments in Minnesota to the institution. A lawyer named Darius H. Starbuck journeyed from Forsyth County, North Carolina, where he had held a thirty-seven-year-old African American man in 1850. On July 3, 1856, just five months after the establishment of Sherburne County, he bought land in Big Lake at Township 33, Range 27, Section 15. He then returned to North Carolina.[38]

Starbuck was born to parents who did not own enslaved people, and neither of his parents came from slaveholding families, but he became an instant slaveholder in his adult years and actively held slaves for more than a decade. In February 1840 an acquaintance of his wrote his will and named him an heir to a family of slaves. Starbuck was not to receive the slaves until after his friend and his widow died, and he had to promise to emancipate them when legally possible. However, four years later, he purchased the family from the couple. He allowed the couple to use the enslaved family's labor until they both died, but he stipulated that he would not free the slaves until the monetary value of their labor matched the price he paid for the slaves. His new human possessions were the patriarch Syphax, his spouse Letty, and their three children. Syphax may have helped to build Starbuck's estate in 1851, which was one of the first mansions of Winston, North Carolina.[39]

By owning five slaves, Starbuck was elite among local enslavers. As with Guilford County, Forsyth County relied very little on slave labor for its economy. The county's population was 86.5 percent "white," 12.1 percent enslaved, and 1.4 percent free African Americans. Barely one out of ten of the county's farmers owned slaves, and half of those masters held no more than two slaves. With the average slave population at 3.76 per household, Starbuck possessed more human chattel than most of his neighbors did.[40]

In 1851 Starbuck worked with C. E. Shober in Salem, North Carolina, on the Fayetteville and Western Plank Road Company, chartered in January 1849. His colleague in the company, George Mendenhall, handled the company's branch in Jamestown. Plank roads, built with cheap timber, improved travel between locations not yet serviced by railroads, but they were expensive to maintain. The company contracted with slaveholders from the Appalachian Mountains on a monthly and yearly basis for labor. Enslaved women received lower monthly wages from the company than their male counterparts did.[41]

Contrasting with his stable investments, Starbuck experienced turmoil with his political associations and struggled to find a party to reflect his beliefs throughout the 1850s. In 1852 Starbuck attended North Carolina's Whig convention as a delegate, but the Whigs were in a weakened state by then and split into factions. Four years later he gravitated to the American Party, which sought to unite the conservative Whigs and pro-union Democrats. This faction differed from the Republican Party, which had abolitionists among its members and consequently little support in the southern slave states.[42]

During this time Starbuck participated in several transactions involving ownership of unfree laborers. As administrator for the estate of David King of Forsyth County, North Carolina, Starbuck facilitated the sale to the county of "One Negro Slave Charles" for $1,375 on August 1, 1853. After having bought land in Minnesota that year, Starbuck remained engaged in slavery. A church recorded him as owning a female slave as of October 1857: "Nancy Adelia, a single woman, property of Darius Starbuck." Also, he continued to handle transactions concerning slaves named in wills. In 1858, he offered for sale a deceased person's land and slaves. Advertising "14 Likely Negroes," Starbuck promised in his notice, "These are a CHOICE lot of NEGROES, and among which are some good COOKS and

NURSES." He did not add to his holdings through marriage; he married a northern woman from the free northern state Pennsylvania in 1853.[43]

Throughout the late 1850s, Starbuck struggled to find political organizations that supported both slavery and the cohesion of the Union. The American Party fell apart, but he moved on to the Opposition Party. At one of the Opposition's conventions, the delegates declared, "We yield to no portion of our fellow citizens in our determination to maintain our common rights in slave property, and this can be better effected within the Union than by its destruction." Starbuck and the party would have barely one year to plead for unity before his home state seceded from the Union to join the proslavery Confederate States of America.[44]

◆

The elite slaveholders who acquired land in Minnesota were not invested in developing the territory for the long term, but some of the planters attempted to maintain a physical presence in the Northwest without settling permanently there. In the 1850s, southerners' trips to Minnesota increasingly became seasonal excursions. A Minnesotan writing to a New Orleans newspaper remarked in 1857, "I was surprised on coming here to find so many southerners who have made Minnesota their permanent home, and the still greater number who have become largely interested in her future growth and prosperity and who reside here a part of the year." Some of the elite southerners who stayed temporarily in Minnesota made annual trips to the territory, and they arrived in the Northwest every spring or summer and departed in the fall or winter. Moreover, they conducted different businesses in Minnesota than in the South, and they essentially became bi-regional American commuters.[45]

CHAPTER FIVE

Commuters

In the mid-1850s, two enslaved women more than a thousand miles apart in the South were among many women who underwent extreme humiliation while realizing their worst fears: being sold on an auction block. One woman was in New Orleans, Louisiana, and the other was in Port Tobacco, Maryland. The auctioneers forced the women to strip bare, and potential buyers approached their potential purchases to thoroughly inspect their bodies. The customers checked for fresh and dried flesh wounds in the shape of whip lashes, for the number of markings showed how obedient the slaves were. The attendees also studied the human merchandise for signs of illness, trying to determine how many years of labor might be wrung from them. This particular method was not always foolproof, because some slaves avoided sale by pretending to be grossly ill. But the customers had no other means to decide on whom to buy.[1]

These two women were sold when their owners, Robert Dyson and Thomas B. Winston, took advantage of advancements in transportation to make a change in lifestyle. More steamboats began sailing between the South and the Northwest in the mid-1850s, and the frequency and affordable cost of the voyages allowed a new type of southern investor to emerge—the bi-regional commuter. This type of traveler differed from those of previous years in Minnesota. The presidential appointees may have typically left Minnesota during the winter months, but they eventually returned because of their appointments. Some elite planters, like Henry Dawson, would stay in Minnesota for summer vacations and not engage in any business ventures beyond real estate purchases, because they already received income from their plantations. In contrast, commuters such as

Dyson, Winston, Morgan May and his nephew Theobald Forstall, and former territorial secretary Joseph Travis Rosser started businesses in Minnesota and lived in the Northwest during the spring and summer to run
them, and they returned to the South to manage the interests they still
held there in the fall and winter. They remained southerners while actively
integrating themselves financially and socially in Minnesota.

As commuters, Winston, Dyson, May, Forstall, and Rosser sought as
much wealth as they could from the South and Minnesota at the same
time. Both places were equally important to them, and they divided their
time between their southern, slave-populated homes and their northwestern business offices. For some, these efforts reaped immediate professional dividends. Winston used his wealth from slave labor to ascend
quickly into the territory's business class, Dyson rose to prominence in
the territory's Democratic Party, and Rosser worked to regain footing in
that party. However, after all three men began spending more time in Minnesota and less time in the South, they decreased their personal inventory
of unfree laborers. As commuters, they relied less on slave labor than did
full-time southerners. Their laborers watched their slave communities
gradually disintegrate with sale after sale. Winston and Rosser started the
1850s holding slaves but ended the decade without them. Dyson inherited
enslaved people from his father in the mid-1850s but liquidated his holdings by 1860 as he engaged in cross-regional business endeavors. These
men could clearly see that the return on investment was greater in real
estate than enslaved labor.

◆

Born in 1811 in Henrico County, Virginia, Thomas B. Winston was one
of the oldest commuters between the South and Minnesota. He was well
into his forties when he decided to try a bi-regional lifestyle, but by then
he was already experienced in relocating and reestablishing himself professionally in new environments. In his early adulthood, he had left Virginia for New Orleans, where he worked as a merchant. Wealth from
slavery helped him to ascend into the upper class of his new hometown.
In 1837 he married into an elite slaveholding family in New Orleans; his
bride, Margaret Shall, was the daughter of George Shall, who held forty-
three slaves.[2]

Winston himself became a slaveholder before reaching the age of thirty,
and he used his wealth to punish anyone threatening his holdings. When

one of his slaves boarded a boat destined for New York, Winston sued the vessel's captain for $1,200—$400 for the cost of recovering his fugitive slave and $800 for the slave's value. By 1850 he owned twelve African Americans. At the time his family consisted of himself, his wife, and their daughter and two sons, so the household's composition averaged at least two slaves per Winston family member.[3]

He constantly bought and sold African Americans throughout the early 1850s. In January 1852 he offered for sale a twenty-five-year-old male "SUPERIOR House Servant" who had been with the family for ten years. The price was $1,200. In November he offered a "house servant for sale." In August 1853 he requested to buy "a Small Negro Boy . . . ten or twelve years of age," and he promised a "fair price" for "an extra smart one." After selling another slave early in 1854, he offered his twenty-two-year-old enslaved woman Frances and her two-year-old daughter for sale together for $1,800 in April. He called Frances a "first-rate General House servant, acclimated, and in fine health," and he claimed that she could earn between forty and fifty dollars per month as a hairdresser. Late in the year he bought another enslaved person, but then in early 1855 he sold one.[4]

He had a method to his constant buying and selling. He purchased pre-adolescent slaves like the "Small Negro Boy" but sold slaves in their twenties. Winston's child slaves stood a good chance of paying off well as investments. Their inability as infants and toddlers to work for him delayed the recouping of his investments in them, but they were worth more money as they became stronger and performed more labor while approaching adulthood. They attained their peak in monetary value when they reached their twenties, and Winston then sold them for a profit. By offering Frances and her daughter together, he showed some concern for maintaining family ties at his household. On the other hand, his purchases of children ripped them from their parents or adult caretakers on other plantations.

Winston left New Orleans in June 1855 to spend the summer and fall in Minnesota. Arriving in St. Paul by August, he immediately found his way into the state's power structure. He bought shares in the two-year-old St. Paul Mutual Insurance Company, and that month he attended a shareholders' meeting, held to elect the company's board of directors. Although new to Minnesota, Winston won election to the board. His fellow victors ran across the political spectrum, from the current Democratic governor Willis Gorman to St. Paul's Whig mayor (and Minnesota's past and future governor) Alexander Ramsey. They all were rich, and Winston became part of the network of Minnesota Territory's most economically and politically powerful people.[5]

Winston then joined a wave of investors buying and selling real estate in the territory in the mid-1850s, and some of his wealthy contemporaries were part of the trend. He became a shareholder in the new city of St. Peter, which Governor Gorman had helped to establish. He purchased an entire block and nine lots of various blocks in St. Peter in Nicollet County and acquired eighty acres in the former town of Centralia in adjacent Le Sueur County. Lots in the territory often sold at around a hundred dollars each. The sales of Winston's "SUPERIOR House Servant" and his mother-daughter pair—valued at a total of three thousand dollars—would have allowed him to buy about thirty lots.[6]

Winston spent the winter of 1855–56 in New Orleans, where he immediately resumed participation in the slave-trading business. A Mississippian placed an advertisement in the New Orleans *Daily Picayune* announcing, "I want to purchase a Cotton Plantation, Negroes, &c., situated on the Mississippi River, somewhere between Memphis and Vicksburg." The petitioner placed his name below the request, and below his name was that of "Thomas B. Winston." The new Minnesotan was brokering the transaction instead of buying slaves himself. He distinguished himself among his fellow Minnesotan elites by assisting in the purchasing of slaves after joining the territory's upper class.[7]

That same winter he tested the extent of his political influence in Minnesota Territory. He sent Mayor Ramsey a letter enclosing a "skeleton of a charter," and he praised his own draft as "beneficial to the Middle Classes or Men of small means in all our Western states." He wrote, "I hope you will have the charter get through the Legislature, & I will put the machinery in motion as soon as I return, if too much engaged hand it to some good influential member." Less than three months later, Minnesota Territory's legislature approved a proposal establishing the charter of the St. Peter Company, and Winston was named in the new law as one of the incorporators. He now had the attention not only of the territory's chief executive but also its lawmaking branch.[8]

The enslaver was still in New Orleans at the time of the bill's passage, but Winston returned with his family by boat to St. Paul in May 1856. Meanwhile, the *New Orleans Crescent* newspaper began printing advertisements in which he asked his fellow southerners to invest in Minnesota.

Winston touted the territory's growth, and he predicted even more after southerners began coming to St. Paul "either as a source of investment for the future, or as the great 'Summer Home' of health and recreation." He wrote that Minnesota's status as a territory contributed to its growth: "I suggest the propriety and public policy of our remaining a Territory for a few years, without manifesting too much eagerness to assume the mantle of State sovereignty. Our progress is rapid, but healthy and permanent, and we can afford to be called political infants, while we are enlarging and developing the bone and muscle which are to give us energy, vigor and power when we arrive at manhood."[9]

Before he left St. Paul for another winter in New Orleans, he invested in the new town of Nininger, which Mayor Ramsey's brother-in-law John Nininger had established. Advertisements in Minnesota's newspapers started promoting the new community during Winston's holiday in the South. In the meantime, his publicity for Minnesota continued to appear in the New Orleans press. In March 1857, when the Supreme Court's *Dred Scott* decision legalized slavery in Minnesota Territory, the verdict gave new

Nininger, Minnesota, about 1890

context for Winston's year-old arguments for Minnesota to delay statehood, because prolonged territorial status now meant prolonged legal slavery.[10]

Upon Winston's return to Minnesota that spring, he purchased forty acres in Scott County. However, his faith in real estate was soon shaken, for his two major land investments collapsed before the end of the year. The St. Peter Company lost an ambitious campaign for its city to become the territory's new capital, and the town of Nininger struggled to survive. Concerning the latter, Winston rallied his fellow investors in July, asking them to meet with him to discuss "the advancement of the town, if not . . . the profit of its 'original founders.'" But by September he had lost hope in the project, and he began writing lampoons of Nininger. That same month a devastating nationwide economic downturn—the Panic of 1857— further doomed his investments.[11]

After that traumatic year Winston spent less time in Minnesota. As his real estate plummeted in value, he faced personal losses. His daughter died in 1857, his wife passed away the following year, and his sons went to school in Germany. He still lauded Minnesota, placing a new advertisement about it for the New Orleans press in 1859 and purchasing forty acres in Anoka County in May that year. On the other hand, he left the state to travel to Europe that summer, and he returned to the United States to Missouri instead of Minnesota for health reasons. While recuperating he wrote his will, which asked that Alexander Ramsey—now the governor-elect of the new free state of Minnesota—serve as an executor of his property in Minnesota.[12]

◆

Morgan May was originally from England but immigrated to the United States in the early 1850s. He lived in New Orleans, where he invested in real estate in Louisiana and married the daughter of a slaveholder, thus joining the slave economy through matrimony. His bride on that day in 1853 was Louise Polk, and her father, Samuel W. Polk, had owned at least three slaves. Back in 1825 Polk had put three of his unfree laborers up for sale. One was twelve or thirteen years old, the second was fifteen, and the third was twenty-four; in the French-language notice, he bragged that the youngest excelled in housework—a "bonne servant de maison."[13]

May began commuting between Louisiana and Minnesota at around the same time as Winston. By 1856 May started living in Stillwater during

the spring and summer, and he brought some of his in-laws from New
Orleans to the Northwest. They also had ties to slavery, and their business enterprises in Stillwater further rooted the city in the ownership
of people. He partnered with his wife's nephew Theobald Forstall to operate a grocery store. At age twenty-six that year, Forstall was more than a
decade younger than May, but he had had to mature quickly. During his
childhood he, his siblings, and his parents had resided at his slaveholding
grandfather's estate. His parents and grandfather died between the time
Forstall was fifteen and nineteen years old, and he stayed at the estate
with his siblings and widowed grandmother until he began commuting
with May. In the summer of 1857, May took his wife, his mother, and
Forstall to the St. Croix Hotel in Stillwater, and the store, May & Forstall,
continued operating there.[14]

May's group of commuters changed significantly over the next two
years but stayed linked to slavery. In New Orleans in December 1857, his
wife died suddenly at age thirty-two. After one more season of business
in Stillwater in 1858, May gave up his share to Forstall, who then named
the enterprise solely after himself. Forstall engaged in Stillwater's affairs
by editing the city's Democratic newspaper and running a failed campaign for the recorder's office. While in New Orleans in the winter of
1858–59, Forstall married Anna Eliza Walton. Her parents owned slaves,
and one of them—a sixty-year-old woman named Rosina—had nursed the
bride in her infancy. When Forstall returned to Minnesota, he brought
Anna, her mother, and at least two slaves with him. Rosina, who had in-
sisted on joining the Forstalls and Anna's mother, was one of them.[15]

Minnesota existed as a free state when the Forstalls and Rosina disembarked from their boat to dry land at Stillwater, and the presence of the
slave generated controversy in town despite its long history of prominent
slaveholders. Some abolitionist women confronted Rosina soon after her
arrival and told her that her presence in a free state made her a free person, and they tried to convince her to exercise her legal emancipation by
abandoning the Forstalls. Rosina, however, angrily refused their sugges-
tion and threatened to scald them if they did not quickly flee her presence.[16]

Forstall nurtured a reputation in Stillwater as a supporter of slavery
through other means besides his ownership of Rosina. He penned proslavery editorials for the *Democrat*, and he ironically criticized democracy itself. As a rival newspaper later recalled, "Forstall was a monarchist

in principle and always contended that the people were not capable of self-government." In addition, he caught the attention of Minnesota governor Henry Sibley, who still managed some of Pierre Chouteau's land while in office. The governor appointed Forstall to serve on the state prison's board of inspectors in 1858.[17]

Forstall decided to leave the free state permanently in 1860 and return to New Orleans. In one of his last acts of public service, he participated in a jury in April that year. By then, Minnesota's residents had elected a Republican governor to replace Sibley, and public hostility to slavery increased statewide. As sectionalism grew, Forstall took his wife, his mother, and Rosina back to Louisiana, and Rosina consequently lost her legal freedom upon departing Minnesota. By the following January, Forstall joined a business in New Orleans and left Minnesota and Morgan May behind.[18]

◆

Robert Dyson of Maryland followed a different path than did May and Forstall, but he too became a part-time resident in Stillwater in these years. In 1850, when he was twenty-three, his widowed father—a medical doctor named Bennett Dyson—announced that his son had joined his medical practice in Nanjemoy, Maryland, as an associate. That same year Robert began his lifelong involvement in politics by attending his county's meeting of members of the Whig Party. Meanwhile, his sister Sarah married Nanjemoy resident Samuel W. Adams, and the groom involved himself in the affairs of the bride's extended family for years afterward.[19]

Also shaping Dyson was his family's involvement in slavery. Dyson's father became a large slaveholder in a short amount of time, doubling his holdings from fifteen slaves in 1830 to thirty-two in 1840. Ten years later, thirty-six slaves labored for the Dyson household. Dyson's sister married Adams that year and joined his household of fourteen slaves. Dyson himself, in contrast, seemed to distance himself from the practice. He married a Massachusetts-born woman named Ann Elizabeth "Agnes" Healy in Baltimore in October 1852; her parents still resided in the free state of Massachusetts.[20]

With his father's sudden death in 1855, Dyson became an instant enslaver. Not yet thirty years old, he assumed control of the family estate and became the head of the home and the family medical practice. With Adams's help, Dyson also managed the execution of his father's will. The document stipulated that Dyson was to inherit eleven of his father's slaves; the inheritance had a collective monetary value of more than four thousand dollars.[21]

Dyson spent the next year trying to establish himself in Maryland without his father's presence. In March 1856 the Maryland legislature named him as one of the founders of the Charles County Mutual Insurance Company, a business that included insurance policies on the lives of slaves. Ultimately he decided to leave Maryland. That November he announced that he would sell his 225-acre farm at a place called Eagle's Nest and most of his own personal property at the Nanjemoy estate on December 15—"Negroes excepted."[22]

Although the state of Maryland allowed for manumission, Dyson chose to keep some enslaved people and sell others. In February 1857 he advertised his intent to sell a "NEGRO MAN." However, a man named Edwin Adams wrote the notice, which suggested that Dyson was not in Nanjemoy at the time. Later that year Dyson's wife spent time in Minnesota, and he may have already left Maryland with her when the advertisement for the sale appeared in the local newspaper.[23]

Like Samuel W. Adams, Edwin held slaves, and both Adamses held strong views about the practice. While negotiating Dyson's slaveholding affairs, they volunteered to help the community of Nanjemoy deal with local issues concerning slavery. They joined the Mutual Self-Protecting Association of Nanjemoy, which proposed to intensely monitor the local free African American population and make sure that "all free negroes and mulattoes, now living in a state of idleness" began earning a living. If the ex-slaves could not prove that they made enough money to support themselves and reside in permanent homes, the committee saw fit to place them in slavery and to help law enforcement remove "free negro and mulatto children" from their impoverished families. Thus, the Adamses were more inclined to keep Dyson's slaves in bondage than to liberate them.[24]

While still holding on to his Nanjemoy home, Dyson set his sights on Minnesota Territory. By October 1857 his wife, Agnes, resided in Minneapolis with the Karns family, but Dyson chose not to extend the family's medical practice there. Instead he established a real estate agency in Minneapolis, and he promoted it in the newspaper of his hometown. As of April 1858, when he wrote the advertisement, slavery was still legal in Minnesota. Therefore, Dyson's notice had the potential to attract slaveholders in Charles County, Maryland, to purchase land in the territory.[25]

Dyson's advertisements, *Port Tobacco Times and Charles County Advertiser*, May 6, 1858. *Courtesy author*

In the newspaper issue publishing that advertisement, another notice from Dyson appeared directly below the one for his agency. It declared his intent to sell another of his slaves: "For Sale: A Young Likely NEGRO WOMAN will be offered at private sale during May Court in Port Tobacco." The announcement constituted one of the few times that a person who identified as a resident of Minnesota announced in print that he intended to sell any of his slaves in the South. The advertisement for Dyson's agency listed its location in Minneapolis. Whether or not other commuters conducted similar sales after establishing themselves in the Northwest, Dyson's openness about the sale illustrated how confident southerners felt about practicing slavery in the South while conducting business in Minnesota during the *Dred Scott* era.[26]

After May 1858 Dyson stopped promoting his real estate agency, and he severed his business ties to Minneapolis. He went to Maryland to sell his slave, but after returning to Minnesota later that year he resided not in Minneapolis but in Stillwater. Dyson resumed his medical practice, establishing an office in the Minnesota Hotel, on the same street as the grocery store of fellow Stillwater slaveholder Theobald Forstall. The doctor practiced homeopathy, whose popularity was spreading in New England at the time. He promoted his treatments in the *Stillwater Messenger* from October 1858 to November 1859.[27]

Dyson's presence in Stillwater increased the city's connections to slavery. He advertised his medical office in the *Messenger*, which also printed notices about Forstall's store. The antislavery newspaper was thus taking in money from slaveholders. Also, by practicing homeopathy in Stillwater, Dyson introduced the city to an alternative medical practice that slaveholders had recently started to apply to their slaves. Various plants were used as medicines from the Upper South in Maryland to the Deep South in Louisiana, where Samuel S. Boyd's planting partner Rice Ballard tried using homeopathy on slaves at some of his plantations.[28]

The doctor ingratiated himself successfully and quickly with Minnesota's Democratic Party. By the time he relocated to Stillwater, Minnesota was transitioning into statehood. The change in status meant that the federal government would no longer choose Minnesota's leadership, and the new state outlawed slavery within its borders. For supporters of slavery in Minnesota, the Democratic Party best reflected their interests. Although no Minnesotans actively pushed for legal slavery in the state, local Democrats encouraged their fellow residents to allow southerners interested in northwestern investments to keep slaves during their stays in the state. With the offices of governor and lieutenant governor in contention in 1859, Minnesota's Democratic Party held a convention that year to choose its candidates. Dyson attended the meeting as a delegate from Washington County.[29]

Republicans won the state election, and by 1860 Dyson and his wife were back in Nanjemoy. With no home of their own in Maryland, they lived with the Adamses. The Dysons held no slaves when they returned to the South, but they did not have to do so. Adams alone kept thirty-eight enslaved people in 1860—more than Dyson's father had ever claimed. In a sense, Dyson's resettlement in Maryland was a return to the large-scale slavery he had seen in his youth on an even grander scale. Later in 1860 a newspaper in Port Tobacco published Adams's call for an overseer who was experienced in "the management of negroes."[30]

◆

After the humiliating political defeat inflicted by his fellow Democrats in August 1857, former territorial secretary Joseph Travis Rosser effectively became a commuter. He went back to his home state of Virginia from time to time over the next year for various reasons. As of September 1857, he still resided in St. Paul, according to the territorial census. However, in November Rosser arrived at Brown's Hotel in Washington, DC, and he remained on the East Coast through the winter months. He stayed busy in the nation's capital and discussed territorial matters with officials there. On February 11, 1858, he testified to Congress about land sales in Minnesota.[31]

Exactly three months later, in May 1858, Minnesota officially achieved statehood, and it entered the Union as a free state. Rosser's proslavery views had no legal support there anymore. Nevertheless, the slaveholding Virginian remained committed to reestablishing himself professionally in the Northwest. He left Virginia again for Minnesota and arrived in St. Paul in June. "It looked like old times yesterday morning," a newspaper wistfully reported. Rosser seemed to have goodwill remaining among some Minnesotans since the paper noted, "We were glad to welcome him."[32]

On the other hand, Minnesotans had not only moved on from Rosser's proslavery politics but also gravitated toward the very politics he bitterly and violently opposed. Morton Wilkinson, whom the former secretary had pummeled in a fistfight, mounted a campaign for the US Senate in 1858, and he won the election that fall. Rosser did not run against him, but Wilkinson's victory among Minnesotans meant a symbolic rejection of Rosser's besting of him in fisticuffs for the honor of the South. After all, Wilkinson won the same office for which Rosser could not even receive a nomination from his fellow Democrats.

Rosser left St. Paul for the winter but returned to Minnesota months later to start a new life once more. In a departure from his previous six summers in Minnesota, he left behind his longtime northwestern home of St. Paul to try his luck in another community. In April 1859 the *Belle Plaine Enquirer* referred to the town of Mankato in Blue Earth County as Rosser's "new home," and he resumed his law practice and moved his law library there. Meanwhile, he reentered local politics by redefining himself as a private resident of a free state instead of a slaveholding federal employee. At the urging of some local Democratic and Republican newspapers, he entered that year's congressional race.[33]

A hoped-for victory promised the best of both worlds for him: the chance to return to political prominence in Minnesota while living near his family in Virginia whenever Congress met. Local Democrats, however, were underwhelmed with the former secretary, and Mankato's newspaper did not even announce his candidacy. He participated in Blue Earth County's Democratic convention that year, but he lost the party's nomination for Congress to a popular Irish American named Jim Cavanaugh. Having failed to receive his party's support for the second time in two years, Rosser never ran for public office in Minnesota again.[34]

The Democrats had a problematic relationship with Rosser by the time he ran against Cavanaugh. The former secretary remained sensitive to slights, and by 1859 he violently defended himself against fellow Democrats. Early in the year, he and a fellow Democrat named William J. Cullen argued about a local political figure while aboard the steamboat *Frank Steele*. Cullen called Rosser a "dirty dog," and the former secretary punched him in the face before waiters broke up the fight.[35]

More humiliation awaited Rosser and his fellow Democrats before the end of the year. His foes were on their political ascent. In October 1859 voters elected Republicans to serve as governor and lieutenant governor. Republicans also won all of the elections in Blue Earth County, which meant that Cavanaugh lost the congressional race to Republican opponent William Windom. The former secretary was now a member of the state's minority party, and its decline had just begun.[36]

Rosser still had enough political clout to attend the state's Democratic convention as a delegate in January 1860. However, he caused divisiveness during the proceedings when he proposed that former governor Willis Gorman, as president of the state party, nominate Stephen Douglas— a moderate candidate on the issue of slavery—for president on behalf of the entire state party. The half of the members opposing slavery left the convention in protest. Those who remained chose Rosser as one of the delegates for that year's national convention. The division at the state convention, however, was merely part of the party's discord nationwide.[37]

At the national convention held in Charleston, South Carolina, some southern delegates who held strong proslavery views recoiled at the presence of Douglas and his supporters. He had spoken out against possible

secession by southern states from the Union, and his position angered the
"fire-breathers" of that region. Consequently, at the convention he lacked
the two-thirds vote needed to win the nomination. The party met in Baltimore six weeks later to try to secure a nomination, but Douglas's certain
victory there prompted delegates from the Deep South to abandon the
meeting and nominate fellow southerner and vice president John C. Breckinridge later in Virginia.[38]

Rosser, however, was not part of the group that split from Douglas.
Despite the former secretary's hair-trigger temper, he agreed with the candidate's moderate stance on slavery. Rosser attended the Douglas Democratic convention session of August 30 in Raleigh, North Carolina. He gave
a speech near the end of the proceedings, criticizing the party's secessionists and praising Douglas. By doing so, he was breaking not only from
fellow southerners but also from Breckinridge, who, like Rosser, was a
southern investor in Minnesota's real estate. Rosser's role as convention
delegate marked the last time that he would politically represent Minnesota in any capacity.[39]

After the Charleston convention, Rosser stayed in the South and returned
to Virginia. Minnesota was a solidly Republican state, and he lost considerable political leverage by dividing the state's Democrats. In leaving
Minnesota for South Carolina, he abandoned his property in Minnesota
and the people to whom he owed money. People had given him small
loans throughout his years in the Northwest, and they saw his extended
departure from Minnesota as an opportunity for repayment. They seized
his belongings from his Mankato home and sold them all—down to the
Cenci painting Alexander Wilkin had gifted him in 1853.[40]

Thomas B. Winston, Morgan May, Theobald Forstall, Robert Dyson,
and Joseph Travis Rosser achieved varying degrees of professional success as slaveholding commuters. Winston managed to become part of
the elite in both the South and the Northwest, but he had labored since
1855 to appeal to Minnesotans. May and Forstall found success as grocers
in Stillwater, but locals were wary of the slaves they brought with them.
Dyson achieved remarkable political success in Minnesota in a shorter
time than Winston, but the doctor did not have the same relationships
with powerful state leaders that Winston had. Rosser, meanwhile, had once
been a powerful leader in Minnesota and knew the state's leaders on professional and personal levels, but he never became Minnesotan enough
to win over the state's voters in elections. He was too openly proslavery,

and his violent defenses of the South and his constant attempts to retain power transformed him from a potential Democratic leader to a desperate opportunist.

Henry M. Rice, now a former Chouteau & Company employee, by the mid-1850s had figured out how to become a non-slaveholding Democratic leader in Minnesota while remaining loyal to proslavery Democrats. He made no attempt to introduce legal slavery to the Northwest, but he encouraged slaveholders to invest there. Some of the property they bought came from Rice himself, and he continued to enrich himself from slaveholders for years after leaving Chouteau's firm. As Minnesota developed and grew with dollars from plantations, Rice received the credit for the state's new cities and expanding communities. Moreover, he managed to do so while commuting between Minnesota and Washington, DC— without throwing a single punch.

CHAPTER SIX

Rice's Network

After Henry M. Rice left Chouteau & Company in October 1849, he no longer depended on the St. Louis slaveholders in the partnership for income. Rice retained his trading post, and the Winnebago Outfit's agent Sylvanus Lowry also quit Chouteau's firm to stay under Rice's supervision at the post. As an independent entrepreneur, Rice continued to foster business relationships with people associated with the slave trade.[1]

He built a hotel, the American House, in 1849, which earned a reputation among other St. Paul hotels for welcoming southerners. Levi Dolbear, his wife, and their four children arrived from Natchez in November 1854 and stayed through the winter. Dolbear invested in three hundred acres near St. Paul, and the following spring he started advertising property for sale in Natchez newspapers. His agent, named in the notice, was Natchez resident L. M. Patterson. Dolbear's associate not only held slaves but also actively sold them while working for him, and Patterson occasionally hosted slave auctions at his "auction store." Just above Dolbear's advertisement in one newspaper was an announcement by Patterson of an upcoming private sale of "two LIKELY NEGRO WOMEN, good field hands, acclimated, and fully guaranteed."[2]

Dolbear returned to Minnesota in the next year for another visit, and he sent another advertisement from St. Paul to Mississippi, expressing more confidence in his business. "Permit me to call your attention to the great inducements which the growing prosperity of this city and territory presents to capitalists for investment," he began. "Having examined most of the land in and about Saint Paul, I flatter myself that I am able to make

Henry M. Rice, about
1863

good and lucrative investments." Among his slaveholding references were
New Orleans resident H. S. Buckner, Natchez citizens F. A. W. Davis and
Frederick Stanton, and banking brothers Joshua and Thomas Green of
Jackson, Mississippi. Another reference—the firm Calcote & Pollock—
sold slaves and other merchandise; it offered "two likely Negro men, good
cotton pickers and fully acclimated" for sale in 1854. Dolbear's most pres-
tigious reference was Mississippi's former governor John A. Quitman,
who held almost four dozen slaves at his home in Natchez and more than
one hundred elsewhere in the state.[3]

Despite Dolbear's enthusiasm, few southerners traveled to Minnesota
in the early 1850s, and even fewer were as wealthy as Chouteau and his
slaveholding partners, whose Minnesota land investments were handled
by Henry Sibley. Without accessibility to powerful enslavers, Rice could
not develop his own proslavery business network in any way that matched
or surpassed that of his former employer. In 1849 he gained his only
prominent relationship with a slaveholder, through marriage. That year

he agreed to give money to his mother-in-law, Rachel Whitall, to help her settle a matter of "very great necessity." Her husband, Rice's father-in-law, was a yeoman master, holding only one slave—a fifteen-year-old boy.[4]

But Rice sought business relationships with enslavers beyond his wife's family in order to maintain his prominence in Minnesota, and he found them in the US Congress. Slaveholders from the slave states served in the House and the Senate, and many of them were among the elite planters of their states if not of the entire country. As a territory Minnesota did not have a senator or representative; a delegate elected by territorial residents represented them in Congress. Minnesota's delegate lacked some of the privileges of senators and congressmen, but serving in the position allowed one to interact with multiple powerful slaveholders, all in the Capitol with him at the same time.

Rice's old American Fur rival Henry Sibley had served as delegate ever since the establishment of Minnesota Territory in 1849. Rice had failed to wrest the position from him in the 1850 territorial election. In 1852 Sibley vacated the office and made an unsuccessful bid for governor, and Rice ran again for the position of delegate as the Democratic Party's candidate. He handily defeated his opponent Alexander Wilkin, representing the Whig Party. The winner rode a wave of Democratic electoral victories, which culminated in the election of Franklin Pierce to the presidency. Pierce would also select Democrats for land offices and the executive branch of Minnesota Territory in 1853.[5]

When Rice arrived in Washington, DC, to serve in Congress, slavery became more visible to him, unavoidably. For the first time in his life, he lived for an extended period of time in an area that legally permitted slavery. More than 3,600 slaves resided in Washington, constituting six percent of the city's population. In contrast, Minnesota was a free territory with a much smaller slave population; the territory itself was so small that the number of Washington's slaves was about half of Minnesota's entire population. As a result, slavery must have become more remote and abstract to Rice whenever a congressional session ended and he returned to the Northwest.[6]

Enslaved people were present in multiple aspects of Rice's everyday life in the District. They were sold there, and they walked in chains through the city from the slave states of Maryland, Delaware, and Virginia to markets farther south. As the free population grew, slaves became increasingly unhappy with their enslavement, and Rice could witness firsthand the desperate condition of people from whose labor he indirectly profited. On any given day, residents could witness enslavers beating and whipping enslaved people in the streets of Washington. They worked all over the city—laboring in restaurants, aboard carriages as drivers, and in the homes of Rice's congressional colleagues. The slaveholders coming to his Washington home for parties may have had slaves drive them there and then wait outside his estate in their coaches until the festivities ended hours later. Any slaveholders he invited to his Minnesota home may have brought one or two body servants or nurses on the trip with them.[7]

After his inauguration Rice successfully sold land to his new slaveholding colleagues in Congress, and with their money he contributed to the development of many of Minnesota's institutions. With his election, Rice began to meet enslavers of the Old South—comfortable, wealthy people who were at least second-generation masters instead of cautious and risk-averse newcomers to slavery. Rice almost exclusively invited people who had inherited slaves from their parents to spend some of their vast riches on Minnesota, and he helped to connect the territory to massive plantations that had already exploited slave labor for generations.

As a former agent of the fur trade, Rice had worked with both northerners and southerners. His fellow agents were other northerners without slaves, and his employers were the enslavers of Chouteau & Company. Moreover, his electoral victory demonstrated significant support from his non-slaveholding northwestern constituents. Therefore, Rice made a deliberate choice in developing business associations with slaveholders after becoming a delegate. His own ties to slavery may have endeared him to his southern colleagues in Washington. His marriage to an enslaver's daughter was four years strong by 1853. Above all else, he was a Democrat, and his abstention from slavery did not clash with his endorsement of the party's extension of slavery into territories such as Minnesota. Thus, he had tremendous potential to cultivate relationships with slaveholding legislators.

Representative James L. Orr of South Carolina was an obvious choice for Rice to befriend. He was raised in a modest slaveholding household; his parents possessed at least eighteen slaves during his early childhood. As an adult he held fourteen slaves in his home state as of 1850, and he acquired at least five more over the next ten years. As Rice entered Congress in early 1853, Orr took on the leadership of the House Committee on Indian Affairs. Consequently, the southerner had to familiarize himself with the areas where Indigenous nations lived, which included Minnesota.

Rice facilitated a land transaction for Orr, whom he called "a gentleman of the highest standing in our party and one that I am desirous of
obliging." He wrote to a federal official to arrange "land warrants for 160
acres . . . assigned to Hon. Jas. L. Orr of South Carolina."[8]

Two of Rice's congressional colleagues from Kentucky—John Breckinridge and Beriah Magoffin—visited Minnesota Territory. While on
an extended stay in 1854, the two became "purchasers of property," as a
St. Paul–based newspaper put it. The paper noted that October, "These
gentlemen have been with us but a brief period, and propose to make, at
present, only a brief stay." However, the announcement presented the
Kentuckians' purchases of land as beneficial events for the territory. "Min-
nesotians have reason to be glad when they receive such accessions,"
beamed the newspaper.[9]

James L. Orr, between
1855 and 1865. *Library
of Congress, Prints &
Photographs Division*

Rice's wife, Matilda, played an important role in wooing his southern colleagues to the Northwest. She welcomed slaveholders into the Rice home in Minnesota while he was away in Washington, DC. Charles W. Pairo, who held a slave in the nation's capital, took his extended family with him to pay a visit to Matilda in 1853, and she recorded their stay in a letter to her husband: "I intended writing you last week the news of the election, but a house full of company prevented me. Mr. Paro [sic], his sister, niece and sister-in-law spent nearly a week with me." Taking pride in her talents as an entertainer, she reported, "They were delighted with the country and thought me a remarkable housekeeper."[10]

Rice's facilitating of northwestern real estate transactions for slave-holding colleagues had political ramifications. As Rice convinced his fellow legislators that free territories possessed great monetary value, they were seeking ways of opening areas that prohibited slavery to wealthy masters like themselves. Although the Missouri Compromise of 1820 had banned slavery in Kansas and Nebraska, southerners in Congress successfully pressed for a new law allowing residents of those territories to decide for themselves whether to enter the Union as free states or slave states. One of the few northern supporters of the Kansas-Nebraska Act was Rice, and his advocacy further aligned him to the slaveholding wing of the Democratic Party—the wing that he recruited for real estate in his own free territory. Thanks in part to Rice's efforts, the federal government negated its own thirty-four-year-old protection in the North against slavery, and Minnesota suddenly became vulnerable to entering the Union as a slave state.[11]

◆

Rice's association with slaveholders tainted all of his business ventures with money from slavery. He was a powerful and popular figure in St. Paul, where he donated some of the land for what became Rice Park and established several enterprises. These businesses combined with his land interests there to tie the territorial capital's economy to payments from slaveholders. He provided funding to keep the *St. Paul Daily Democrat* afloat and countering the point of view of the competing *Pioneer*, which his rival Democrat Henry Sibley funded. In 1853, Rice was also an incorporator of the St. Paul Mutual Insurance Company, as was his former Chouteau & Company colleague Charles W. Borup, and slaveholding commuter Thomas B. Winston joined the company in 1855.[12]

During that same year, members of the growing Republican Party in Minnesota sought to replace Rice in Congress. The party, which opposed the extension of slavery to territories, portrayed him as a supporter of slavery. That year a Republican candidate named William R. Marshall unsuccessfully tried to unseat Rice. A local pro-Republican newspaper argued that a vote for Rice was a vote for the Democrats who supported the Kansas-Nebraska Act and its possible extension of slavery to territories. On the other hand, a vote for Marshall was a vote "to confine slavery to its legitimate limits, and never to let it spread one-eighth of an inch in Territory now free." (The Republicans' support for prohibition did not earn them many votes from the German immigrants who were flooding into the territory, and that issue may have been more powerful in determining the election's outcome.)[13]

In any case, Marshall also had a tie to slavery. He was the son of a yeoman slaveholder in Boone County, Missouri. His parents held one slave in 1830, when Marshall was five years old. Soon thereafter the family moved to Illinois, and they stopped owning slaves. Marshall's family, therefore, had no operating connections to slavery when he relocated to Minnesota in the early 1850s and when he began serving as the University of Minnesota's first librarian in 1851. Slavery's history among even Minnesota's Republican candidates demonstrated the extent of the practice among the territory's early residents.[14]

Rice's relationship with slaveholding congressman William Aiken Jr. of South Carolina proved beneficial for territorial higher education. In the summer of 1856, Rice arranged for Aiken to purchase a bond for the University of Minnesota, thus linking a slaveholder financially to the territorial government. Aiken bought $14,925 in bonds, $10,000 of which went to the university's building contractor.[15]

With his investment Aiken stood to help alleviate the school's poor condition. The University of Minnesota was not much to look at in 1856. The territory had closed it two years earlier, and it had only been in operation between 1851 and 1854. The university moved to a new site in 1854, and it began building a new facility—Old Main—on that land. However, construction of the building cost more money than the university's facilitators possessed, and the extended period of construction exacerbated the institution's debt. Old Main remained unfinished in 1856, but the territorial legislature permitted the university to issue $40,000 in bonds. Aiken's loan, therefore, constituted more than 40 percent of the $36,200 raised.[16]

For the benefactor, becoming a slaveholder was a rite of passage. One day in his early adulthood, William Aiken sailed with his father and namesake on a river near Charleston. Enslaved oarsmen navigated the increasingly swampy water while bringing the father and son to a marshy island in the river. The slaves stopped the boat, and the father directed his son's attention to the five-thousand-acre land mass in front of them. The senior Aiken then announced the island—named Jehossee—as a gift to the junior Aiken, saying, "Here are the means; now go to work and develop them." The son did just that, assuming total control of the island by 1830.[17]

Aiken transformed Jehossee into a thriving rice plantation and became the largest slaveholder in the state. He spent $13,000 yearly to maintain

William Aiken Jr., between 1855 and 1865. *Library of Congress, Prints & Photographs Division*

his plantation and populated the island with more than seven hundred slaves. The master quartered his slaves in plain, wooden houses, reserving an enormous Gothic Revival mansion for himself and his family. The slaves took care of more than two hundred animals and grew two thousand bushels of corn and four thousand bushels of sweet potatoes per year. The slaves' work on the 1,600 acres of Jehossee reserved for rice cultivation annually earned $50,000 in sales of rice. The island lay on a waterway that provided access not only to Charleston, South Carolina, but also to Savannah, Georgia, thus giving Aiken ease of shipping to multiple markets.[18]

Aiken attempted to encourage community among his laborers while enslaving them. He encouraged marriages between enslaved couples, although none of the unions were legally binding. On the other hand, he did not provide complete liberation, and some slaves rejected their enslavement in preference for freedom. One of Aiken's fugitive servants reached New Hampshire, according to a South Carolina newspaper, and was still "in hot haste for Canada."[19]

Remote and swampy Jehossee lay sixty miles away from Aiken's home in Charleston, where he kept still more slaves. His three-story Charleston mansion housed an art gallery, among other things, and its grounds comprised an entire city block, with kitchens, stables, a shelter for the carriage, slaves' living quarters, and an open work area. Aiken's holdings of slaves at the mansion, largely working as domestic laborers, more than doubled from seven in 1850 to nineteen in 1860.[20]

Aiken's slaves at Jehossee and Charleston provided the wealth that enabled his investment in the University of Minnesota, which in turn helped to expand and resurrect the university. Builders added a fourth floor to the lone campus building in late 1857, and a local newspaper grandly predicted: "This edifice will be one of the most magnificent granite structures in the whole north west." The school then reopened in 1858. The New York Herald saw Aiken's interest in northwestern investment as a gesture of intersectional goodwill. A writer for the newspaper expressed hope that such purchases between the North and the South would decrease feelings of sectionalism or "dissolution excitement."[21]

Not everyone was pleased with Aiken's loan. Critics of southerners' investment in the Northwest did not distinguish his philanthropy from other southerners' purchases of real estate. To opponents, Aiken and others were greedy opportunists, not content making money only in the South.

The *Hinds County Gazette* in Raymond, Mississippi, said that southern investors should invest in the South, which needed the money to stay independent of the North. Similarly, the *Freeman's Champion* of Prairie City, Kansas, said that southern investment in the Northwest revealed that slavery was not as profitable as southerners had claimed. Otherwise, why would they invest outside of the South?[22]

By the fall of 1856, Minnesota's press was paying attention to the slaveholders staking their claims to the territory. The *Minnesota Pioneer and Democrat*, the new paper supported by Rice, identified Aiken and Breckinridge among the "many prominent parties [who] have made desirable locations in the immediate neighborhood" in St. Paul. Reporters did not express concern about the presence of the investors, because they did not see legal slavery as a likely outcome of the investments. Nevertheless, the identification by the local papers of Aiken and Breckinridge as St. Paulites showed that Rice's slaveholding network in Minnesota had begun gaining traction.[23]

◆

For several weeks in late 1856 and early 1857, newspapers in New York reported alleged bribery and corruption concerning congressional land schemes. One congressman would call for a *New York Times* reporter to be fired for his January 9, 1857, report, but then Representative Robert Treat Paine of North Carolina said that a colleague had offered him a $1,500 bribe to vote in favor of a bill about land in Minnesota. Paine said he would name the colleague if the House formed a committee to study the paper's charges. It did so, and South Carolina's James L. Orr was one of the two Democrats named to the committee.[24]

Rice, who considered Orr an advocate for the interests of the Northwest, was concerned about the negative press coverage and for good reason: he stood to lose the confidence of his slaveholding acquaintances in their investments. He wrote to the enslaver early in 1857 to seek his assistance in spreading goodwill about Minnesota—and to complain: "Dear Sir, In consequence of false reports having been spread over the country in regard to Minnesota Land Bills, the reputation of the Territory and her citizens has received an injury almost incurable." In reference to a report that Congress was preparing about the controversy, Rice suggested, "I would therefore respectfully submit to you, if in the report about to be made (should the charge that has been made not be true), that it should fully vindicate the territory and her citizens, this to me appears to be the only course left in which reparation can be made." He concluded by lamenting, "Should a doubt remain as to the course pursued by our citizens, I cannot expect, neither do I desire, that my request be entertained. Very Respectfully and Truly Yours, H. M. Rice."[25]

That committee found that the reporter James W. Simonton had acted "recklessly," and it called for his firing. It resolved that Representative Orsamus B. Matteson of New York be expelled from the House of Representatives for corruption concerning land in Des Moines, Iowa. Representative Francis S. Edwards of New York was expelled for having tried to bribe Paine concerning land for a railroad in Minnesota in December 1856. William W. Welch of Connecticut was also expelled, for corruption in another matter. No Minnesota resident was involved in corruption, and the territory was indeed vindicated.[26]

Rice's slaveholders occasionally made unfortunate business decisions. Orr invested in the ill-fated town project of Nininger. He was not alone as a slaveholding shareholder; George Clitherall and Thomas Winston had also sent their plantation dollars toward the cause. Nininger's failure did not affect Rice, because he had not invested heavily in it despite solicitations from its founders. Also, Nininger's founder, Ignatius Donnelly, primarily drew supporters from Whigs and Republicans like himself. Nevertheless, the town's struggles showed at least one of Rice's supporters that investments in Minnesota Territory were not guaranteed to pay off.[27]

Still, as a Democrat, Orr prioritized party loyalty over loyalty to region. In late 1857 he publicly lauded his party's northern members for their work in expanding slavery in recent years. In a letter to a colleague, he credited northern Democrats with helping southern slaveholding Democrats in passing the Kansas-Nebraska Act and therefore "establishing the doctrine of non-intervention with Slavery by Congress." He hoped that the northerners would also assist slaveholders in making Kansas a slave state.[28]

◆

Henry Rice's network of slaveholders evolved in the late 1850s. He retained his relationships with slaveholding congressmen after his term as delegate expired in 1857, but his absence from Washington, DC, made him more reliant on visitors to Minnesota. In addition, the resignations of Aiken and Breckinridge from Congress in 1857 left Rice without two powerful southern advocates for Minnesota's interests. Fortunately for the former delegate, he still owned the American House hotel, and it continued to attract southerners. George Mendenhall's nephew R. J. Mendenhall traveled from North Carolina to stay there as he started recruiting southerners to Minnesota.[29]

Some southerners in Congress offered support for Minnesota's development throughout the 1850s after Rice's term ended, and he rewarded them for their gestures. He arranged for Minnesota counties to be named after Breckinridge (although it was spelled "Breckenridge") and Robert Toombs of Georgia. Toombs had purchased land in Minnesota by the time he was the lone southern senator to side with northerners to approve the bill to admit Minnesota into statehood in the spring of 1857. On March 18, 1858, Minnesota established Toombs County (later renamed Wilkin County) and Breckenridge County (later renamed Clay County). Both of these supporters were raised by slaveholding parents and, therefore, had Old South money and influence to invest in the territory.[30]

Rice could do only a limited amount of work to bring southerners to Minnesota, especially while out of Congress. Therefore, to nurture his network of masters, he started buying land in the nation's capital and selling it to his slaveholding colleagues there. In the middle of 1857, Breckinridge and Rice joined with Stephen Douglas to invest in real estate in Washington. Each of the three built a house on that land, planning to live in their new homes while working in the city as elected officials. Breckinridge sold a woman and her child for $1,100 in November 1857, while the homes—later dubbed Minnesota Row—remained under construction. Thus, money from human trafficking helped to fund one of Rice's investments during his public service to Minnesota.[31]

Some of his former colleagues continued to invest money in Minnesota, even when out of office. In the summer of 1857, both Aiken and Orr traveled to the territory again. Aiken had just completed nearly twenty years of public service—from South Carolina's legislature and governorship to the US House of Representatives—and suddenly had the time to travel. Like other tourists of means, he lodged at the Fuller House, an opulent hotel in St. Paul. From there he took a short trip to visit the Falls of St. Anthony. The falls were a popular, cooling tourist attraction for southerners suffering from summer heat.[32]

Orr, on the other hand, remained an active congressman, and he helped Rice to enlarge his network of enslavers while in office that summer. The congressman visited Minnesota Territory with a fellow South Carolinian named Augustus M. Smith. In July they bought eight lots in Stearns County from John Wilson in lower St. Cloud. Slaveholders had bought much of the northern part of St. Cloud the previous year, so the purchases by Orr and Smith brought a greater portion of the city under slaveholding ownership. The two South Carolinians also acquired twenty lots in Benton County, thus enriching Sauk Rapids's Democratic leader George W. Sweet. In all, they invested $4,300 while on the trip.[33]

By involving Smith in the purchases, Orr linked central Minnesota with one of South Carolina's most politically powerful planters and one of the state's largest slaveholders. Smith had been raised in South Carolina's elite planter class and had witnessed the family's growth in wealth during his teenage years and early adulthood. His father served in the South Carolina legislature and on the board of a local railroad. The elder Smith's holdings in slaves doubled from fifty-four in 1840 to 110 in 1850, and he still held slaves at his death in 1855. As an adult, the younger Smith kept 135 slaves at his home in Abbeville County, thus continuing his father's tradition of large, elite planting. He also helped sell off eighty of his late father's "Cooks, House Servants, Seamstresses, Blacksmiths, and first-rate Field Hands" at a public auction.[34]

Smith saw land acquisition as a means to expand his wealth, and he purchased real estate in the South as well as in Minnesota. In 1859 he bought five thousand acres in Jefferson County, Arkansas, and organized them into two plantations. He purchased the Good Hope Plantation in Orangeburg, South Carolina, but moved all of its slaves to his two new Arkansas plantations, placing about fifty slaves at each of the Jefferson County locations the following year, thus bringing his total holdings of slaves to around 250. He acquired an enslaved boy named Westley from his mother's estate that year. Smith turned thirty-three years old in 1860, making him one of the youngest slaveholders in Rice's network.[35]

In eastern Arkansas, where rivers provided fertile soil, youth was no detriment to acquisition of wealth for any planter wanting to pursue it. European American men in their twenties became rich after establishing their plantations in that part of the state, and the riches could grow exponentially in as little as two years. This trend took place in the 1840s and 1850s, and Smith caught the end of the plantation boom. Nevertheless, he nearly matched his South Carolina holdings of slaves in Arkansas after barely one year.[36]

Smith's slaves suffered from the relocation. At the time, no railroad line directly connected Orangeburg to Jefferson County, Arkansas, and no boat could travel from South Carolina's coast to landlocked Arkansas. As a result, the Good Hope slaves likely spent part if not all of their journey in coffles, fastened together. While the specifics are not known, the circumstances of such travel have often been described. Men, women, and children were chained together and forced to walk, led by guides on horseback. The slaves reluctantly soiled and wet themselves while walking and were denied bathing privileges day after day. If they boarded a railroad car that took them part of the way, they sat packed tightly together and suffered each other's stench. Upon arrival in Jefferson County, Arkansas, they would have been given a chance to bathe—but only to prepare them to start work.[37]

Smith acquired a young, strong, and resilient slave community when he bought the Good Hope slaves. They were a close-knit unit because their family ties at the plantation extended to the eighteenth century. Nine-tenths of the slaves were under fifty years old, and a third were children under ten. Therefore, nearly all of the slaves had reached their peak of monetary worth or would eventually attain it. Also, the slave couples had durable relationships and produced large families, but most of the families began with births from teenage girls.[38]

As of 1860, Smith was as rich in land as in slaves. His real estate possessions totaled $200,000 in value, and his personal estate reached $250,000. His Arkansas slaves especially were a gold mine for him. The average price of an individual slave in that state more than doubled from $485 to $1,000 through the 1850s, and a skilled slave could sell for as much as $2,000. Thus, Smith established plantations in Arkansas at exactly the most opportune time for him. Meanwhile, the lots he co-owned with Orr in Minnesota comprised part of the $200,000 in real estate, and he gave the territory one of its few financial links to Arkansas.[39]

Orr, Aiken, and Smith were part of the wave of southerners visiting Minnesota Territory immediately following the US Supreme Court's *Dred Scott* decision of March 1857. With the new legalization of slavery in the territory, more enslavers traveled northwest that year than in 1856. The post-verdict uptick reflected a greater sense of ease among slaveholders about spending time in Minnesota and their willingness to diversify their holdings of land beyond the South. Twice as many slaveholding investors bought land in St. Cloud in 1857 as in 1856. Also, although no enslavers purchased lots in McLeod and Scott Counties in 1856, some of them did in 1857.[40]

While in Minnesota with Orr and Smith in mid-1857, Aiken reportedly cashed eight thousand dollars of his bond with the university. The transaction marked one of the few times that a public institution in Minnesota directly paid a slaveholder. The interest he earned on his investment helped support him, his family, and his plantation. Some of what the University of Minnesota repaid him went toward renovating his mansion in Charleston.[41]

Aiken's withdrawal amounted to half of his bond, thus still leaving about seven thousand dollars for the university's continued use. But because the school did not receive enough funding from tuition fees to remain open, the institution operated for just six months in 1858 before closing again. Further, the investor was both lucky and unlucky in his timing. He pulled out half his money just a couple of months before a national financial calamity—the Panic of 1857. The economic recession that followed lasted well into 1859. The university's reopening was in jeopardy—and so was the remainder of Aiken's loan.[42]

The country's rebound from the economic panic did not help. The school made embarrassing national news in 1859 for hemorrhaging money via construction. The completion of one wing of the campus building cost $49,000, but two-thirds of the edifice was yet unfinished. "This costly structure is going to ruin, no care being taken of the premises," complained one reporter, "all the doors being wide open, and the snow has drifted into the building and melts on warm days through the floors." Aiken's hometown newspaper called the facility "a melancholy ruin."[43]

Nevertheless, Rice found another person with ties to slavery to invest in the university. In 1853, as an adolescent, Isabel Kall of Washington, DC, had visited Rice's wife, Matilda, with her mother and slaveholding uncle in Minnesota. Having become a wealthy woman in her early twenties as of 1857, she purchased a university bond of seven thousand dollars. While her transaction supplied most of the money that Aiken would retrieve, the university now owed money to two benefactors of slave wealth.[44]

◆

Rice's political power as a delegate served his network well, but his coalition suffered in his absence from Congress in 1857. His previous recruits returned to Minnesota that year, and the *Dred Scott* decision gave southern trade in Minnesota new life. But Rice's successor as delegate, although a fellow Democrat, did not nurture relationships with congressional slaveholders during his time in office. The Democrats in federal positions in Minnesota Territory were appointed by President Buchanan, whose candidacy Rice did not initially support. The former delegate's power in Minnesota began to weaken.

Minnesota's entrance into statehood on May 11, 1858, gave Rice the opportunity to return to Congress and revive his network. With statehood, the position of delegate transitioned into a seat in the US Senate. The term of the delegate then serving ended with statehood, after just fourteen months, and the incoming senator was to then serve fifty-eight months, as if finishing a full six-year term in the Senate. Rice won Minnesota's first senatorial election, and Robert Toombs—the slaveholding senator from Georgia—presented Rice's credentials to Congress when he

Clement C. Clay, 1859.
Library of Congress,
Prints & Photographs
Division

took the oath as the new state's senator. The Senate accepted, and Rice officially became Minnesota's first senator on May 12.[45]

Although Minnesota transitioned from a slave territory to a free state, the new status did not deter Rice's networking any more than the Northwest Ordinance and Missouri Compromise had during the territorial years. He soon added to his coalition. Clement C. Clay of Alabama visited Minnesota, and he bought 1,800 acres of land in Pine and Chisago Counties by 1861. When seeking advice on travel to the Northwest, he wrote to Rice. Few Alabamians visited or relocated to Minnesota because of their distance from the Mississippi River and other major waterways that connected to Minnesota; consequently, this link with Clay helped to open Alabama to the Northwest. Also, the Clay-Rice relationship introduced the territory to significant Old South money and power from Alabama. Clay was the son of a US senator who owned more than forty slaves during Clay's childhood.[46]

By the time Clay served with Rice in Congress, the Alabamian had become a slaveholder in his own right but paled in wealth in comparison to his father. In 1850 the younger Clay owned land next to his father's plantation and held four slaves alongside his father's ten. Ten years later the junior Clay held one fewer slave, but the senior had gained four more. The son was typical of Madison County, Alabama, slaveholders, because two-thirds of them kept at most ten slaves. The father, meanwhile, was part of the elite one-third, owning more than ten unfree laborers, but as slaveholders both father and son comprised part of the majority of Madison's population. They both engaged their slaves in raising Madison's staple crop of cotton, but while in Congress the junior Clay had to manage his slaves from afar.[47]

Rice's success with his network was largely limited to St. Paul and Washington, DC. Although his acquaintances bought real estate throughout Minnesota, he did not control the politics in the communities where those purchases took place. Orr bought land in central Minnesota in the town of St. Cloud in 1857. The political boss of that part of the territory was Rice's former protégé Sylvanus Lowry, who used tools similar to his mentor's in gaining and maintaining his leadership there.

CHAPTER SEVEN

Lowry's Network

In the spring of 1857, a slaveholder moved from Tennessee to Minnesota, bringing two enslaved people to serve him in his new home. The master had recently inherited his laborers from his father, who himself had acquired people from his aunt. As the master prepared to leave for the Northwest, he sold the three slaves that did not accompany him, thus dissolving a slave community that had belonged to his family for three generations. The two traveling with him, a woman and her small child, had no community but each other in Minnesota. Their home community, which had taken at least half a century to develop, was no more.

The enslaver arriving in Minnesota, Thomas P. Calhoun Jr., had recently entered the ministry through the Cumberland Presbyterian Church of Lebanon, Tennessee. His father-in-law, also a Cumberland Presbyterian minister, operated a branch of the denomination in central Minnesota in the new city of St. Cloud, and his wife's family invited him to settle in Minnesota. The master's brother-in-law owned all of the land in the northern third of the city, and the in-laws lived there and built the church there. With the slaveholder's arrival in St. Cloud, the father-in-law had a partner to help with the church, and the brother-in-law had an investor who could buy land from him—with money earned from the sales of slaves.

Sylvanus Lowry was the brother-in-law. He had worked for Chouteau & Company for only one year before leaving it with Henry Rice in 1849, but in that short time he learned from Rice about generating personal income by recruiting southern slaveholders to make investments in the Northwest. Lowry funded his rise to political and economic prominence in St. Cloud in the late 1850s with income from slaveholding church

Sylvanus Lowry, about
1860

members who purchased his real estate. Like Rice, Lowry invited slaveholding acquaintances to buy land from him, and many of St. Cloud's
early political leaders rented land from him.

Lowry was well accustomed to the influence of enslavers beyond the
South even before his brief association with Chouteau, because slavery in
both the South and the Northwest shaped his childhood. His father—a
clergyman—held a slave in Kentucky in 1830, when Lowry was five years
old. Three years later President Andrew Jackson sent the father—and thus
the entire Lowry family—to Wisconsin Territory to teach Ho-Chunk people
in a mission school. During the minister's seven-year tenure there, he and
his family shared a military outpost—Fort Crawford at Prairie du Chien—
with slaveholding military officers. From 1832 to 1834, Second Lieutenant
Thomas Stockton held a St. Louis enslaved woman named Rachel at the
fort, and she gave birth to her son James Henry there in 1834.[1]

After Rice and Lowry left Chouteau in 1849 to independently trade
furs, Lowry stayed in Rice's employment in Watab, a trading post on the

Mississippi in central Minnesota, until the early 1850s. He established himself politically and geographically in central Minnesota before turning thirty years old. In 1853 Minnesota's new territorial governor, Willis Gorman, appointed Lowry to the position of adjutant general. Lowry left the office before the end of the year, but he would often be addressed as "General Lowry" for the rest of his life. In 1854 he claimed a portion of land about eight miles to the south of Watab and called it Acadia. He owned most of Acadia for the rest of his life, but he controlled it politically for only a short while.

In 1856 Lowry's claim officially became the northern section of the city of St. Cloud, subsequently known as "Upper St. Cloud" and "Upper Town." His family members and acquaintances from Tennessee, many of whom owned slaves, bought lots from him. Most of his clients were commuters, but some elites and migrants also conducted business with him. As local author William Mitchell recalled decades later, southern slaveholders brought enslaved people from the South to St. Cloud between 1855 and 1858. The slaveholders who bought the lots were more likely than Lowry to foster the area's proslavery politics.[2]

General Lowry's brother-in-law Thomas P. Calhoun was the first of the Tennesseans to buy real estate in northern St. Cloud. In August 1855 he visited St. Cloud and purchased a land claim from one of Lowry's neighbors for eight hundred dollars. It consisted of 320 acres and included a

US Land Office in St. Cloud, about 1858. Photo by E. F. Boyd.

farm at the Sauk River, to the west of the river's mouth. His purchase came on the heels of his first acquisition of slaves. When Calhoun's father died in April 1855, the son inherited at least two hundred acres of land and slaves Mary, Cherry, Lucinda, and Jo.[3]

Although Calhoun followed his father into the ministry, he worked even more extensively in the church with Lowry's father—Reverend David Lowry. Calhoun ministered with both his father and father-in-law at the Cumberland Presbyterian Church in Lebanon, Wilson County, Tennessee. The denomination's doctrine resembled Calvinism in that it included the belief that only God could draw people to Christ and that God initiated a person's steps to salvation. Cumberland Presbyterians felt obligated by their faith to educate enslaved people and to help them achieve spiritual salvation. Shortly after Thomas Sr.'s death, the junior Calhoun attended the denomination's General Assembly with Reverend Lowry and served as the gathering's treasurer. Calhoun also served as the secretary of the denomination's board while his father-in-law was a board member.[4]

Early the following spring, Calhoun returned to St. Cloud and purchased land from his brother-in-law. By that time General Lowry had been president of the town council in St. Cloud—a position akin to mayor—for only twenty days, having been appointed to the position by members of the council. The residents of the city at the time were almost exclusively migrants from New England and immigrants from Scandinavia and Germany, and General Lowry stuck out as a southerner. On the other hand, he was wealthy, and he had ties to powerful members of the Democratic Party. St. Cloud was established as a city that year, and Lowry was its first town council president. Consequently his selling of land to a slaveholder after starting his appointment tied St. Cloud's government to the institution of slavery from the city's founding.[5]

Reverend Lowry further connected slavery and the church to his son's community early that summer. On June 20, 1856, General Lowry filed a plat for his two-year-old claim and called it "Lowry's Addition." It consisted of forty-two blocks—a total of 420 lots. That same day General Lowry received a visit from a group of his father's colleagues, who acquired more of his land. Jordan Stokes, who sat with the minister on the Cumberland University board of trustees, bought twenty-five lots in Lowry's Addition—including all ten lots of a single block. Stokes owned eight slaves; the Tennessee press called him "a lawyer of distinguished ability and large practice" and a "gentleman of the finest order of intellect." Days later Stokes bought two lots of land in the southern part of St. Cloud from local resident John W. Tenvoorde.[6]

On the first of July, General Lowry sold land to his wealthiest customer. Robert Looney Caruthers, a founder and instructor of Cumberland University and a Tennessee Supreme Court justice, sat with Reverend Lowry on both the trustee board and the Cumberland Presbyterian Church mission board. Caruthers paid $3,485 for more than forty lots in Lowry's Addition on July 1, 1856. The following month he paid $500 for nine additional lots. Between 1850 and 1860, the valuation of his real estate holdings in Tennessee and Minnesota quadrupled from $42,000 to $169,000; his personal estate grew to $110,000. He held eleven enslaved people in Tennessee in 1850, and he acquired eight more over the next decade.[7]

Judge Caruthers had other pursuits besides the ministry. He owned a textile mill in Tennessee and used slaves to run it. He also co-owned a plantation in Yazoo County, Mississippi, with fellow Tennessean James W. Hoggatt. The partners held a total of one hundred slaves there—about five times the number Caruthers owned in Lebanon. The plantation's land value was $15,000 in 1860, and the items there—including the enslaved people—totaled $105,622 in value. Since neither owner of the plantation lived in the Yazoo Delta, they employed R. B. Loftin, an illiterate man, to serve as the overseer.[8]

The partners chose to invest in one of the most fertile parts of the South. The Yazoo's rich soil and temperate climate meant a constant pace of field labor for the area's slaves through all four seasons. The Yazoo Delta led the nation in cotton production, yielding at least five times as many pounds of cotton per acre as the average of the South itself. Moreover, Caruthers and Hoggatt operated their plantation in plush times. In the 1850s cotton production increased by at least six hundred percent in the Yazoo Delta, and plantations there boasted an average value of $30,000.[9]

The judge's long career in government service extended into his real estate activity in Minnesota. Born in 1800, Caruthers rose from the position of Tennessee house clerk in the 1820s to state's attorney in the early 1830s and Tennessee representative in 1835, as a member of the Whig Party. After a term as US representative in Washington, DC, he returned to his home state and began his term as a justice of the Tennessee Supreme Court. He was still on the state bench when he bought land in St. Cloud.

The other Tennessean slaveholders buying property in St. Cloud were colleagues of Stokes and Caruthers in the Whig Party and served as

delegates for Tennessee's branch of the party. On June 23 a young wid-
ower and Mexican War veteran named John F. Goodner of Alexandria,
Tennessee, made his purchase of seven lots for $600, and he eventu-
ally built a warehouse on one of his lots. He owned two enslaved people
in 1850 and five in 1860. On June 25 Stokes's brother William B. Stokes
bought two hundred acres of land from local farmers John and Miriam
Becker for $2,070. After working some time as a hog trader in the 1840s,
he served as a Tennessee state legislator and owned between seven and
ten slaves in that state. In addition to his real estate in Stearns County, he
acquired seven thousand acres in Kanabec and Isanti Counties in Minnesota Territory.[10]

By July 8 the Stokeses returned south to Tennessee, and Goodner and
Caruthers joined them soon thereafter. Only Calhoun and Reverend Lowry,
who had arrived before the others, remained when summer ended. Some
of the Tennesseans stayed in St. Cloud long enough to build homes for
themselves in the South's popular Greek Revival style, but their one-story,
wide-veranda houses were ill suited for blustery and frigid winters. They
eventually developed a reputation among central Minnesotans as absentee landowners. County historian William Mitchell described William
Stokes as a "non-resident" and noted that Tenvoorde "took charge" of the
slaveholder's claim in his absence. The second floor of Jordan Stokes's
warehouse on St. Cloud's upper levee served as the meeting place of the
North Star Lodge of Masons well into the 1860s, and local resident L. A.
Evans set up a store in the building.[11]

The last sale General Lowry made that summer to an enslaver was to
his father. On July 12 the elder Lowry paid a thousand dollars for land.
Unlike the other Tennesseans, the minister stayed in the city after the
summer ended, and he remained there for the next eight years. Although
the Cumberland Presbyterian Church did not recognize him as an official
missionary to St. Cloud, he set about establishing a church of that denomination there. The general allowed his father to use one of his warehouses
as a worship space.[12]

By the end of September, the year's tourism season neared its end.
However, one more Tennessean traveled to St. Cloud, and he played an
important role in Acadia's development. Judge Caruthers's nephew William A. Caruthers arrived in St. Paul on September 30 and stayed there for
a week. He then left for St. Cloud on a six-horse stagecoach, and General
Lowry and a northern Democrat named Christopher C. Andrews shared
the ride with him. General Lowry and the young Caruthers, who was

often addressed as "Colonel Caruthers," got along well enough for the former to welcome the latter as a houseguest on October 10.[13]

Colonel Caruthers tried hard to recruit Tennesseans to Minnesota. He wrote a letter from St. Cloud to a Tennessee newspaper to extol the city's virtues and marvel about its rapid growth. "One year ago St. Cloud contained two log huts, now a flourishing village of six hundred inhabitants, with a fine steam mill, two fine hotels, large store houses, mechanic's shops of every description, forwarding houses and cottages of every style and taste, invite inspection," he bragged. "One year ago lands that could be had by 'squatting' upon are now selling at from three to seventy-five dollars per acre." He advised farmers to bring their horses and cattle with them in order to break up the prairies, and he claimed that oxen were worth $125 to $200 per yoke. On cold weather, he reassured, "I have suffered less than I did in the South during our ordinary winters. It is all humbug that Southerners cannot stand this climate." Minnesota had "less poor land and more rich than any State or Territory in the Union," "the best timbered prairie region in the world," "the best watered country in this Union," fruit in abundance, "coal and rich copper mines," "game and wild fowl of every kind," and "educated, enterprising, enlightened" people. He started a land agency in St. Cloud and advertised it in newspapers back home.[14]

Few took him up on his sales pitch to buy land in St. Cloud. However, being Judge Caruthers's nephew did have one benefit. James Buchanan, who served in Congress with the judge, became president of the United States in March 1857. That same month the new president appointed the colonel as land register at Sauk Rapids. As the nephew of Acadia's largest investor, the colonel represented the interests of the Tennesseans. At the time Minnesota was still a federal territory, and Colonel Caruthers's appointment demonstrated the White House's willingness to protect wealth from slaveholders in federal lands.[15]

◆

General Lowry received more than twelve thousand dollars from sales of land to enslavers in 1856, and he put it to use in St. Cloud. He had a business of forwarding and commission—dealing in pork, bacon, grain, and flour. The money also went toward the maintenance of his warehouses and his pony express enterprise. He served as the town council president throughout 1856, maintaining business relationships with slaveholders while carrying responsibility as a government official to keep slavery out of a free territory.[16]

However, all of his income made little difference to his health, which grew precarious. He fell ill in early 1857 and temporarily left the country to recuperate, recruiting Thomas Calhoun to move to St. Cloud and manage his farm in his absence. The minister arrived with his family and one of his slaves by May 1857. By then two months had passed since the Supreme Court's *Dred Scott* decision legalized slavery in all territories—including Minnesota. As a result, Calhoun was under no legal obligation to free the enslaved people he brought to the Northwest—a pregnant woman named Mary Butler and her child.[17]

Mary was born around 1825, a slave of John Calhoun of Wilson County, Tennessee. Mary's parents were the Calhouns' slaves Street (born around 1786) and Sylvia (born around 1796); her older brother Carroll was born around 1823. She and her family were passed down to John's widow Agnes upon his death in 1830, and then to her nephew Thomas Sr. after her death in 1851. When Thomas Sr. died in 1855, his son Thomas Calhoun Jr. inherited Mary, who by then had a child.[18]

According to antislavery journalist Jane Grey Swisshelm, Mary's child died on the frigid trip up the Mississippi River. She gave birth to a son named John in August 1857, and in the following month, the territorial census identified both Mary and John with the surname "Butler"; previous documents of the Calhoun slaves had not provided last names. Because the *Dred Scott* decision made slavery legal in Minnesota from March 1857 until it became a free state in May 1858, Mary's legal status as a slave meant that John was born a slave in Minnesota. After Minnesota became a free state, Mary and John remained with the Calhoun family.[19]

Her child's death compounded Mary's losses. As Calhoun prepared to depart Tennessee, he had sold away the other enslaved people that he had inherited from his father. Cherry, who was the community's matriarch, and her daughters Lucinda and Elizabeth went to another slaveholder in Wilson County. Consequently, Mary, who had been able to lean on several slaves for support and a woman in her fifties for wisdom, had to adjust to becoming the only adult slave and thus the oldest slave in St. Cloud. She also had to respond to the new needs of her captors in a new environment while seeing to the needs of her newborn baby.[20]

Mary's new home had frigid winters, but it resembled the home she left behind in terms of division of labor. Enslavers in Lebanon generally did not work if they did not have to do so. They designated all the labor to the slaves. The unfree raised the cattle, tilled the lime and clay soil, and grew the corn, oats, and wheat. Similarly, General Lowry's household consisted of the Lowrys, his parents, the Calhouns, Mary and her son, and some European immigrants who worked as servants and farm laborers.[21]

During Thomas Calhoun's time in St. Cloud, he involved himself in local enterprises. He acquired a boat and rented it out to a St. Cloud resident's ferry business. He also helped his father-in-law with the church. In May the Cumberland Presbyterian Church board elected to start a church in St. Cloud, and the announcement took place at about the same time as Calhoun's permanent relocation to the city. The denomination never officially named a missionary to St. Cloud's congregation, but Calhoun and Reverend Lowry made such a declaration superfluous because of their voluntary ministry in the church's name there.[22]

Without payment for ministerial work, Calhoun needed to seek income by other means, and he followed his brother-in-law's example of real estate. Calhoun made thousands of dollars after moving to St. Cloud by selling his inherited land in Tennessee to slaveholders. In 1857 he received $5,467 in sales to his brother Samuel and his Wilson County neighbor William M. Provine. On the other hand, with these sales Calhoun was also distancing himself from the South. When Calhoun briefly returned to Wilson County to sell 195 acres to Samuel on June 27, the minister identified himself not as a local but rather as "Thomas P. Calhoun of the County of Stearns, Minnesota."[23]

As another annual season of tourism descended upon Minnesota, more Tennessean slaveholders came to Acadia. The company Allison, Anderson, & Company purchased two lots from General Lowry. Andrew Allison, who traveled to St. Cloud to make the purchase on behalf of his business, served with Judge Caruthers and Reverend Lowry on the Cumberland University board of trustees and the Cumberland Presbyterian Church mission board. Allison and Judge Caruthers had once been partners in a cotton yard firm in Lebanon, and the two of them and Jordan Stokes were stockholders in the Tennessee Manufacturing Company. Also, the Lowry family's clients began recruiting their own slaveholding acquaintances to St. Cloud for visits and real estate transactions. Goodner's brother-in-law James Nesbit Cartwright bought two lots in St. Cloud, and Colonel Caruthers sold two lots to Tennessean Sampson McClellan.[24]

Competing land barons in central Minnesota took advantage of Lowry's absence from St. Cloud by attracting the southern arrivals. John Wilson, who owned the middle section of St. Cloud, sold some property to South

Carolinians Fountain F. Beattie and James Orr for a total of $2,500. In Sauk Rapids, Beattie and Orr bought land from George W. Sweet for $3,300. After General Lowry returned in late summer, Judge Caruthers purchased land from him. Earlier that year Wilson succeeded General Lowry as the town council president, thereby replacing one profiteer from slaveholder wealth with another. John Tenvoorde, who had sold to a slave-holder the previous year, won the office of treasurer.[25]

The first sign of tension concerning the presence of the Tennesseans in St. Cloud emerged violently that summer, when a traveler from that state lodged with his slave at the Stearns House. The slave tried to escape with help from at least one ally, but, according to the city's *Advertiser* newspaper, "law and order people" thwarted the attempt, and one person suffered an injury by slingshot in the fracas. The new police force's protection of slavery constituted one of the first major actions of law enforcement in the year-old city of St. Cloud. Both the *Dred Scott* verdict and the Fugitive Slave Act were the laws of the territory, and the officers were obliged to uphold them.[26]

St. Cloud received its first major press coverage in the country because of the slave's failed escape attempt, and newspapers portrayed the city as friendly to slavery. The incident became a rallying point nationwide, primarily for people opposed to territorial slavery. Periodicals from Chicago to Boston reprinted the *Advertiser's* report, and some editors added their own antislavery comments to it. The press in Minnesota did the same. The *St. Paul Times* criticized the *Advertiser's* point of view, saying that "here a fugitive slave pants for freedom, and a soulless newspaper calls his attempted rescue 'an outrage on our laws'!" At the time government officials were preparing for a constitutional convention in Minnesota, for the territory to transition to statehood, and the *Times* cited the disturbance at the Stearns House as a cautionary event for the delegates to remember as they deliberated. "Humanity is waiting breathlessly for their action," exclaimed the paper, "and let one of the first things they do be to pass a law declaring that our atmosphere shall hereafter spurn the kidnapper and the slave hunter and that no man shall ever again be worked and sold and flogged upon our soil."[27]

The negative press coverage had little effect on the Tennesseans' exploits in Minnesota, and Colonel Caruthers spent his second year in town nurturing his political power. During General Lowry's absence for most of 1857, Caruthers effectively replaced him as leader of the Democratic Party in central Minnesota. He chaired a meeting in St. Cloud to discuss the St. Paul newspaper reports of the city's ruins. Six months later he joined Wilson and St. Cloud resident James Shepley in publicly supporting both President Buchanan and the Kansas-Nebraska Act at a gathering in Acadia. The event marked the first political meeting in St. Cloud, and the politics of Lowry's Addition became the politics of St. Cloud at large. When the federal government moved Colonel Caruthers's land office from Benton County to Stearns County that month, he placed his new headquarters in Lowry's Addition.[28]

The Cumberland Presbyterian community also expanded beyond Lowry's Addition. In January 1858 Reverend Lowry's church moved out of his son's warehouse to Wilson Hall, built by John Wilson in the middle of St. Cloud. When Calhoun was not preaching, he sought more investment opportunities in real estate. That same month he paid $3,221 for 214 acres in Tennessee from his slaveholding brother P. B. Calhoun, who at the time lived in Texas.[29]

A new newspaper called the *St. Cloud Visiter* [sic] reported on the church's relocation and other local events. The editor, Jane Grey Swisshelm, had arrived in town the previous June from Pennsylvania. She was a nationally known antislavery activist, but she relied on money from General Lowry, Wilson, and the land agency Beede & Mendenhall to launch her St. Cloud paper. Slaveholders had paid all three sponsors for real estate over the past year or two; thus, Swisshelm's antislavery periodical existed in part because of money from slave labor. This irony demonstrated the extent to which St. Cloud's enterprises were funded by real estate sales with absentee slaveholders.[30]

Swisshelm encountered significant hostility among Minnesotans toward her open opposition to slavery. The issue had been a continuing point of controversy in the territory. As early as 1851, a St. Anthony newspaper warned, "Let abolitionists, negrophobists, and all farmers of Negro riots understand that Minnesota is not a congenial soil for their fanatical doctrines.... [N]ot a score could be found in the Territory who would not stand by the Fugitive Slave Law." In the years after that, slaveholding federal appointees gained control of politics in central Minnesota, and residents across the territory voted business associates of slaveholders into government offices. Meanwhile, Tennesseans owned the portion of St. Cloud that generated the most business. The melee at the Stearns House in 1857 did not bode well for Swisshelm's attempt to bring abolitionism to the city.[31]

The journalist indeed soon fell out of favor with the proslavery local elites. Swisshelm had promised General Lowry that in exchange for his patronage, she would support President Buchanan. Lowry kept his word and funded her newspaper, but in print she criticized both the practice of slavery and the commander in chief—by praising him with ferocious sarcasm, thus honoring the letter of her commitment. In response, three of Lowry's allies, assisted by two others, destroyed her printing press. Swisshelm, ignoring death threats, soon acquired a new press, and she resumed her critiques of slavery and its local supporters in her new newspaper—the *St. Cloud Democrat*.[32]

Swisshelm's business relationship with Lowry ended, of course, but she continued to rely on business associates of slaveholders for financial support. Beede & Mendenhall continued to advertise in her newspaper.

Jane Grey Swisshelm,
about 1860

Charles Mackubin, who—like Mendenhall—was an enslaver's son who made real estate deals with slaveholders, coauthored a pitch for land in Breckenridge, a town on the Red River named, with misspelling, for John C. Breckinridge. Swisshelm also printed notices from the Stearns House, whose proprietor had allowed her to speak at his hotel—and still welcomed enslavers and their slaves as guests.[33]

She was selective in her targeting of slavery's proponents, and her choices demonstrated her primary concern with slaveholders acquiring political power. She frequently addressed General Lowry, Colonel Caruthers, and Samuel Hays; after all, they held public offices and led the local branch of the Democratic Party, which supported slavery's territorial expansion. On the other hand, her first address in response to the destruction of her press took place in the Stearns House. Charles Stearns, the hotel proprietor and the namesake for the county, was a supporter of hers, and he advertised in her newspaper. She used her paper to try to prevent slavery's local and federally appointed supporters from controlling local government, but profit among St. Cloud residents (even her friends and allies) from the slave trade's wealth received little mention if any.

For the 1858 tourist season, Judge Caruthers once again emerged as the primary slaveholding investor of central Minnesota. In the first ten days of May, he bought two thousand dollars in land from his nephew in both Lowry's Addition and Sauk Rapids. As a result, Colonel Caruthers had two thousand dollars more to spend on his political pursuits in St. Cloud, and the judge owned even more of central Minnesota.[34]

On May 11, 1858, Minnesota became a free state. For locals dependent on business with enslavers, the transition created a problem. They worried that enslavers would refrain from visiting Minnesota if the visit meant the freeing by law of any accompanying slaves. Therefore, free statehood threatened the survival of local hotels like the Stearns House, and land agencies stood to have fewer southern clients.

Nevertheless, at least one enslaver bought real estate in Minnesota during the summer of 1858. In August a man named William Davis Bone, who resided in DeKalb County, Tennessee, paid a hundred dollars for one lot of land in lower St. Cloud. Bone had been raised by slaveholders; his parents kept four enslaved people when he was a teenager. In 1856, at age twenty-five, he lost both of his parents, and he may have inherited at least one slave from them. In 1850 his father had held two fifteen-year-old enslaved girls, and in 1860 one of the junior Bone's three slaves was a twenty-five-year-old woman. The same year he bought real estate in St. Cloud, Bone spent a larger sum building his own house in DeKalb County. Although he held a small number of enslaved people, he was more invested in Tennessee than in Minnesota.[35]

Bone's very presence in Minnesota that year reflected the strength of General Lowry's slaveholding network, which had expanded beyond Lowry's control. John F. Goodner likely accompanied Bone on the trip from Tennessee to Minnesota. Both men were from DeKalb County, and early that summer Goodner went to St. Cloud to start a lien on property before lodging at a hotel elsewhere in Minnesota for the remainder of the season. At the very least, Goodner served as a financial mentor to the young Bone by bringing him along to Minnesota and showing him opportunities to spread his wealth beyond slavery in Tennessee.[36]

Meanwhile, Thomas Calhoun created controversy in his response to Minnesota's new legal prohibition of slavery. Calhoun's slaves Mary and John were now legally his ex-slaves, but the minister did not officially free them. Rather, he caused a stir in town in June 1858, when he removed the two enslaved people from St. Cloud and, reported the *St. Cloud Democrat*, returned them to Tennessee. He had traveled to Wilson County with them in order to witness the county clerk's recording of his sale of land to his neighbor Provine on June 14. Because Tennessee did not permit slaveholders to free slaves within its borders, Calhoun legally left them in the South as slaves. The Fugitive Slave Act permitted any enslaver to retrieve any slaves in the North or the Northwest and bring them back to the South.[37]

The incident provided Swisshelm with her first local story about slavery, and her reporting about the transaction allowed her to apply her antislavery stance to Minnesota. She claimed that Calhoun had told her of his hatred of slavery and his plans to free his slaves in Minnesota. She was therefore confused by his taking Mary and John, both legally free, to a slave state that did not permit manumission, and she made a point of noting baby John Butler's birth in the North. She asked Calhoun in her *St. Cloud Democrat*, "May I therefore, for the sake of the prosperity of Zion, call upon you to explain this matter?"[38]

Swisshelm unsuccessfully attempted to pressure her adversary into dialogue with her by using hyperbolic statements about the issue's importance. She stated that the country awaited details from Calhoun, thus making the transfer of Mary and John a national issue about slavery. Without citing evidence, she wrote that "in this community . . . in many parts of

Swisshelm's home and office in St. Cloud, about 1860

the country your answer is awaited with deep interest." Calhoun, however, refused to publicly engage with her, and she refrained from press-
ing him further. The story was dead by the end of 1858.[39]

Free statehood and Swisshelm's reports caused little damage to Lowry's Addition. A new slaveholder owned part of the city that June, when
John B. Johnson joined the business Allison, Anderson, & Company. In
the fall, George Sweet chaired the district's Democratic convention. Colonel Caruthers's choices for candidates for the new state legislature won
the party's nominations, but none of his candidates claimed victories in
the general election. Instead, two antislavery Democrats and a Republican won representation of the district. Still, Caruthers's ability to lead the
local Democrats showed how powerful he had become in central Minnesota after just two years in the region.[40]

Nevertheless, more hardship awaited the Lowry's Addition community in the following year. Calhoun died in a road accident in February
1859, and his death resurrected the controversy about Mary and John
Butler. St. Cloud resident Christopher C. Andrews, who had become a
friend of the Lowry family, admitted in the *St. Paul Pioneer and Democrat*
that the deceased was a slaveholder who "had three or four slaves in

Tennessee," and he recalled that Calhoun allowed them to stay enslaved there "at their request . . . retaining what they earned and living in comfort." More importantly, Andrews wrote, "One accompanied his family in Minnesota," thus confirming that Calhoun indeed owned a slave in the free state. On the other hand, according to Andrews, the minister allowed her to return to Tennessee because "she became disoriented away from her acquaintances and desired to return," and he even handled her travel expenses. By describing the disappearance of Mary and John from St. Cloud in this manner, Andrews tried to definitively answer Swisshelm's unresolved query of whether his friend had sold the mother and son as slaves in Tennessee.[41]

Swisshelm addressed the validity of Andrews's remarks, noting that there was no proof of the claims, only his own word. To avoid any criticism that she was soiling a dead man's reputation, she observed that Andrews had initiated this discussion and that she was merely responding to him. Her central question to him was, "Did Mr. Calhoun, according to his promise, emancipate this woman?" She inquired about evidence, "Are her free papers here? Did he take the necessary precautions to prevent that freeborn Minnesota baby from being reduced to slavery?" Reinforcing the point about the Butlers as local slaves, Swisshelm referred to John as "the little boy born, perhaps in his [Calhoun's] kitchen." She tied the fate of the mother and son to the fate of the state's status concerning slavery: "The people of Minnesota have a right to know whether this is slaveholding soil and whether men may here raise babies for the Southern market." She continued to take up the issue for many weeks after her first response to the late clergyman's friend. "Come, Brother Andrews, report about the woman who was not returned to bondage," Swisshelm jibed. "Where is she if she is not in bondage, and where is the baby?"[42]

The editor also dragged General Lowry into the controversy. She routinely alleged that he supported slavery, especially after his client Shepley destroyed the press of her first newspaper. At times Swisshelm blamed Lowry himself for the destruction. In addition, she claimed that his hosting of Calhoun's family at his house made him an accomplice to the minister's enslaving. With Calhoun's death, General Lowry bore the full brunt of her anger over local slavery.[43]

Lowry's Addition soldiered on despite Swisshelm's barbs, and the political leadership of the Tennesseans and Democrats in central Minnesota remained secure. In April Reverend Lowry won election to St. Cloud's board of supervisors. Later in August Minnesota's Democratic Party nominated General Lowry for lieutenant governor. That fall Shepley was elected town council president, Andrews became a state senator for Stearns County, and Benton County's electorate awarded George Sweet the position of state representative. General Lowry lost the election for lieutenant governor, thus denying Lowry's Addition statewide political influence, but Stearns County residents had chosen him over his opponent. Indeed, General Lowry took the antislavery activist's comments in stride. "Mrs. Swisshelm is still spouting, I see," he wrote to his wife from Washington, DC, that year. "I hope she enjoys herself, for she does not hurt me; and, lone as I am, her gun is too dirty to reach me."[44]

However, some signs of weakness in Lowry's Addition were emerging. In 1859, for the first time since 1855, no new or returning Tennesseans bought land in St. Cloud during the tourism season. The Panic of 1857 had caused land values to plummet, and the real estate industry had not fully recovered in the two years since then. General Lowry still owned 223 of the 420 lots he had platted. Tennesseans collectively owned more than half of the remaining lots, thus placing slaveholders and the proslavery Lowry in control of three-fourths of northern St. Cloud. Judge Caruthers alone possessed one-eighth of Lowry's Addition. By the end of 1859, it was clear that Minnesota could not rely solely on a constant flow of individual slaveholders to keep the state in good financial health, and locals looked to southern financial institutions such as banks for help.

CHAPTER EIGHT

Bankers and Insurance Agents

The life of an enslaved person was one of constant valuation, for an enslaver defined a slave's existence as both a person and property. However, not all appraisal of slaves took place at dramatic, heart-rending auctions; some valuations were more mundane. Any expensive endeavor a slaveholder wanted to undertake required a financial assessment of his human inventory, because he needed to know how much money he could afford to lose in his venture. In these cases, enslaved people still underwent the ordeal of having to provide evidence of good health, but they were not in danger of being sold, and the inspections took place in offices instead of on auction blocks.

Unless slaves pretended to be sick to avoid being purchased at auctions, they could exercise very little agency over their own monetary value. If an enslaver wanted to start a new business and he offered his enslaved people as collateral, a banker determined the slave's value. Banks in the South carried credit from larger banks from the East Coast and Europe to the slaveholders, and the southern banks accepted the lending risks in exchange for a portion of the interest. Slave mortgages were very common in the United States by the time Minnesota Territory was organized.[1]

Enslaved people sailing up the Mississippi River from the South to Minnesota were likely insured when they accompanied their masters for vacations and business trips. A slaveholder or a business arranging to insure an enslaved person had to contact an insurance agent, who calculated how much money to charge as a premium for the life of the slave. The agent asked the customer a series of questions about the slave's health and then subjected the slave to a health examination. Enslavers often hired doctors to conduct medical examinations on slaves and then sent the reports to insurance agencies, which determined insurance rates. Agents insured enslaved people for as much as two-thirds of their market value.[2]

Minnesota was hardly an anomaly in the United States, for banks nationwide depended heavily on money from slave labor. Banks in New England financed slave plantations in the South, helping planters afford to purchase land and slaves. Brisk business from slaveholders also stood to benefit northerners. Northern institutions supported cotton production, using cotton fabric to make clothes in textile mills throughout the free states. In New York City, companies produced boats for shipping the raw goods that slaves grew, and they constructed warehouses for storing those goods. The city grew so economically dependent on cotton for survival that even that northern metropolis threatened to secede from the Union in 1861.[3]

Some of the enslavers who bought land in Minnesota worked in finance, and they brought their experiences in judging monetary values and in negotiating agreements when purchasing real estate in the Northwest. Most of these buyers traveled to the Northwest once or twice to see and buy property and then returned to the South, but some stayed permanently in Minnesota to monitor their interests. Many of the southern financiers in Minnesota were bankers who extended credit to people. Other financiers worked as insurance agents. The initial investors in Minnesota came largely from the Upper South, but they began to arrive from the Carolinas and Tennessee after the *Dred Scott* decision extended legal slavery to Minnesota. By the mid-1850s both central and southern Minnesota had multiple cities, and their rapid growth drew southern financiers. Aetna Insurance, which insured slaveholders, had branches in Shakopee and Belle Plaine, Minnesota, and both branches advertised in local newspapers.[4]

These investors had a personal interest in protecting slavery because of their own holdings of slaves. Older bankers and agents generally kept more enslaved people than their younger counterparts and had more money to spend on land in Minnesota. Younger bankers and agents used real estate in Minnesota to geographically expand their financial portfolio beyond slavery. Some of the younger men had grown up with slaveholding parents but chose to concentrate their wealth fully on real estate. Nevertheless, regardless of age, the financiers named slaveholders among their references in newspaper advertisements, especially in southern periodicals, using those names as devices to attract people to buy land in Minnesota.

The year 1857 started out with promise for slavery's financiers connected with Minnesota but ended with loss and turmoil, and developments in the financial industry caused the turn of events. When the US Supreme Court legalized slavery in Minnesota Territory in March 1857, bankers and insurers stood to benefit significantly from the verdict. As more slaveholders came to the Northwest with slaves, insurers likely saw an uptick in policies on unfree laborers sailing up the Mississippi to Minnesota. The territory's banks could also enjoy increased business as more slaveholders purchased local real estate. For nearly the entire summer of 1857, financial institutions took advantage of Dred Scott's impact on Minnesota's trade with slaveholders.

Just before summer ended, on August 24, the New York branch of the Ohio Life Insurance and Trust Company collapsed. The business's failure precipitated a months-long economic panic—later known as the Panic of 1857—that affected bankers and insurers throughout the country. Northern and urban areas, whose economies were deeply dependent on these financial institutions, suffered far greater financial ruin than the plantation-driven South. A city's merchants, manufacturers, and businessmen, large and small, participated in a daily hum of commerce that required constant loans and repayments; in a panic, money stopped moving. In the immediate aftermath, northerners appeased southern financiers in order to keep businesses afloat, and southerners used support for slavery as leverage for conducting business. On the other hand, the plummeting of land values in the North and the Northwest meant that fewer southerners would travel to Minnesota to buy land. As fewer southerners sailed northwest with enslaved people, insurance companies had fewer slaves to insure. In addition, the southern bankers who had purchased land in Minnesota before the panic lost money on their investments. Their misfortune made some Minnesotans even more desperate to curry their favor by presenting themselves as welcoming to slavery, but Minnesota's entrance into the Union as a free state jeopardized that effort.[5]

◆

The bankers and insurers who invested in Minnesota in the wake of Dred Scott represented some of the nation's most powerful financial protectors of the practice. Many of them worked for financial institutions that had extended credit to slaveholders or insured enslaved people for generations. Other investors had familial or professional ties to those institutions. Bankers that poured money into clients' slave plantations also funded northwestern lots, and insurers of slaves' lives also sought to protect claims to real estate. For both groups, profits at the expense of slaves' lives fueled their interests in Minnesota—especially central Minnesota.

The Bank of Cape Fear, established in 1804 by the North Carolina legislature, extended credit to enslavers for generations. Its presidents and stockholders also owned slaves. The cashier and teller from the Raleigh, North Carolina, branch of the Bank of Cape Fear served as directors of the North Carolina Mutual Life Insurance Company, which insured slaves in that state and in Alabama, Georgia, and Virginia. Enslaved people accounted for half of North Carolina's wealth. Before the late 1850s, the company did not reimburse masters or physicians for medical examinations of slaves, and most of the reports given to the company were flawed if not deliberately inaccurate. Among the company's clients were James C. Sproull & Company, Boatwright & Miot, Freeman and Houston, and Dickinson, Grant & Gauze; all of them insured slaves. North Carolina Mutual disbanded during the Civil War.[6]

James A. Bradley and Israel G. Lash, employees of the Bank of Cape Fear, bought land in McLeod, Meeker, Sherburne, Sibley, and Stearns Counties. Bradley came from a plush background. His father held thirteen slaves in 1820 and twenty-two the following decade. Bradley held nineteen slaves at his home in Wilmington, North Carolina. He paid $650 for A. J. Bell's land in McLeod County on July 17, 1857. Bradley was the bookkeeper for the Bank of Cape Fear from as early as 1851 to as late as 1861. Although he owned enslaved people, he offered to hire "a Negro Man accustomed to any work with the axe" for the spring, summer, and fall of 1856. Bradley set up a temporary office in Minneapolis and advertised in the local press to his fellow North Carolinians: "Notes on the Commercial Bank of Wilmington, North Carolina, will be redeemed at the office of the subscriber, in currency on Exchange on New York at currency rates."[7]

Lash grew up in a financially prosperous household and used that prosperity to strengthen slavery. His father held twenty enslaved people in 1820 and almost twice as many two decades later. As a young adult, Lash grew and sold tobacco, and he made and sold cigars. By the 1850s he had become a banker too, working as a cashier at the Bank of Cape

Fear. He held at least thirty slaves in Forsyth County and trained them in mechanical labor. They were collectively worth $80,000. He had little regard for family units among his laborers. One enslaved man named Wesley lived apart from his daughter and her mother, both of whom resided with another master. Also, in his capacity as a banker, Lash protected other slaveholders in North Carolina. He loaned more than $5,000 to a slaveholding widow in 1861 so she could pay her debts without selling any of the slaves she wanted to someday pass along to her children.[8]

Lash was not the first enslaver from Forsyth to travel to Minnesota. Darius Starbuck preceded him and purchased real estate in Sherburne County in 1856. The following year, on August 10, Lash bought land in the same county. It was the only investment he made in central Minnesota.[9]

A bank in South Carolina further supported masters' ownership of central Minnesota, in part because of the state's efforts to compete effectively against other slave states. By 1857, Hamburg, South Carolina, had been a thriving town by the Savannah River for at least two decades. It engaged in a commercial rivalry with its neighbor across the river—Augusta, Georgia—for business and for residents. Both cities had slave markets that attracted slaveholders from the same part of the South. More than thirty miles east of Hamburg, residents of Edgefield, South Carolina, could choose among three markets for buying slaves: Augusta and Hamburg to the west and, equidistant, Charleston to the east.

The South Carolina legislature passed a bill in December 1835 to "Establish and Incorporate a Bank in the Town of Hamburg." The new law allowed the bank to "have, purchase, receive, possess, enjoy and retain, to it and its successors . . . chattels . . . to an amount not exceeding, in the whole, three times the amount of the capital stock of the said corporation." Bank of Hamburg founder Henry Shultz started the bank because of his grudge against Augusta. Cotton boomed in the 1850s, and the Bank of Hamburg profited.[10]

Fountain F. Beattie, whose father held at least one dozen slaves, was one of the bank's original commissioners. His F. F. Beattie & Company was worth $75,000 and had credit comparable to that of the Bank of Charleston, and Beattie himself had a personal estate of $90,000. He was still affiliated with the bank when he arrived in Minnesota in July 1857 and purchased lots in Benton and Stearns Counties. He bought $2,300 in land from George Sweet of Sauk Rapids, allowing Sweet to use money from a slaveholding banker to develop the city. John Wilson did not make as much money from selling land in lower St. Cloud to Beattie, but that money allowed Wilson to pursue business interests.[11]

When Allison, Anderson, & Company in Tennessee bought $400 of land for the company from Sylvanus Lowry in St. Cloud, the sale brought at least two slaveholder-run financial institutions into St. Cloud's economy. Andrew Allison was not only a partner with Thompson Anderson but also an official of the Tennessee Planters Bank in Nashville. Anderson, meanwhile, had a business interest beyond the partnership, and it tied St. Cloud to the protection of the monetary value of slaves. The Tennessee legislature established the Tennessee Marine and Fire Insurance Company in November 1853. Anderson was not an original commissioner, but by 1857 he headed the company, which provided coverage for the transit of "Negroes against the dangers of the River."[12]

Slaveholding financiers also owned real estate in Stillwater, Minnesota. Thomas R. Smith and Levi Joy of Bolivar, Tennessee, bought land in Washington County in 1857. They returned to Bolivar after making their purchases, and they became involved in protecting the interests of other enslavers. In 1860 Tennessee's legislature named them among the incorporators of an insurance company bearing similarities to the Phoenix Insurance Company, which had branches throughout the country and provided insurance policies for enslaved people in transit.[13]

Despite having lived in the same town in Tennessee, Smith and Joy were unlikely business partners, sharing very little in common. Smith was born and raised in Maine, and he held no enslaved people before leaving home for Tennessee at age nineteen in 1849. He married into slavery in 1851; his bride's father held ten slaves in 1850. By the following decade, Smith himself owned as many African Americans as his father-in-law had in 1850. Joy, in contrast, was a child of slaveholders and raised in Bolivar. His mother held five slaves in 1850, and he doubled that number for himself in 1860.[14]

When the partners of the Missouri-based commission business Tillman, Rozier & Company acquired land in Stillwater, the city became further connected to the South's financing of slavery. Senior partner Charles Tillman was one of fourteen wealthy residents of St. Louis to bail out their neighbor James H. Lucas's bank after the Panic of 1857. Both men comprised part of a small demographic in the city: immigrants from France who were rich slaveholders. Tillman's payment to Lucas allowed that minority to retain its financial hold over St. Louis.[15]

Lucas was a lawyer, and his bank comprised only a portion of his business interests. He prioritized real estate and owned a significant portion of land in St. Louis. In addition, he served as the vice president of the local branch of Globe Mutual Insurance, thus making money from insuring slaves in Missouri. Unlike Tillman, however, Lucas was not a first-generation slaveholder. His father acquired enslaved people in the United States after having immigrated with his family from France. Thus, Lucas had slavery-based income on which to build after reaching adulthood. On the other hand, he built his slave community almost from nothing, because his father decreased his own holdings of slaves over the years and expressed support for gradual abolition. The elder Lucas recalled that as Missouri prepared for statehood in 1820, "I expressed an opinion that it would be proper to limit the importation of slaves to five years or a short period from the date of the Constitution [of Missouri]." Critics labeled him an "emancipator," which was, he said, "the worst name that can be given in the state of Missouri."[16]

Because of support from Tillman and others, Lucas survived the panic remarkably unscathed. As of 1860, the banker and insurer owned $3.5 million in real estate, and his personal estate totaled $225,000. His eighteen slaves comprised part of the latter, and at least three of them linked Lucas even more to land in Minnesota. Years earlier, in 1849, Lucas had bought three enslaved people from fellow St. Louis resident John F. A. Sanford, who was a partner of Pierre Chouteau, Jr. & Company and thus would become part owner of real estate all over Minnesota. Following the threads of these financial interactions shows the web of interconnections with slaveholder wealth. When Sanford took money from Lucas for unfree laborers, he gained funds from a southern bank and an insurance company that he could use to manage or increase Chouteau properties in Minnesota. One decade later, Lucas used money from Tillman—part of which came from investing in Minnesota—to survive the Panic of 1857.[17]

The enslaved people that Lucas purchased from Sanford may have personally known Minnesota's most famous slave, Dred Scott. Sanford managed business affairs for his sister Irene Emerson, who inherited Scott upon her husband's death in 1843. She hired him out until 1846, when she brought him and his family with her to St. Louis, and they resided with her father Francis Alexander Sanford. The elder Sanford owned five slaves, four of whom he had bought with his son John's money. After the patriarch died in 1848, Sanford handled his father's estate. Thus, the three slaves he sold to Lucas months later had likely belonged to his father. If this is so, as Scott waited for his case's outcome, he had to watch three members of his slave community leave to serve another master.[18]

✦

Meanwhile, a new generation of southern financiers emerged from the South and made its way to Minnesota as the visits by enslavers peaked. This younger wave came of age in slave-owning households and took advantage of the opportunities that wealth from slavery provided them. They had watched the slaves work in their childhood homes, serving the parents, and they had observed their parents whipping those servants, and buying and selling them. They had seen how slaves treated them with deference, whether the servants were older or younger than they were. The lessons they learned from childhood were as old as American slavery itself, and they were merely the latest people to be socialized in the practice and expected to continue it themselves.

However, these young observers did not follow their elders' example in the enslaving of Africans. After they finished their college education, they became well-to-do professionals in urban areas. Also, they grew up in a context of slavery as an institution of violence that meant danger not only to the slaves but to the slaveholders themselves. Many in this younger generation were children when Nat Turner led a slave revolt in Virginia in 1831, and they reached adulthood when John Brown attacked supporters of slavery in Kansas in 1856.

Although these new financiers did not fully engage in slavery, they still used the riches from their families' involvement in the practice. They relied on slaveholders to financially back their endeavors in the Northwest. They named slaveholders as business references, and they promoted their enterprises in southern publications. They set up business offices in Minnesota's cities, living in hotels or rooming houses. Thus, when they relocated to the Northwest, they served as couriers, finding ways to bring slaveholders' wealth from their parents and parental acquaintances in the South to urban areas in Minnesota.

In 1856, at age twenty-six, Oscar Stephenson arrived in St. Paul from Virginia and advertised his services as a "Commissioner of the State of Virginia" in the *Enquirer* newspaper in his hometown of Richmond: "Money Loaned and Invested. Taxes Paid and Collections made throughout the Territory." His choice of newspapers for promoting his bank

guaranteed that slaveholders would at least read the notice. The two advertisements directly above his called for "Negro Hiring."[19]

Stephenson typified the young southern financier in Minnesota. He
was exposed to slavery before reaching adulthood but held no enslaved
people of his own before moving northwest to Minnesota. However, his
parents, Thomas and Caroline, did not provide much wealth for him, for
he had no recorded values of real estate or personal estate. Nor did he
reside with his parents as a young adult; rather, at age nineteen he worked
as a schoolteacher in another county in Virginia, living with a couple who
owned twelve slaves. Like many of his fellow young investors, he earned
a law degree in the South but set up a law practice in Minnesota. His law
degree came from the University of Virginia, and he worked as a lawyer
in St. Paul by the fall of 1857.[20]

Also from Virginia came the nephew of a prominent slaveholding
banker. Job G. McVeigh relocated to Minnesota at age twenty-two in 1857,
and the *Alexandria (VA) Gazette* first published his notice early the following year. His uncle was William N. McVeigh, who headed the Bank
of Old Dominion and served on the board of directors for the Potomac
Insurance Company, which issued policies on slaves. Both he and a slaveholder named J. W. Brackenbrough served as young Job's references.[21]

George Mendenhall's nephews worked for banks and insurance companies connected to slavery in North Carolina. R. J. Mendenhall came to
Minnesota in 1856 at age twenty-eight and started a bank that same year
with a previous business associate named Cyrus Beede. Beede & Mendenhall advertised in the *Standard* of Raleigh, North Carolina, promising,
"Will make investments, loan money at western rates." Among the partners' slaveholding references were Walter Gwynn, former North Carolina governors William Graham and J. M. Morehead, and then-governor
Thomas Bragg.[22]

Beede & Mendenhall lured several southerners to the Northwest almost
immediately. In April 1856 two slaveholders from R. J.'s hometown traveled to Minnesota to visit and invest. His brother Cyrus Mendenhall provided more than $11,000, and W. A. Caldwell, himself a cashier of the
Farmer's Bank in Greensboro, invested one thousand dollars in R. J.'s
firm. More family arrived the following year. R. J. wrote in his diary in
mid-1857, "Aunt Delphina, Uncle George, [and two others] came to see
me. . . . They all left some money to be loaned and invested as we might
think best." That same year at least three southerners came to Minnesota

Richard Junius
Mendenhall, about 1893

from R. J.'s home county of Guilford in North Carolina to acquire real
estate from him in Stearns County, and two of those three held enslaved
people. Abel Gardner, whose father owned one slave, purchased one lot
for $250. Brothers C. E. and F. E. Shober jointly bought another lot for
$300. Back in Guilford County the former brother kept one African Amer-
ican enslaved, and the latter held three. Years earlier two of F. E.'s slaves
were a boy he fathered and the woman who birthed the child.[23]

Although Beede & Mendenhall convinced some slaveholders to acquire
land in St. Cloud, the firm never translated its commercial success into
political power. The partnership's clients did not purchase nearly as many
lots and acres in town as all of the Tennesseans who bought real estate.
Sylvanus Lowry had sold many of his lots in Lowry's Addition to his relatives and acquaintances before the arrivals of the North Carolinians, and

he owned more of St. Cloud than Beede & Mendenhall did. Although the partners sold several lots in the southern part of the city, their success did not undermine John Wilson's role as the leader of that part of St. Cloud. Also, the agents lived and established their business office in Hennepin County, and their only presence in St. Cloud was in the land they wanted to sell. Lowry's status as central Minnesota's most powerful, proslavery political leader remained secure.

◆

Henry Rice courted the finance world when seeking to build his post-Chouteau network of enslavers, and at least one slaveholder from that world formed a relationship with him. In Maryland his acquaintance Charles W. Pairo owned and operated the Banking and Exchange House of C. W. Pairo. In January 1852, when William Nourse joined the bank, it became the firm Pairo & Nourse. "Land warrants purchased and sold. Interest at the rate of six per cent, per annum paid on deposites [sic] when left for thirty days or longer," the partnership announced. Both Pairo and Nourse owned slaves. Rice was in Washington, DC, as territorial delegate for only a few months before convincing Pairo to visit Minnesota in the summer of 1853.[24]

In the early 1850s Pairo was an agent for Baltimore Life Insurance. The company insured enslaved people at the time, and most of them were domestic laborers. Baltimore Life was the South's most lucrative life insurance company. Its agents were reluctant to insure slaves during the company's first years in the 1830s, but by 1850 more than half the business there consisted of policies on slaves. It then started frequently advertising its coverage of the unfree.[25]

Pairo also involved himself in matters concerning African Americans who were not enslaved. In 1854 and again in 1855 he donated twenty-five dollars to the African Colonization Society. The ACS advocated the sending of free African Americans away from the United States, seeing no place in America for free African Americans. As someone who made his money pricing enslaved people, Pairo literally and figuratively found no value in ex-slaves and free people. If no one could invest in them, they served no purpose in the country, as far as he was concerned.[26]

Pairo's work as a financier became endangered during the Panic of 1857, and his involvement in Minnesota real estate may have partly caused his predicament. The firm Pairo & Nourse collapsed just three weeks after the panic began. Although the bank's location—Washington, DC—legally permitted slavery, the economy of an urban area was far more vulnerable to financial panic than a place dependent on plantation labor. Pairo and Nourse ended their association with Baltimore Life. One local newspaper blamed the bank's suspension on the partners' excessive investment in "the West."[27]

To survive the panic, Pairo sold some of his personal property. Pairo's home in Georgetown had a view of the Potomac River, stables, outhouses, a greenhouse, and a house for his carriage. When he sold it in 1857, he, his sister Sophia Kall, and his niece Isabel Kall went their separate ways and lived in different homes. He also liquidated his holdings of enslaved people.[28]

When Pairo & Nourse failed, the fate of the partnership's properties in the Northwest became uncertain. The firm owned real estate in Ramsey County. By the time of the collapse, Pairo's acquaintance Rice was out of Washington, DC, and out of politics and thus had no direct access to power in order to help alleviate his associate's distress.[29]

◆

After the Panic of 1857, southern financiers in Minnesota struggled to attract new investors in land. None of the land agents put advertisements in southern newspapers after 1858. Stephenson and Mendenhall stayed in Minnesota, practicing law and banking, respectively, but young McVeigh returned permanently to Virginia. Slaveholding visitors to Minnesota after 1858 were mostly tourists, commuters, and relatives of migrants. The arrivals generally were not interested in buying real estate, and the few who did purchase lots at that time were either financiers or their relatives.

Both the Panic of 1857 and Minnesota's free statehood as of May 1858 had the potential to repel slaveholders from the Northwest, but some of them maintained their financial interests in the region. Israel Lash relied in part on his midwestern holdings to keep himself financially secure after the panic started. He bought land in Sibley County from Henry Brainard for a thousand dollars on August 2, 1858, and people mortgaged some of Lash's land in the following year.[30]

R. J. Mendenhall followed in his uncle's footsteps by transporting slaves out of North Carolina, and he guided some of them to the Northwest. He brought African American boys to his home in Minnesota, but they failed to achieve full free citizenship in their adopted homeland. His first transplant was a teenager named James Reed, who arrived while Minnesota was still a territory. St. Anthony resident Emily Grey recalled that Reed voluntarily lived without a consistent home during his time in the city. Later, in the fall of 1858, R. J. returned from a visit back home with an eight-year-old boy named Jerry Sears. R. J. had to show free papers for the boy in order to travel through New York en route to Minnesota, because the state of New York forbade European Americans from traveling through the state with slaves. After their arrival, however, R. J. treated Sears in ways that suggested a continuation of enslavement. Although the census of 1860 listed the boy by name as if a free person, his name appeared simply as "Jerry"—not unlike the millions of African American

Jeremiah "Jerry" Sears,
about 1860

slaves identified without surnames in wills and slave inventories in probate courts nationwide. Sears did not attend school at all in Minneapolis— like other enslaved people, he was deprived of education.[31]

Both R. J. and his business partner remained tied to slaveholders individually and professionally for years. While in Greensboro with new bride Abby in the spring of 1858, R. J. stayed overnight with his slaveholding brother Cyrus Mendenhall. In the following year, Cyrus Beede moved into a property in Minnesota that Abby dubbed "the Shober House," suggesting that one or both of the Shober brothers of Guilford County had acquired the property when visiting Minnesota back in 1857. Three years later R. J. served as a land agent for his brother, arranging for him to buy real estate in Minnesota.[32]

R. J. also remained tied to North Carolina in a sentimental sense. In the late 1850s, he and his wife built a palatial, three-story house on Nicollet Avenue in Minneapolis, which they named after the county of Mendenhall's youth. A long path took travelers from the street to a loop in front of the estate, and trees bordered the loop from the inside. To the right of the house lay a greenhouse, where the Mendenhalls pursued an interest in horticulture. "Today we have moved to our new country home, which we call Guilford Place," announced an entry in the family diary.[33]

Although Cyrus Mendenhall himself visited Minnesota to buy land, he remained committed to his own financial ventures in North Carolina. He headed the Farmers' Bank of North Carolina as of 1859, thus becoming president of the same bank where his traveling companion Caldwell was the cashier. Mendenhall acquired lots in Stearns County in October 1860 and in Wright County between November 1860 and March 1861. He purchased from local residents instead of southern migrants, and both counties were among the last in Minnesota to benefit from a significant influx of cash from a slaveholder before the Civil War began in April 1861.[34]

By the time Cyrus Mendenhall went to the Northwest in 1860, he was significantly experienced in determining the monetary value of unfree laborers. In the 1850s he helped to establish the Greensborough Mutual Insurance Company, and he served as the company's attorney into the 1860s. The insurance company promised: "Slaves insured on reasonable terms." Another advertisement said that the company catered to "those desiring an insurance upon their own lives or the lives of their slaves." Greensborough Mutual Insurance Company canceled any slave policy duplicated at another company, and it nullified any policy for a slave who died because of inadequate care or medical treatment.[35]

Cyrus Mendenhall also participated more directly in slavery. Like his uncle, Mendenhall married a daughter of a prominent planter. His father-in-law was Abram P. Staples, who held more than one hundred slaves in Patrick County, Virginia. Staples died in the 1850s, and his daughter Nancy likely inherited some of his slaves afterward. Mendenhall himself held no slaves in 1850 but, after marrying Nancy, was listed in 1860 with forty-six slaves. On the other hand, more than half of the couple's slaves were fugitives, which suggested that Cyrus and Nancy shared Uncle George's willingness to liberate members of his labor force whenever possible.[36]

Meanwhile, Mendenhall additionally encountered slavery through agricultural pursuits that supplemented his income. He ran the West Green Nurseries and Gardens in Greensboro with S. W. Westbrook, who himself owned slaves in Guilford County. As the 1860s began, Mendenhall benefited from rather fortunate timing. He won election to North Carolina's House of Commons in August 1860, shortly before his departure for Minnesota. When he made his last purchase in Wright County in March 1861, the country was one month away from engaging in a civil war, and his home state was two months away from officially joining the enemy nation. Thus, he became one of the last slaveholding southerners to buy real estate in a country from which his home state would soon secede, and his land would become part of a country that his home state would try to militarily conquer.[37]

Cyrus Mendenhall was certainly not the only southerner in Minnesota to have been caught off guard by the eruption of conflict. Some of his fellow southerners had been vacationing in the state in hotels at the time. For years the hotels had served as sanctuaries for slaveholders wanting to bring enslaved people to the Northwest, and Minnesotans tried to preserve that reputation for the state's hotels even as sectionalism intensified in the late 1850s and early 1860s. The Kansas-Nebraska Act and the Dred Scott decision had allowed proslavery sentiment to strengthen among southerners and their political allies in the Northwest. Minnesotans spent the first years of statehood quarreling about just how much slavery was too much for a free state, but southern investments complicated the debate. The slaves themselves and a presidential election would accelerate the debate's conclusion.

CHAPTER NINE

Hotel Guests

Every spring from the mid-1850s to 1860, slave communities of some plantations anticipated an unsettling annual ritual. The master of the estate summoned no more than three slaves and forced them to travel to Minnesota with him for the summer season. Each trip caused disruption among the enslaved people left behind, who had to adjust to the absence of the traveling slaves and then adapt again upon their return in the fall. The chosen slaves, meanwhile, struggled to resist the temptation to try to become free in a free state, and they grieved the loss of their opportunity for emancipation when returning to the South with the master at summer's end. Minnesotans rarely interfered with the slaveholder-slave relationships in their hotels, and their apathy left slaves with no recourse but to forego the realization of their legal freedom. Thus, every fall throughout the South, some slave communities consisted of newly heartbroken laborers who had turned away from the "Promised Land" of the Northwest, past sojourners who knew the new returnees' pain, and laborers who had never left the "Egypt" of the South—all working alongside each other.

Enslavers visited the free state at their own risk. Beginning in the territorial period, dozens of free African Americans in St. Paul helped slaves accompanying their vacationing owners to leave them and escape to Canada. They assisted in bringing to St. Paul some fugitives who had successfully fled the South and reached Galena, Illinois. They arranged for enslaved people to depart by boat and by horse for Canada, and they asked slaves of tourists in local hotels if they wanted to be liberated. These free African Americans remained active well beyond the date of Minnesota's entrance into the Union as a free state.[1]

Slaveholding tourists, recalling past experience, gambled that they would retain their slaves while in the Northwest. After all, they and their slaves had been welcomed when Minnesota was a free territory and during the fourteen months of legal slavery after the *Dred Scott* decision. Local merchants benefited financially from tourists' patronage, and the tourists counted on them to turn a blind eye or to keep silent when confronted with slavery. They acted as if their investments in the state insulated them from having to manumit their slaves, and Minnesotans had not given them any reason to behave otherwise.

Because Minnesota's African American population had not previously sought legal freedom specifically within the state's borders, slaveholders held another kind of advantage. Before the war, most of the free African Americans in Minnesota had spent years in freedom in Illinois, Indiana, and Ohio before coming to Minnesota. Very few had arrived as fugitive slaves directly from the South; runaway slaves tended to escape to free states in the Midwest and North and to Canada but not to western and northwestern states. Moreover, Minnesota had just recently been a slave territory from 1857 to 1858, giving fugitive slaves even less incentive to seek freedom there. As a result, free African Americans in Minnesota did not have resources in place to help enslaved people on their enslavers' summer vacations to transition to freedom. The territory and state did not even have an official mechanism by which to produce "free papers" for enslaved people who petitioned for them.[2]

Slaves of tourists had to form their own slave communities at the hotels where they lodged. While their owners dined or chatted among themselves, the enslaved people may have had opportunities to talk with each other about life in slavery. They may have compared stories about traveling in second-class accommodations aboard steamboats on the Mississippi, or they perhaps discussed what labor they performed back in the South. Riverboat captains tended to hire free African Americans to serve the passengers, and the slaves on board may have never seen anyone who looked like them but was not enslaved. They likely remarked to one another about the coolness of Minnesota's climate, the absence of plantations full of crops like cotton and rice and tobacco in the Northwest, and the near-invisibility of slaves already in Minnesota. The ways in which Minnesota's free African Americans associated with the state's European Americans more as fellow residents than as servants probably did not escape the slaves' attention.[3]

Some of the European Americans who came to Minnesota from the North tried to capitalize on its popularity in the South as a tourist attraction. The novelty of access by water to Minnesota's scenery attracted both southerners and East Coast residents. In addition, Minnesota's summers, warm as they are, offered considerable relief from tropical heat in the South; lakes and rivers provided beauty as well as cool breezes. In 1849, Henry Rice built a three-story hotel in St. Paul and named it the American House, also known as the Rice Hotel. In 1852 newspaper editor Joseph Goodhue of the *Minnesota Pioneer* called the territory "an exhilarating luxury" for a southerner and his "debilitated wife and pale children, almost gasping for breath." The Winslow House, a five-story limestone structure, opened in St. Anthony in 1856, and its owner, J. M. Winslow, who had come from the East Coast to build the hotel, situated it by the Falls of St. Anthony to bring in tourists. At first, people from within the state were the majority of the guests. Sylvanus Lowry stayed there in June 1858, and one of the landowners in Lowry's Addition—J. F. Goodner—lodged there during a return visit to Minnesota two months later.[4]

Winslow sold his hotel to New England resident Christopher Woodbridge McLean in July 1858. The new owner had already acquired properties in Boston, but the Winslow House was a risky venture, largely since the country was still reeling from the Panic of 1857, and few investments of any kind had strong prospects for success. Also, Minnesota had become a free state two months before McLean bought the hotel, and the new status put the state's attractiveness to southern tourists—especially slaveholders—in jeopardy.

However, McLean was accustomed to risk and took the gamble. Born in October 1828, he had experienced a life full of instability in the three decades before his acquisition of the Winslow House. His father died before McLean reached the age of ten. His mother remarried in 1838, but McLean's stepfather was killed in the Mexican War in 1847, when McLean was still a teenager. Tragedy struck the young man even more directly two years later; his first marriage ended with his new wife's death after only five months. He remarried in 1850, and the couple had three children as of July 1858. Even the purchase of the Winslow was tinted with loss, for their second child had died three months earlier.[5]

The new owner made a more determined effort than his predecessor to lure southerners to the hotel in the free state. He advertised in southern newspapers during the tourism season; one issue of the New Orleans

Henry Rice's American House, on the corner of Wabasha Avenue and Fourth Street, St. Paul, about 1873

The Winslow House, St. Anthony, about 1870

Times-Picayune placed his advertisement directly to the right of a notice of a slave sale. Within a month of McLean's takeover, enslaver John F. Goodner of Tennessee was the new owner's first southern guest. Goodner was no stranger to Minnesota, having traveled to St. Cloud in 1856 to buy land from Sylvanus Lowry, and he made a return trip there to facilitate a lien for more property in June 1858. But two months later he stayed at the Winslow before returning to the South. McLean's approach earned a positive if inaccurate comment from the Sauk Rapids *New Era*: "The energetic and popular proprietor Mr. McLain [*sic*] and his accomplished lady, hailing from the South, give to the Winslow a tone and southern air which we like." Mrs. McLean, like her husband, was a New Englander.[6]

McLean drew even more southerners to the Winslow in the summer of 1859, and more of them began noting the enslaved people accompanying them when signing the register book. Tourists traveled to the hotel from Kentucky, Louisiana, Mississippi, and Tennessee. And among them "several southerners . . . had their negro servants with them," according to correspondence from the hotel to a Memphis newspaper. Five of the guests in August—Judge James Howry of Mississippi; William E. Butler, William H. Long, and W. C. Stovall of Tennessee; and returning tourist Henry S. Dawson of Louisiana—collectively enslaved more than one hundred people. Butler owned land forty-five miles northwest of St. Paul, and he intended to build a summer home there. A local resident told him that slaveholders could keep slaves there and that anyone trying to coerce slaves to abandon them would be "instantly mobbed" by Minnesotans. In the following month, Dawson and Stovall and two "servants," as Swisshelm's *St. Cloud Democrat* put it, visited more of the state and stayed at the Stearns House in St. Cloud.[7]

Three enslavers signed in their slaves by job title in the Winslow's register book that summer. Their boldness in announcing their fellow travelers reflected the confidence they had in Minnesotans respecting the privacy of the guests' slaveholder-slave relationships. They did not use the word *slave* to identify their human property, but the anonymity given to them spoke volumes as to their enslavement. After all, the federal slave schedules similarly identified slaves only by the names of their enslavers. Signees included L. G. Beise and family "and nurse" from New Orleans, Mrs. A. P. Beers and child "and servant" from New Orleans, and A. T. Burnby "and servant" from Kentucky. The Kentuckian held four slaves back home.[8]

BIRTHS.

On Friday, August 31st, a son to C. P. Brainard.

On Monday, the 3d inst., a son to J. E. West.

On Tuesday, the 4th inst., a daughter to O. Taylor.

LIST OF ARRIVALS AT THE

STEARNS HOUSE
For the Past Week.

C. T. STEARNS, Proprietor.

W Garcelon..St Ant'ny	C Leather...............do
J R Moneton...........do	J Spencer...............do
M Sherin................do	J Richardson.........do
J H Shepley...........do	P Corrilas..............do
P Miles.................do	R Strout...Minneapolis
J Armstrong...........do	M Shootz...Ft Aber'bie
H Greenleaf....St Paul	E E Payne.Payn'sville
J P Chamberlain.....do	P L Gregory.Alex'dria
G Pomeroy.............do	T H Barrett...........Ill
F O Hazen...Monticelo	H S Dawson & servant..
N Myrick......Traverse	Lousiana
d'Sioux	T Kershaud........Miss
D Wood....Sauk River	T L Clarke............do
W Bosworth....Marion	V H Rodes............do
C Warner.. ....do	W C Smedes.......Tenn
Muyor..........St Louis	A T Burnby & s'vnt.Ky
E Spencer...Red River	A G Bacon............do
R W Furlong........do	E O Hamlin..S'k Ra'ds
J Taylor..............do	Capt Nelson.U S Army

Abstract of Meteorology.

As kept by O. E. Garrison for the Smithsonian Institute, Washington. For August, 1860. Reported Monthly for the DEMOCRAT.

St. CLOUD, MINN. Lat. 45° 45'. Lon. 94° 23'.

Thermometer.

Highest degree,	Lowest degree	Range	Warmest day	Mean of ditto
90°	45°	45	5th	80°

Cold'st day	Mean of do.	Mean Monthly	No. observations
12th	54.66	65.56	42

On September 6, 1860, the *St. Cloud Democrat* noted that Henry Dawson and his "servant" stayed at the Stearns House—as did several other southerners. *Courtesy author*

With the arrival of fall in 1859, Minnesota completed its second tourist season as a free state. Henry Sibley was the governor for both of those seasons. While serving in office, he managed land in Minnesota for slaveholder Pierre Chouteau Jr. As late as September 1859, Chouteau recorded one of Sibley's transactions on his behalf in his ledger book in St. Louis. Beholden to the interests of slaveholders, Sibley did not enforce the state's prohibition of slavery. When Sibley declined to run for reelection in 1860, he had given the state a reputation for tolerating enslaved people and their captors within its borders.[9]

Southern visitors expressed appreciation for the state's efforts to woo them. A correspondent for the New Orleans *Times-Picayune* wrote from the Winslow in early 1860, praising the facility for its hospitality to southerners: "None enjoyed things more apparently than the guests from Louisiana, Mississippi, and other southern states, quite a number of whom contemplate returning here this year, and probably a host of new tourists from the 'sunny' (but alas! hot) South will visit us this summer for the first time."[10]

As the 1860s began, Minnesota entered a political transition. Some Democrats who had permanently relocated from the South won seats in the state senate, and they used their service to promote the causes of their fellow southerners. Democrat John S. Prince, who managed some of Chouteau's real estate in Minnesota, won St. Paul's mayoral election, and he continued to work for the slaveholder after assuming the office. On the other hand, Alexander Ramsey became the first Republican to serve as governor, and several members of the party won seats in the Minnesota legislature. As local Republican victories significantly chipped away at the Democratic Party's control of governmental appointees, guarantees for the protection of slavery in the state were threatened.[11]

Governor Ramsey tried to minimize sectional discord in his capacity as the leader of a free state tolerant of slavery, and he refused to discuss any possible bold action to eliminate the practice in Minnesota. He offered a rhetorical sop to his fellow Republicans in his inaugural address, calling slavery "an institution so manifestly fraught with insecurity and weakness." On the other hand, when speaking against growing threats to secession, he said that "we can never encourage, threaten nor permit the sundering of those political ties that make of our United States a great, prosperous, powerful nation." Thus, his first speech as governor prioritized unity over abolition.[12]

Democrats may have appreciated the Republican reassurances, but the election had consequences for several of President Buchanan's appointees. George Clitherall, Charles Wagner, and William Caruthers resigned their positions early in 1860, and by February Buchanan had nominated successors. Wagner was in Washington, DC, working as a federal clerk by June. Clitherall, Caruthers, and Wagner sacrificed their social stature

Alexander Ramsey,
second governor of the
state of Minnesota,
about 1860

in Minnesota to retreat to the South—to states run by their own party. They could return to slavery, and they could claim to have stood on principle—rejecting service to an antislavery party—when arriving back home. However, they returned to states full of Democrats who had never left the South, and the former appointees faced the task of transferring their political capital from a free state and maintaining it in a slave state.[13]

Samuel Hays—the Virginian appointed to St. Cloud's public moneys office—stayed with the Democrats in Minnesota, but he ran afoul of the party's national leader. Buchanan fired him, reportedly for opposing his choice of Democratic candidate for president. Hays's older children were in Virginia, but he himself had no property there to which he could return. All of his wealth lay in the Northwest, and he remained in Minnesota to nurture it. He continued to operate his gristmill, which remained popular among the locals. His wife and youngest child stayed with him in St. Cloud, as did his slaves Chloe and Ellen.

By 1860 the debate over slavery in Minnesota centered on whether the state's hotels should serve as sanctuaries for southern guests wanting to bring slaves with them while visiting the state. Republicans were already against the extension of slavery into new territories and opposed the extra-legal protection of slavery in a free state. The Democratic Party supported slavery in territories, but some local Democrats did not want slavery legalized in Minnesota. The Democrats who supported the tourists' practice considered the slaveholder-slave relationship sacrosanct wherever the enslaver brought it, and they believed that Minnesotans had no business in interfering with such a relationship—even in their own free state. In the meantime, tourists likely put insurance policies on slaves accompanying them to Minnesota in that hostile political climate—to cover any losses not only from travel by water but also from any uprisings like the Stearns House disturbance of 1857.

For the duration of the legislative session of 1859–60, the state's pro-slavery and antislavery lawmakers engaged in political quarrels related to the institution of slavery. One of the first tests of the legislature stemmed from an event that took place hundreds of miles away and weeks before the legislators met. Abolitionist John Brown had led both slaves and free people on an unsuccessful raid on a federal arsenal at Harper's Ferry, Virginia, in October 1859, and people responded differently according to political affiliation. Democrats and some Republicans spoke against Brown, but abolitionist Republicans tended to express solidarity with Brown and then consider him a martyr after his execution. When the 1859–60 legislative session began weeks later, in December 1859, Senator William Sprigg Hall introduced resolutions that strongly denounced the raid and anyone supporting it. In the Minnesota House, however, a representative felt compelled to respond by adding a condemnation of people wanting secession if a Republican became president.[14]

Toward the end of the session, perhaps inspired by the economic difficulties that continued after the Panic of 1857, Minnesota's supporters of slavery tried to legalize the practice by codifying the state's unofficial acceptance of tourism-based slavery into law. By March 1860 six hundred residents of Stillwater, St. Anthony, and St. Paul signed a petition asking the state legislature to legalize slavery just for southern tourists. They argued that by "allowing citizens from the South, while remaining temporarily in this state for health, pleasure, or other purposes, to bring with them and hold within the state for a period not exceeding five months, any slave or slaves whom they may deem it necessary to retain with them as body servants, for their comfort and convenience," according to the petition's text, "the interest and welfare of the citizens of Minnesota would be promoted." The signers included "Democratic editors, Lt. Governors, Land Office men," and others. Senator Charles Mackubin, originally from the slave state Maryland, presented a bill that championed their cause. Although he had chosen to live without slaves, that did not mean he opposed the institution. Slavery had given him a childhood of privilege, and it supported his widowed mother and siblings. Moreover, his fellow native Marylanders William Sprigg Hall and Harwood Iglehart— his business partners and, in the case of Iglehart, his cousin—still participated in slavery, as did their families. With Mackubin's proposal he was asking Minnesota to respect the practice that gave his friends and family a living. A similar bill was introduced in the Minnesota House of Representatives by Daniel A. Robertson, an ally of Henry Rice.[15]

The patience of state legislators of both parties regarding local slavery had worn thin by then, but one-fifth of the lawmakers—each one a Democrat—voted for the bill. The senate rejected Mackubin's proposal, 29 to 5, and the vote revealed a political split between its Maryland-born members. Hall voted against it despite his history as a slaveholder, thus opposing his fellow southerner and real estate partner. The house also dismissed the proposal, 51 to 18, but among those who voted for passage were local profiteers from slavery. Representative George W. Sweet of Benton County had sold thousands of dollars in land to enslavers just three summers earlier, and Representative Oscar Stephenson—a native of Virginia—had promoted his Minnesota-based business in a southern newspaper. The vote symbolized the last stand not only for legal slavery in Minnesota but also for the legislative power of slavery's supporters. After the legislature adjourned in March 1860, Hall, Mackubin, Stephenson, and Sweet never returned to it.[16]

◆

Despite the failure of the bill to legalize seasonal slavery, southern tourism still thrived in Minnesota. Leaders of the state's growing institutions operated within this context, seemingly with no hesitation. On June 26 and July 25, the University of Minnesota's board of regents met at the elegant Winslow House. The 1860 tourism season was underway, and the attendees were surrounded by slaveholding tourists. Days before the first university board meeting, the first of the season's guests to sign in slaves, Dr. E. M. Lane of Mississippi, registered his "Col'd Boy" and "Col'd Girl," two of his eleven slaves.[17]

Three more enslaved people were signed in before the university board's second meeting there on July 25. By then Richard Christmas of Issaquena County, Mississippi, arrived at the Winslow with his family and their slave Eliza Winston. Signing in as "C. R. Christmas wife child and nurse," they stayed in Minnesota for months that year. The Christmases, like many of their fellow planters in Issaquena County, left the plantation management to others, took a slave away from the plantation, and hoped for the best during their holiday. More than 150 slaves kept working the fertile fields of the Christmas plantation.[18]

Enslavers occasionally did not sign on behalf of their accompanying slaves in the Winslow guest book. Stovall signed only his own name in August 1859, and Dawson registered just for himself and his family in July 1860. By leaving out their servants, they took a precaution: they were in a free state led by a Republican, and the Stearns House disturbance had happened when Minnesota was still a slave territory. The slave revolt led by John Brown on Harper's Ferry had taken place mere months earlier. With the slaves left off the registry, the slaveholders did not have to worry that local authorities or antislavery crusaders would read the words "servant" or "nurse" and then demand to interview them.[19]

The hotel registrations inspired constant local press coverage throughout the summer. The *St. Anthony Express* reported in late June, "The Winslow House in this city is rapidly filling up with visitors from the east and south." Two weeks later the St. Anthony *Falls Evening News* boasted, "[The Winslow] is doing an active business, and is winning high encomiums from its guests." Newspapers published by Democrats reassured southerners that Minnesota's new free statehood need not worry them. The *Minnesotian and Times* told potential slaveholding tourists that "we assure our Southern friends that they are always welcome to visit us and to bring their servants with them. No one will ever molest them." William Wood, in the Sauk Rapids *New Era*, attempted to respect the state's free status while awkwardly cautioning Minnesotans not to enforce it. "We don't believe in Slavery, and rejoice that Minnesota is a free State," he began, "but when people come up here from the South, and, relying on the honor and good faith of our people, bring along with them their servants, we don't think it looks well nor do we believe it right for us to interface and coax off these servants and then raise the 'hue and cry' of Slavery in Minnesota." Thomas Newson, who edited the *St. Paul Times*, promised on July 14 that Minnesota would not interfere with any slaveholding that southern tourists brought to the state. Southern guests in Minnesota were elated and sent copies of that issue down to their plantations to spread the word in the South about northwestern, proslavery hospitality.[20]

In contrast, that summer the pro–Republican Party newspaper *Minneapolis State Atlas* published "Is Minnesota a Free State?" In Minnesota, the paper said, "men who, pretending to act as officers under the laws of this State, engage in the disgraceful and detestable business of kidnapping free men for the purpose of forcing them into slavery." Slaveholding tourists, it said, were "openly disregarding the constitutional law of our State, and bidding defiance to, and insulting the sentiments and feelings of our people." The editorial directed less anger to the visitors than to "those infamous beings who live in our own State, and who, in order to secure a few dollars of Southern money are willing to see the constitution of Minnesota trampled underfoot, and the feelings of our people outraged by the introduction of negro slaves in our very midst." The commentary asserted that African Americans became free within the borders of the state and "shall be protected to the full extent of the law by our state." It further warned tourists, "When you voluntarily bring your human chattels into Minnesota, they will exercise their own discretion as to remaining with and going back with you."[21]

Among those tourists were Martha Terry Prince, her children, and her slaves. Born in 1823, Prince was raised in a wealthy plantation society in Mississippi. Her father, William Terry, ran one of the most successful plantations in Carroll County. Both she and her sister married into the Prince family, whose patriarch William Berry Prince had founded the town of Princeton in Washington County, Louisiana. The town peaked in 1836 with a courthouse, a bank, a railroad, and six hundred people— mostly educated, well-mannered, wealthy, and of great social prominence. The state legislature, however, added land to Washington County in 1839, and the formation of Issaquena County from part of that addition in 1844 hastened Princeton's decline.[22]

By that time the Prince family had escaped Princeton's troubles by relocating to nearby Claiborne County, where Prince and her husband held twenty slaves in 1850. Her husband's death sometime during the decade left her to raise their five children alone. By the end of the 1850s, she resettled her family in Yazoo County. Then on July 4, 1860, her sickly mother-in-law, Catherine Prince, drew up her will, leaving her enslaved young man Thompson and "servant man Green" to Martha Prince's children. Catherine died four days later.[23]

Martha Prince was in Minnesota less than two weeks later for the sake of health. Two of her children were sick, and her doctor had advised her to take them to the Northwest to recuperate. She brought them to the International Hotel in St. Paul and took at least three family servants with her to attend to them. The vacation was to provide therapy to the sons as the family grieved the loss of their matriarch.[24]

The slaves traveling to Minnesota likely came from families with multi-generational ties to the Princes. In Claiborne County, Mississippi, enslaved people who worked as domestics were descendants of earlier slaves owned by the master's ancestors. Without the family connections, enslaved people in Claiborne were consigned to plantation labor, cultivating cotton for their entire lives. Moreover, the county's planters tended to assign their slaves to work on small farms adjoining the plantations, especially if relatives of the planters owned those farms. Prince's hotel slaves were still on work duty in Minnesota but as body servants in a milder summer climate instead of as field hands pricking their skin on cotton bolls in oppressive heat.[25]

Even on vacation, however, the Prince family could not escape from suffering loss. On July 17 Prince's servant Henry Sparks disappeared from the International with two free African American employees of the hotel, who had been counseling him on his own new legal freedom as of his arrival in Minnesota. The three found refuge at another hotel nearby, but a group of European Americans found them and sent Sparks by boat to the South. The incident initiated a new debate among Minnesotans about local slavery. According to a correspondent for the newspaper *New Orleans Delta*, St. Paul residents claimed that Sparks had left in broad daylight, of his own accord. The antislavery press, however, reported the event as the kidnapping of a freed slave. Also, Governor Ramsey expressed outrage at Sparks's treatment and ordered an investigation of those who sent him away, but St. Paul mayor John Prince (no relation to Martha Prince), still employed by a slaveholder, claimed that he had asked local law enforcement not to involve itself in matters concerning Sparks.[26]

In addition to the trauma of the publicity surrounding Sparks's departure, his owner soon suffered the indignity of a writ of habeas corpus,
given to her by Minnesota Supreme Court chief justice Lafayette Emmett.
Attorney George Nourse had asked for it, assuming that she knew of her
estranged servant's whereabouts and that she would confess his location
under oath. However, as he prepared to question her, she stated through
her own lawyer that she had not been in contact with Sparks since his
departure from the International and that she wished for the writ's dis-
missal. Emmett believed her and granted her request.[27]

Shortly afterward Martha Prince left the hotel with her family and slaves
and spent the rest of her Minnesota summer in St. Anthony. She signed
in at the Winslow House on July 22 in her own name and with "3 children
and 2 svts." The Christmases and their slave were still there, and they
became better acquainted with Prince while at the Winslow together.[28]

The Sparks incident inspired acts of vigilantism among local opponents of slavery, and Prince's relocation to the Winslow did not protect her
against further controversy. According to the St. Paul Pioneer and Democrat of July 22, Ramsey County's sheriff and more than a dozen men
came to the Winslow for Christmas's slave, and some in the party said
that "they were also going to arrest some of Mrs. Prince's negroes, who
have been living in the vicinity since the affair at the International Hotel
in this city." The paper surmised, concerning the search party, that "what
they most desired was to insult the [Christmas] family." However, no one
was apprehended that day, and the Mississippians continued their stay in
St. Anthony with their "servants."[29]

The Christmases had felt enough confidence in Minnesotans' tolerance of slavery to mark "nurse" in the hotel guest book, but they knew
they were potential targets of opponents of slavery. They developed a new
ritual with their nurse, Eliza Winston. Whenever the family detected the
approach of an abolitionist group wishing to abduct and then liberate enslaved people, the Christmases ordered their nurse into the woods to hide.
She always obeyed, but she did remain near the hotel each time and tried
to make herself conspicuous to any wandering abolitionists. "I did not go
very far, hoping that they would find me," she later wrote.[30]

◆

Some tourists had no illusions about tolerance in Minnesota toward
slavery. In correspondence dated August 19, 1860, a writer told the New

Orleans *Times-Picayune*, "The Winslow House . . . is filled with Southern people. Gentlemen, with their families, are here from Louisiana, Mississippi, Kentucky, and other southern states: spending their money with livery stables, boatmen, shops and hotels, much to the delight of the grateful recipients, who, whatever they may think of us as men and women from slave territory, have a great respect for our purses, if not our persons."[31]

Two days after the writing of that letter, Minnesota's de facto slavery faced its most formidable challenge. The Christmases and Prince, who had temporarily left the hotel for a short trip together down the Mississippi, returned to the Winslow on August 21, and the ritual of the woods resumed. However, on that day local abolitionists found Eliza Winston and encouraged her to leave with them. She agreed to do so and then petitioned a district court in Minnesota to grant her emancipation from her master. After she pleaded her case, Judge Charles Vanderburgh declared her free.[32]

The Winslow's owner, C. W. McLean, stood outside the courthouse after the verdict and proposed to kidnap Winston and return her to Christmas. He also reportedly was the first to come forward after the trial and said, "If the owner wants to have that nigger, let him say the word and he shall have her. There are plenty of us ready to take her!" He led a mob toward the home of one of the local men who guided the emancipation effort, but Winston remained free in spite of the backlash. McLean's remarks and his gathering of a mob revealed his desperation to protect his clientele and his business. The hotel had flourished that summer, and eleven more slaves were signed in during the four weeks between the University of Minnesota meeting of July 25 and Winston's emancipation on August 21.[33]

McLean's vigilantism proved futile. Half of the guests in hotels in the area left within one day of the verdict, and one observer predicted that soon no lodgers would remain. McLean and the Winslow especially suffered. Throughout the summer southern investors had been arranging to buy the Winslow, but they reneged after the Winston incident. Local journalists wrote angry passages about the financial damage and about the ingratitude of antislavery Minnesotans toward southern patronage. One writer noted, "St. Anthony has lost thousands of dollars by this infamous transaction." Another fumed, "All the money now in this country has been brought here by Southerners." This writer said that "the hotel and boarding-houses [had been] crowded with them" but that the verdict had resulted in a "general stampede" of slaveholding tourists back to the South.[34]

When Martha Prince heard about the court decision, she not only joined the "stampede" but also voluntarily separated herself from her servants. She instructed her remaining two slaves to immediately depart from Minnesota, but they begged her not to abandon them—or so a Nashville newspaper reported. She persisted in her order, and they fled into the woods nearby. She and her children then returned to Mississippi in humiliation, having lost hundreds of dollars in valuable human chattel while on vacation. At the very least, her directive to her slaves allowed her to save some face as a southerner, for she avoided the indignity of watching northerners remove her property from her.[35]

Southerners shared McLean's anger. One tourist in St. Paul wrote to a Kentucky newspaper that Winston's emancipation provided proof that "there exists here a deep-seated hostility to the South and its institutions." The writer additionally advised, "Southern men should begin to prepare themselves for the 'irrepressible conflict,' which I believe lies but a brief distance in the future." Similarly, a St. Anthony tourist wrote to a New Orleans newspaper, calling the incident "one of the most aggravating outrages and insults which have ever been offered to southerners by the abolitionists." The writer felt sorry for McLean, who had enjoyed a great year of business and had stood poised to experience a "handsome harvest" of tourists in the following year. Instead, "now he has good reason to apprehend his prospects have been seriously clouded by the infamous intermeddling of these abolition scoundrels."[36]

Unfortunately for McLean, pity from southerners could not keep his hotel in business, but he catered to slaveholders to the very end. The Winslow's last registered guests of that eventful season were a Mr. Murdock and family "and servant" of New Orleans, who signed in on November 6, 1860. Shortly thereafter, the Winslow House ended operations for the season. It would never reopen. In December McLean sold the Winslow to another northerner for $35,000. The hotel closed on May 21, 1861.[37]

◆

The judge's decision did not prohibit enslavers from investing in Minnesota or traveling there. Indeed, they continued to visit the state and acquire land. R. J. Mendenhall's brother Cyrus bought $780 of real estate in Stearns County in October 1860, and he acquired land in Wright County the following month. Earlier in the year, the 1860 federal slave schedule recorded him as the owner of forty slaves in North Carolina. As had his father, George Mendenhall, Cyrus returned to North Carolina after making his purchases.[38]

Henry Dawson of Louisiana was lodged at the Winslow House when Winston won her freedom, but he remained in Minnesota in order to facilitate his annual hunting trip in the fall. He returned to the Stearns House in St. Cloud that September and planned the excursion with five other southerners vacationing there. One of them, W. C. Smedes, of Mississippi, had once offered slaves to the Magnolia Plantation owned by S. S. Boyd and Rice Ballard. "You can have Phil and his wife Jane, both stout, able and fully acclimated young slaves for $2,400," Smedes wrote to Ballard. "I will also sell Henry and his family for $4,000. You will find them a very likely family. I will sell the two families, Phil's and Harry's, for $6,200 cash." Hunter A. T. Burnby, who had stayed at the Winslow in 1859, now lodged with his servant at the Stearns House. After the trip ended, Dawson and Thomas Kershaw of the hunting party stopped at the disgraced Winslow on October 2, on their way back down to the South.[39]

Dawson's slave Fielding had killed more game on the excursion than any of the other hunters. The fact that his captor armed him in a free state demonstrated how strongly Dawson trusted Fielding to voluntarily remain enslaved. Fielding indeed did not use his gun to try to convince anyone to honor his legal freedom. Although he had a stronger legal case for manumission after the Eliza Winston verdict, he returned to Louisiana with the Dawsons. As their vessel left Minnesota and sailed down the Mississippi River, Fielding experienced a kind of Middle Passage within the United States—legally transitioning from freedman into slave. Judge Vanderburgh's ruling did not end slavery in Minnesota, after all; even in a free state and within weeks of an emancipation verdict, antislavery law still had its limits in the Northwest.[40]

Senator Clement Clay of Alabama, one of Senator Henry M. Rice's acquaintances and the owner of seventeen enslaved people, reluctantly inaugurated the 1861 tourism season in Minnesota. He had fallen ill while visiting a cousin in Virginia in early 1861. "My asthma has distressed me so much, during my sojourn here with my kindred," he wrote to Rice, "that I am at last constrained 'to go abroad' and seek relief in a cold, dry climate, which is not found in my country. I wish to go by way of my home (Huntsville, Ala.) to Minnesota, where I may stay weeks or months." His wife also urged him to recuperate in Minnesota. "In those days," Virginia Clay-Clopton later recalled, "the air of that far western state was supposed to have a phenomenally curative effect upon the victims of asthma, from which for years Mr. Clay had suffered an almost 'daily death.'"[41]

After being joined in Virginia by Clay's brother and a friend, who'd traveled there together from Alabama, they all left for Minnesota. They stayed at the International Hotel in St. Paul upon arrival in late March 1861, but they soon left the hotel because of "an unpleasant experience . . . due to sectional feeling." Two young men in the building spotted Clay, and one said, "Clay, the fire-eating senator from Alabama is in this house. Let's mob him!" Local residents later told the Clays that in Minnesota "it was the fashion of the times to denounce the South."[42]

The Clays relocated to the house of George Culver in St. Paul and stayed there for the next month. When the Civil War erupted on April 12, Clay was anxious to return to Alabama. The southerners had to wait until the ice in the Mississippi River broke, but on April 23 the river thawed enough for them to board the boat *Grey Eagle* and sail for home in a new country—the Confederate States of America.[43]

CHAPTER TEN

Confederates

George C. Mendenhall lived a bi-regional lifestyle long after purchasing real estate in central Minnesota. He worked as a lawyer for clients in both the North and the South, and northerners retained the North Carolinian enslaver to serve as the lawyer for two free African Americans accused of kidnapping a slave in August 1859. However, he never had the chance to secure the defendants' freedom. He drowned trying to ford a river in North Carolina in March 1860, before the trial took place. His widow, Delphina, carried on in his abolitionism, working to free the slaves her late husband had inherited from a previous marriage.[1]

Months later, in October, Robert Dyson died in Maryland. He had spent three years traveling between the Upper South and the Northwest, and he lived in Stillwater only one of those years. He had not risen in power in Minnesota to become a member of the city, county, or state elite. Aside from his homeopathic practice and the land he owned in Stillwater, he did not leave much of a mark in his adopted city.

On the other hand, the death of commuting slaveholder Thomas Winston had a much larger effect on Minnesota. In November 1860 Winston died aboard a boat traveling from Tennessee to Louisiana, and he was buried in New Orleans. He left behind hundreds of lots of real estate in multiple counties in Minnesota. Soon after Winston's death, Alexander Ramsey, who had just been reelected as Minnesota's governor, received a letter from Winston's sister, who asked him to grant her late brother's request that Ramsey execute his will. She pleaded ignorance on her own behalf of legal matters, and she claimed that Ramsey was "the one in St. Paul most trusted by my brother to protect the interest of his two sons, now in Germany at school." The governor of a free state accepted the woman's petition and assessed her brother's property in Minnesota. Meanwhile, a district court in Louisiana inventoried Winston's holdings there, which did not include slaves.[2]

In a sense, the deaths of Mendenhall, Dyson, and Winston symbolized the beginning of the end of Minnesota's development through slaveholder patronage. Minnesota's transition from slave territory to free state had not deterred the commuters from investing, and all three of them had decreased their holdings of slaves in order to shuttle between regions. None of them had traveled to the state for months before their deaths, so all were away when the incidents involving Henry Sparks and Eliza Winston took place in the summer of 1860. Unlike the slaveholders who intentionally stayed away from Minnesota, the three bi-regional travelers passed away before they could choose whether to return.

Sylvanus Lowry was in Washington, DC, when 1860 gave way to 1861, but his stay in the nation's capital allowed him to see internal national discord in the city that brought representatives from all states together. He considered war between the North and South to be inevitable. He wrote to his wife of "the whole nation filled with gloom, preparations for war resounding all over at least the Southern land—business all except gun and powder-making stopped." Within a few months he left the nation's capital, and he returned to the Northwest, thus appearing to side with the Union via his presence in Minnesota.[3]

In the late spring of 1861, southern enslaved people accustomed to their owners' commutes or seasonal sojourns to Minnesota prepared for their masters to depart again. They worried about whom the enslavers would choose to leave home and who would remain to adjust without them. They steeled themselves for another summer with only the watchful eyes of violent overseers upon them. They anxiously awaited the pain that came with the annual division of their communities when some of the slaves left with the masters.

The slaves must have felt surprised at remaining together through the spring, but they would soon hear rumors among themselves and learn from eavesdropped slaveholder conversations about the start of the Civil War in April. Their enslavers never left for Minnesota during the tourism season, and the freezing of the Mississippi that fall ensured that they would not travel there that year. The eruption of the Civil War in April 1861 had cut off the southern Confederate states from northern Union states like Minnesota, and Confederate residents busied themselves with defending their states instead of making plans for leisure travel. Rebel slaveholders kept slaves at home to maintain domestic stability during the war. Slave communities became more stable, because the conflict removed the possibility of travel to Minnesota disrupting them. The only separation they anticipated after 1861 was their removal from the masters by the arrival of Union troops, and the slaves looked forward to that possibility.

The Civil War exacerbated sectional tensions that had intensified in Minnesota after the Eliza Winston case the preceding fall. Just before the war began, the new proprietors of the Winslow House, where Winston had stayed before petitioning for emancipation, tried to keep slaveholders from boycotting Minnesota and made one last-ditch effort to bring southerners back to the state in the following spring. An April 3, 1861, advertisement in Mississippi's *Vicksburg Whig* declared that the Winslow House had become the St. Anthony Falls Hotel. Perhaps for name recognition, the ad was attributed to "McLean & Co," and it claimed, "The patrons of this house are nine-tenths from the South." The same promotion appeared in the weekly paper on April 10 and 17. But with the start of the Civil War on April 12, the newspaper discontinued printing the notice.[4]

C. W. McLean and his family left Minnesota for New Bern, North Carolina, where he acclimated himself to the trappings of the region. Within a decade, he acquired a juvenile African American "domestic servant" who shared his surname. After the death of his second wife, he married a local resident whose parents had owned slaves. McLean had, for all intents and purposes, become a southerner.[5]

With the outbreak of the war, Minnesota's relationship with the slaveholding South fundamentally changed. The cross-regional shuttling that Mendenhall, Dyson, and Winston had performed now became impossible for others to duplicate. The tourists McLean had once lured to Minnesota stayed in the South to defend their region—and their rights to enslave other people. Insurance companies lost business during the war, and southerners had no access to their northwestern investments. On the other hand, the relationship between Minnesota and the South survived by a thread, and that thread was the Minnesota real estate that the enslavers owned.[6]

◆

Those southerners who left Minnesota and returned to southern states joined or supported the Confederate army, and many also resumed their

slaveholding activities after having sold some or all of their slaves to move
to Minnesota. They were not so hostile toward the Union as to give up
their claims to land in the Northwest, and some Confederates communi-
cated with Minnesotans during the war for no other purpose than to keep
their northwestern real estate safe. Nevertheless, the ex-Minnesotan rebels would not budge from the Confederacy, and they demanded that Minnesota and the rest of the Union support their right to enslave.

Theobald Forstall's former time as a Minnesota state official and a
Stillwater-based businessman did not hinder his transition to becoming
one of the earliest enthusiasts of the Confederacy. He was already back in
Louisiana when the state joined the Confederacy, and he served in the
New Orleans city council during the war. He ran a shipping business
until the war cut off his market and led him to bankruptcy, at which point
he joined the Confederate army. He reportedly wrote to a friend in Stillwater about his fervor for his new country. According to the *Stillwater Messenger*, Forstall was "exulting over all the reverses sustained by the loyal
armies, defies the power of the loyal citizens, and speaks of our Government as the 'defunct United States.'"[7]

Stillwater's residents wanted nothing more to do with Forstall from that
moment onward. The *Messenger* portrayed him as a traitor to the country
and ungrateful to the city's residents. "For much of his social position
and property, he owes the citizens of this city, who took him by the hand
when he came here six years ago and extended him a degree of encouragement such as has been extended to few, if any young man who has ever
located amongst us," the reporter claimed. Accusing him of "ingratitude,
rebel instincts, and consummate treachery and meanness of Jefferson
Davis and General Beauregard," the writer linked his behavior to the violent practice of owning dark-skinned people. "Such is the barbarism of
slavery," the commentary concluded. Local anger lingered the following
year. When the Confederate army made a specific effort to recruit Creoles
in New Orleans, the *Messenger* expressed similar bitterness: "We presume
a former citizen of this city and, at a former period, editor of the Stillwater
Democrat will be unable longer to resist the call to duty."[8]

Not every former official made as clean a break from the Northwest as
Forstall did. President Buchanan appointee William ("Colonel") Caruthers
returned to central Minnesota in November 1860, after having spent the
spring and summer in Tennessee. He was no longer the land register
in St. Cloud, but he returned to the city to manage the investments of his
family and friends from Tennessee. Republican presidential candidate

Abraham Lincoln had defeated Democrat Stephen Douglas days earlier, and slaveholders in southern states worried about what Republican rule meant for their livelihoods. Caruthers divested some Tennesseans of their real estate holdings, and he helped others secure their claims to local lands. Jordan Stokes gave him power of attorney and, through him, sold some of his land to a local resident on December 1. In contrast, Caruthers transferred his ownership of 160 acres to his father, Abraham, whose purchase of the land for $5,000 made his investment in Lowry's Addition equal in value to that of Abraham's brother Judge Robert Caruthers. William Caruthers then joined the Confederate forces in Tennessee.[9]

J. Travis Rosser was still in the South as of early 1861, and he had less incentive than Caruthers to return to Minnesota after the Civil War began. The new country fired on the Union's Fort Sumter on April 12, and fifteen days later Rosser organized a Confederate corps. On May 11, 1861, the group—nicknamed "Rosser's Rangers"—joined the Confederate army as Company K of the Tenth Virginia Cavalry, and Rosser achieved the rank of captain. In July he was sent to the command of General H. A. Wise at White Sulphur Springs, West Virginia.[10]

Rosser's Confederate service meant that he fought the same country he had once served. The Minnesotans he had governed were his enemies, and he squared off against at least one of them in battle only months after the war began. Among the Union soldiers he faced at the Battle of Bull Run was Alexander Wilkin—Rosser's predecessor as Minnesota's territorial secretary. The battle's fatalities numbered in the hundreds for both sides, but Rosser and Wilkin each survived.[11]

Rosser's defection to the South gave his old critics another excuse to publicly address his shortcomings. A premature obituary in the *St. Paul Daily Press* on May 2, 1863, claimed that he had been killed in battle. The Republican-leaning newspaper expressed concern over whether it had identified the correct Rosser; if so, "there would be no tears shed over his fate, even if his treason had not merited the doom which has befallen him." The paper called Rosser "one of the most incorrigible loafers which were ever produced even in the fruitful soil of Virginia," and the obituary mentioned at length how disliked he was among Republicans in Minnesota.[12]

The former secretary still had a least one ally in his previously adopted state—an ally who, not coincidentally, had supported slavery. Daniel A. Robertson, a fellow Minnesota Democrat and the state legislator who had introduced the bill for legal slavery to the Minnesota House three years earlier, wrote an open letter in which he did not excuse Rosser's Confederate status but offered political context for it. The writer called Rosser a friend and claimed to have less respect for Confederate-sympathizing northerners than for the former secretary, who at least was in the South on the battlefield to fight for the Confederacy. Robertson had a point. Rosser fought in the Battle of Brandy Station just five days after Robertson's letter appeared in the local press, while the well-known local Democrat named Sylvanus Lowry published a pro-Confederate newspaper in central Minnesota.[13]

Rosser worked for the Confederate States of America (CSA) in various capacities throughout the four years of the war. In the Confederate army he rose in the ranks to major in 1862, but he mustered out in 1863 and then became a volunteer soldier. His time in the Northwest influenced his service during the war. By 1865 he also held a government office in the CSA as chief of Indian affairs, and this position likely resulted from his experience in policy concerning the Dakota and other Indigenous nations while secretary in Minnesota.[14]

Rosser died not in battle but at the home of his brother Leonidas in Virginia on March 20, 1865. An obituary in a local newspaper errantly identified the former secretary as "formerly Lieutenant-Governor and afterwards Governor of the Territory of Minnesota." Although Rosser had served Minnesota, part of an enemy nation in wartime, the South at least accorded him the respect of his past positions. In contrast, coverage in Minnesota's press focused on his "treason," and it did not acknowledge his service in a position a heartbeat away from the governor's office. With this omission, while the Civil War raged, Minnesotans began to distance themselves from their history with African American slavery.[15]

By late July 1860, George Clitherall, who had served as a federal appointee in Otter Tail County, returned to Mobile, Alabama, and resumed slaveholding on a reduced scale. He resided away from his wife and family, staying in the home of John and Annie Scott. That year's slave schedule listed three of his slaves as fugitives—an eighteen-year-old woman and boys aged fifteen and twelve, all designated in the 1860 rolls with an "M" for "mulatto"—and a sole remaining slave, a four-year-old boy listed as "B."[16]

After the war began, Clitherall's state joined the Confederacy, and he went off to battle as a volunteer in the Alabama Home Guard. During the conflict he also found work in the new Confederate government, serving in the CSA treasury in New Orleans. Although he did not officially fight in the Confederate army, his wartime endeavors opposed the same government he had served just a few years earlier. Meanwhile, his wife, children, and slaves managed the Clitherall household in his absence, and whatever income from Minnesota remained in their Alabama estate partially contributed to their survival during the war.[17]

Charles Wagner, a former federal appointee in Stillwater, was in Washington, DC, serving in a federal position in the fall of 1860, but when Abraham Lincoln won that year's presidential election, he joined other southern federal employees in resigning. In the Civil War, he was a colonel and headed a regiment in South Carolina. A Minnesotan in the Union Army recognized him during a battle. The *Stillwater Messenger* reported on the encounter by depicting Wagner with the same kind of anti-rebel invective that it had directed at former resident Theobald Forstall. Encouraging Wagner's defeat, and adding an anti–Native American touch, the periodical cheered on the Union, "Our boys will yet get the ungrateful little fellow's scalp."[18]

◆

People who had moved to Minnesota from the South responded to the war in diverse ways. Those who had opportunities for wealth and strong proslavery feelings tended to leave their new lives in Minnesota behind for some semblance of their old lives in the South. On the other hand, Minnesota residents who had adjusted well to life without slavery and who had successful businesses in the Northwest stayed in the region.

Scott County and especially the town of Belle Plaine were barely recovering from the Panic of 1857 when the Civil War took away their southern benefactors, inflicting a severe blow to the local economy. Henry Spain had returned to Virginia with a slave by the time of the federal census of 1860. His son-in-law Joel Alexander Pace remained in Minnesota, but in 1861 he relocated to Virginia and joined the Confederate army the following year. Pace had been one of Belle Plaine's largest investors in real estate and had thousands of dollars' worth of land at the time of the war's outbreak. When he left town, his wealth left with him. His departure effectively ended any development of the property he owned, thus stunting the area's growth.[19]

The war did not completely cut off the South from the Northwest, and some residents of Confederate states managed to sell their Minnesota real estate during the war because Minnesotans acted as proxies for the transactions. In the fall of 1861, a North Carolinian Quaker named Nathan B. Hill moved permanently to the Northwest to start a Quaker community. Hill came to Wright County six months after the war started. He had held one slave in North Carolina in 1850, but he helped enslaved people escape to freedom through the Underground Railroad throughout the 1850s. By the time he and his family left proslavery North Carolina for Minnesota in 1861, he held no slaves. He bought some land in Wright County from his brother-in-law Cyrus Mendenhall in November and purchased more from him three months later.

Mendenhall was in North Carolina at the time, and by then the state had seceded from the Union. However, weeks before Hill's arrival, Mendenhall gave power of attorney to his brother R. J., who remained in Minnesota and conducted the transaction. At the time, North Carolina's Quakers were leaving their homes in Guilford County in droves. The state had grown increasingly hostile toward abolitionists. Years after Hill's move, he became a prominent medical doctor in Minnesota and served as the president of the Minneapolis city council.[20]

During the war Cyrus Mendenhall stayed in Guilford County with his wife's slaves, and he played an active role in defending the state and, by extension, the Confederacy. By the time he sold his land in Minnesota, he had already started a war-related business with two other slaveholders in his county. He partnered with Ezekiel P. Jones and Grafton Gardner to manufacture guns for the Confederate army. Jones held twenty-five slaves, and Gardner owned eighteen. When Hill bought land from Mendenhall, the new Minnesotan helped to fund a business that armed his own country's enemy and financially supported three enslavers' plantations.[21]

Three institutions in Tennessee, which seceded in June 1861, acquired a significant portion of central Minnesota during the war. Slaveholders controlled and funded all three institutions: the Cumberland Presbyterian Church, Cumberland University, and the office of the governor.

In 1861 David Lowry turned over direct ownership of his St. Cloud property to the Cumberland Presbyterian Church, with which he remained affiliated. Judge Robert Caruthers's nephew William had long since vacated the office of local land register, but his presence in St. Cloud enabled him to facilitate this and other major transactions for Tennesseans. However, William Caruthers was a strong southern Democrat in his politics, and Tennessee's secession put him on borrowed time in Minnesota. In July,

as he prepared to depart, he exercised his power of attorney to facilitate the sale of one of Jordan Stokes's lots to Reverend Lowry, specifically
for use by the Cumberland Presbyterian Church. In the following month
Caruthers developed a warranty deed—a deed guaranteeing clear title—
for some of his uncle's land, and he sent a warranty deed from Lowry to
Stokes. Then he returned to Tennessee to fight for the Confederacy.[22]

Judge Caruthers retained most of his northwestern holdings while in
Tennessee. In 1862, when he won Tennessee's Confederate gubernatorial election, his victory meant that the head of a Confederate state owned
a substantial amount of land in central Minnesota. But by the time of his
scheduled inauguration in 1863, the Union had taken control of a significant portion of Tennessee, and Union-friendly officials assumed control
of the state government. Judge Caruthers—a governor in name only, for
a powerless government—never took the oath of office.

In late 1864 the Union defeated the Confederacy at Lebanon, Tennessee, and captured the town. Its residents scrambled to preserve what wealth
they had in the aftermath of Lebanon's devastation. Union forces torched
Cumberland University, which many of the Tennesseans who invested in
St. Cloud had helped to build. Trustees of the devastated school searched
for new sources of wealth, and they decided to claim some real estate in
St. Cloud that Judge Caruthers had purchased eight years earlier with
funds from the university. In November 1864 the trustees sued Caruthers
for that land, arguing that the property "was purchased from S. B. Lowry
with their own funds & for their own use," as the Fourth Judicial District
Court's record of the case put it. According to the plaintiffs, Caruthers's
name appeared on the title but "only as their Trustee, without his having any personal interest therein." The court convened in Minneapolis
for a special term, and Judge Charles Vanderburgh heard the case. Attor-
neys for the trustees appeared in court, but Caruthers did not attend the
hearing. Vanderburgh found in the plaintiffs' favor, and on December 1
ownership of the real estate transferred from Tennessee's Confederate
governor to the university—the third slaveholding institution in central
Minnesota. Seven months later the trustees gave David Lowry power of
attorney to sell the land as he saw fit.[23]

◆

Before the Civil War's eruption, residents of slave states had more access
to legal redress in Minnesota. In November 1860 Israel G. Lash resided

in North Carolina, but he won a major legal victory in Minnesota. He had sued a John McLeod for money due him in accordance with their mortgage agreement from 1858. The district court ruled that Lash was entitled to reclaim his land after a year without receiving a mortgage payment. This verdict was one of the last antebellum, cross-regional acts of justice that favored the resident of a southern, slaveholding state.[24]

The legal tide in Minnesota quickly turned against southerners after the war commenced, and the state's executive branch shed its unwillingness to strongly and clearly condemn slavery in Minnesota. On January 9, 1862, Governor Alexander Ramsey's annual message to the Minnesota legislature blamed slavery for the war, calling the practice "the undoubted cause of all our troubles." He mentioned that some southerners still owned property in Minnesota, and he requested that the legislators pass a bill to prevent rebels from using their land in the state to harm the Union. Only two years earlier, he had spoken of unity across the regions to keep southern business in Minnesota, but now he promoted punishment from the state for sectional secession.[25]

Six days later a state senator introduced a bill prohibiting rebels from using Minnesota's courts. He and his fellow senators passed the bill on January 17, and the house followed suit on February 1 with an amendment about the appeal process to the Minnesota Supreme Court. The senate then passed the amended bill on February 3, and Ramsey signed it into law on Valentine's Day, 1862. Giving no quarter to the Confederacy, the new law identified all residents of rebel states as rebels. As a result, even the Confederate residents who did not support the Confederacy were banned from judicial redress in Minnesota.[26]

Minnesotans immediately tested the law. F. A. W. Davis of Mississippi—one of the earliest southerners to buy land in the state—became one of the Rebellion Act's first victims. Davis had purchased real estate in Minnesota as early as 1854, and he signed a purchase agreement to sell some of it to a Minnesotan. By 1859 the purchaser was delinquent in paying on the mortgage, and Davis began a foreclosure action. The case moved slowly, and with the Rebellion Act's passage, the tenant assumed that Davis no longer had a right to foreclose on him.[27]

Davis sued, and in April 1863 the Minnesota Supreme Court sided with him. The court ruled the Rebellion Act unconstitutional, because residency alone in a Confederate state did not constitute rebellion in and of itself. Davis's victory came as the Union started to win decisive battles of the war. Also, President Lincoln's Emancipation Proclamation was three months old, and the freeing of slaves in the Confederacy left residents of rebel states without some of their most valuable investments. The court's ruling at least allowed those residents to retain the real estate they legally owned.[28]

William Aiken of South Carolina was not as fortunate as Davis. In 1862 Governor Ramsey made liquidation of the University of Minnesota's debt a high priority. In his address to the legislature, he called for "a commission with full power and authority to transfer the lands and property of the University in payment of its debts." Ramsey's concern for the university and his contempt for rebel residents formed a collective threat to the seven thousand dollars that the university still owed Aiken. In February 1862 someone in Washington, DC, wrote to Swisshelm's newspaper to ask, "Would it not be advisable to have the Legislature pass an act confiscating or sequestering the debts due Gov. Aiken, of South Carolina, and other rebels who have loaned money to the University and are now trying to destroy our national existence and reorganize our society on the basis of unpaid compulsory labor?"[29]

Neither Governor Ramsey nor anyone in the legislature declared that the Rebellion Act essentially transformed Aiken's loan into a donation, but other Minnesotans made statements to that effect. In 1863 the report by the university's regents to the legislature stated that Aiken had held an eight-thousand-dollar bond "prior to the present Rebellion," suggesting that after the war started, he no longer possessed the bond. The *Crisis* newspaper of Columbus, Ohio, recognized the Rebellion Act's consequence for Aiken, wryly noting, "That is the way to pay old debts." Even after Minnesota's Supreme Court ruled the law unconstitutional, the university retained the South Carolinian's money.[30]

On the other hand, the Rebellion Act had no effect on money that the state of Minnesota owed to its other donor with ties to slavery. Isabel Kall, who turned twenty-five years old in 1862, resided with her slaveholding uncle, but their residency in the Union city of Washington, DC, excluded her from Minnesota's Rebellion Act. Thus, when she asked Rice in early 1862 for payment of the interest on her bonds, the state had to comply. Rice dutifully sent Kall's request to the Minnesota legislature's committee on university and university lands.[31]

There was, however, a greater problem looming. Uriah Thomas, secretary of the university's board of regents, noted that a mortgage on the university's sole building at the time had secured Kall's bonds and that the bonds—worth seven thousand dollars—matured on June 1, 1862. As a result, according to his letter to the board that fall, "I was especially desirous of liquidating this claim." Thomas failed in his attempt but not for a lack of trying. He attempted to pay Kall with some land that comprised part of the university campus, and he later claimed to have offered "the best available lands at prices to be determined by disinterested parties." Kall declined, however, because she did not want to care for the land and could not afford to pay the taxes on it. Thus, Kall and the State of Minnesota appeared at an impasse. She wanted only the money that the state owed to her, but the financially struggling institution resisted for as long as it could. With the law on Kall's side, the university had to do something to reimburse her to her satisfaction.[32]

The university's board of regents authorized board member John Nicols to travel to Washington to negotiate a payment plan with Kall. A former slaveholder from Maryland, Nicols had joined the board in 1863 but had taken on a minor role before journeying to Washington. Also, in 1863 he was elected to the Minnesota legislature, and his rise to power was a rare victory for southerners in Minnesota during the war. Therefore, when he met with Kall in the summer of 1864, he spoke to her not only on the state's behalf but also as a fellow child of slaveholders. The two resolved the matter, and by late 1864 the university had paid her the seven thousand dollars it owed her.[33]

Minnesota's other prominent settlers from Maryland had different experiences during the war. After state legislator Charles Mackubin's failed attempt to legalize slavery in 1860, he finished his first and only term in the legislature that spring and died suddenly in 1863. Although he never owned a single enslaved person as an adult, his ill-fated proposal was a dissonant note in his life. His cousin Harwood Iglehart initially remained involved in the St. Paul community, joining the Minnesota Historical Society in 1861. He still owned Rosetta Johnson in Maryland, but that state banned manumission from 1860 to 1864. However, he returned permanently to Annapolis during the war, and there he finally freed Johnson in 1864. In contrast to Mackubin and Iglehart, William Sprigg Hall experienced the transition from wartime to peacetime in Minnesota. He resided in St. Paul during and after the war, and the Thirteenth Amendment freed any slaves he still owned in Maryland in 1865.[34]

◆

Samuel Hays of Virginia did not need to wait for the Thirteenth Amendment to free his enslaved people. His slaves Chloe and Ellen were freed when President Abraham Lincoln signed the Confiscation Act on August 6, 1861. The law allowed the Union to seize and claim Confederate property—including enslaved people. Chloe and Ellen still belonged to Hays's son Peregrine in Virginia. Because Peregrine supported the Confederacy, and his slaves were in Minnesota, they were vulnerable to confiscation. The new law effectively ended Peregrine's ownership.

Days later, on August 25, Chloe married Sylvanus Lowry's African American driver William Butler, and Stearns County certified the marriage. Butler was a free African American from Washington, DC, and sometime between 1857 and 1860 he relocated to St. Cloud to work as Lowry's live-in driver. At the time of the wedding, no state recognized the legality of marriages between slaves, and Chloe did not need to divorce Stephen, Ellen's father, as the separation had ended their union. As a result, the county's certification of the marriage recorded Chloe's first act in exercising her own power as a free person. The document essentially served as her "free papers," and it marked the first and sole occasion that the county provided documentation for a local slave's manumission.[35]

For her final act of service to Hays, Chloe cooked all of the food of the wedding feast. She prepared southern cuisine for the attendees before dressing herself for the wedding. After the ceremony she, her new husband, and Ellen, age six, moved to the town of Albert Lea. William Butler raised Ellen as his own daughter, and he and forty-four-year-old Chloe welcomed their daughter Elizabeth's birth in 1863. Hays never held another slave. The era of active slaveholding in central Minnesota came to an end.[36]

The wedding of Sylvanus Lowry's African American servant did not keep Swisshelm from attacking Lowry in her newspaper during the Civil War, but her commentaries had little effect on his political control over central Minnesota. In 1861 he won election to the Minnesota legislature, thus becoming the latest profiteer of slavery to represent central Minnesota as a lawmaker. But the practice was a dead political issue in Minnesota, and one Democratic legislator in a heavily Republican legislative body faced a steep uphill battle in resurrecting it.

That same year Lowry put some of his money toward the establishment of a newspaper. The *Minnesota Union* (later the *St. Cloud Times*) competed with Swisshelm for readership and served as an outlet for a missing voice in the local press—the southern sympathizer. Lowry initially gave editorial control of the newspaper to Christopher C. Andrews, who was also publisher, and Andrews set the newspaper's political tone. Andrews remained loyal to the Democratic Party despite his personal opposition to slavery, and his commitment to the party endeared him to some of the Tennesseans and their allies. In addition to his work with Lowry on the *Union*, Andrews conducted land transactions with an enslaver. He sold one lot of his land to John F. Goodner in December 1860—six months before Tennessee seceded from the Union. Andrews acquired Goodner's power of attorney in November 1861, months after Goodner had joined the Confederacy, and immediately used that power to buy one lot in St. Cloud from him, thus giving money to an active enemy soldier.[37]

As a result, Andrews took pains to state that he did not want a demolished South without slaves but rather an intact union. In that sense his stance resembled the position of Republican governor Ramsey on the issue in 1860. However, unlike the governor, Andrews opposed secession but not slavery. Also, he strongly supported his party, which rejected Republican opposition to the territorial expansion of slavery. He saw his newspaper as a forum for public expression of Democratic views in Minnesota.

GEN. C. C. ANDREWS.

Photographed in Washington, 1865.

Christopher C. Andrews, photographed in Washington, DC, in 1865

The *Union* lamented, "Northern Minnesota, especially, has been without a Democratic press to represent her conservative opinions." Although the editor promised that "the Union . . . will be a Democratic paper," he noted that "we consider it the first duty of a Democrat to stand by his country."[38]

Andrews opposed secession in a geographical sense but not for its own sake. He concluded, "There would be more reason for permitting the Secession States to form an independent government if they were on detached territory." Intolerable to him were "new governments on our borders." He admitted that slavery was the underlying issue for secession, but he faulted the North for its growing hostility toward southerners concerning slavery. "The principal excuse which the disunionists give for withdrawing from the union is that the anti-slavery sentiment in the North had grown so powerful as to endanger slavery and their domestic peace," he wrote.[39]

However, Andrews left the *Union* and fought against the Confederacy, leaving Sylvanus Lowry as the last public voice in central Minnesota for the interests of slaveholders. Lowry was on borrowed time as the state's political climate grew increasingly volatile during the war. He resigned from the legislature shortly after the start of the 1862 session and left the state for the sake of his health, and others took over the *Union*. He returned to St. Cloud the following year, but his health worsened. By then Swisshelm had departed St. Cloud, and no one else kept his name in the press. Meanwhile, in his absence and afterward, residents of Lowry's Addition abandoned their homes to live elsewhere in St. Cloud. With no family, no visiting Tennesseans, and little hope for a revival of fortune for Lowry's Addition, Lowry died of heart disease in December 1865.[40]

◆

Like Christopher Andrews, US senator Henry Rice also tried to consider the interests of slaveholders. He was appointed to the Senate's Committee of Thirteen in December 1860 to help develop a proposal that would convince secessionists to stay with the Union. Among his colleagues on the committee were his business associates Jefferson Davis, Robert Toombs, and Stephen Douglas. On December 27, Rice proposed that the country admit all northern territories into the Union collectively as the free state of Washington and that all southern territories become the new slave state Jefferson. His proposal failed, and the committee disbanded without having successfully adopted a compromise.[41]

One by one, Rice's allies slipped into the Confederacy, and his network collapsed. His South Carolinian business associates joined in that
state's early fervor for leaving the Union. The young Augustus M. Smith,
who had bought land with Rice's friend and congressional colleague
James L. Orr, was the grand marshal of Abbeville County's secession
meeting in November 1860, and he became a Confederate army major
five months later, when the war began. Orr also joined the Confederate
army, and he and Smith served together while still owning their lots in
Minnesota. Smith was killed thirteen months into the war, in May 1862,
at the age of thirty-four.[42]

With Rice's southern acquaintances now in an enemy nation, Minnesota's government rescinded some of the geographical honors he bestowed
on them. Toombs County was renamed Andy Johnson County for Union-
ist governor Andrew Johnson of Tennessee (and became Wilkin County in
1868, when the new president's behavior also displeased residents). Breckenridge County (named, though misspelled, in honor of Kentuckian John
Breckinridge) was renamed for Senator Henry Clay of Kentucky. On the
other hand, Minnesota targeted only places named for the highest-profile
Confederates, such as officials serving in Washington, DC. George Clitherall supported the Confederate effort but had served no higher office than
as a county-level federal appointee in Minnesota before returning to the
South. Thus, the lake and the town bearing his name escaped renaming.[43]

Rice was in Washington in April 1861, but the war affected his relationships with people around the country. He moved out of the neighborhood
he had helped establish with colleague Breckinridge—Minnesota Row—
and settled at a house in Blogden's Row, which lay next to city hall. The
federal government took possession of Minnesota Row on November 5 to
convert the buildings to Union hospital facilities. The houses, once some
of the city's most elite properties and the sites of elegant parties, were for
a time afterward populated by bloodied, mangled Union servicemen.[44]

Southerners expressed distaste for Rice's criticism of their region, especially because he had long sought their patronage. The people he decried
had once bought land from him and stayed in his hotel. Still, he had bro-
ken from his own slaveholding employer Pierre Chouteau Jr. more than
a decade earlier, and the war finished the job of severing his relationships
to slaveholders. On July 21, 1862, Mary Chesnut, wife of a US senator
from North Carolina, wrote in her diary of Rice's changed attitudes. After
recalling how he had once sent her robes made from buffalo hides, she
noted, "I see from his place in the Senate that he speaks of us as savages,

who put powder and whisky into soldiers' canteens to make them mad with ferocity in the fight." Dismissing his alleged claims, she bragged, "We admire coolness here, because we lack it; we do not need to be fired by drink to be brave."[45]

Rice further broke from his network of slaveholders in 1863 by crossing party lines and for an issue concerning the practice of slavery itself. He supported President Lincoln's Emancipation Proclamation, which legally freed the slaves of all Confederate states when it was issued on January 1. Rice had nothing to gain from taking that political stance but rather stood to disrupt stable relationships and lose revenue sources. Slaveholders residing in the Confederacy, dependent on income generated by their unfree workers, faced financial collapse, and Rice could no longer rely on his business relationships with those planters to enrich himself. His approval of the Republican president's measure put him at odds with many members of his own party. Nevertheless, Rice's refusal to conduct business with Confederates differentiated him from Minnesotans like Christopher C. Andrews and R. J. Mendenhall.[46]

Rice's former business partner Henry Sibley remained on Chouteau's payroll when the war began. Sibley's slaveholding benefactor was initially not a Confederate resident, because Missouri was a neutral state at the conflict's outset. Sibley left public office after completing his term as governor early in 1860, and he declined to run for reelection. Thus, during the war, he conducted business with Chouteau as a private citizen. Their last documented financial transactions took place between January and July 1861. Sibley sold more of Chouteau's real estate, and his employer recorded the sales in his ledger. After August, when the Confederate army won a decisive victory in Missouri, no further sales came from Sibley.[47]

Still, Sibley faced a reckoning with his history of tolerance for slavery. By 1863 he had joined the Union army and held the rank of general, and as a Union official he became responsible for enforcing federal law, which included the Emancipation Proclamation. Minnesota had a severe labor shortage during the war, and Sibley requested that Confederate slaves whom the Union army had captured be sent from St. Louis to Minnesota, because he wanted them to work as drivers of mule teams transporting equipment at Fort Snelling. St. Paulites opposed the idea, especially Irish immigrants who felt they would lose jobs to men willing to work for less. Before the army could comply, a commercial steamboat captain, bringing up a load of mules and wagons, found Robert T. Hickman and a number of families escaping slavery in Missouri drifting in a raft on the river and towed it north. So the first shipment up the Mississippi River that spring included forty men, ten women, and twenty-six children—not just former male slaves but entire families. After years of taking money from slave labor without having witnessed the labor itself, Sibley saw the laborers in Minnesota—and saw them with their loved ones.[48]

Of Chouteau's associates in Minnesota, only St. Paul mayor John Prince remained with him from the war's beginning until its conclusion in 1865. He continued to manage Chouteau's real estate in Minnesota after the war started, but his business relationship with a slaveholder did not seem a problem for his constituents in wartime. He won reelection twice during the conflict and stayed in office into 1863. Chouteau's last entries in his ledger book were in 1862, and Prince, as the slaveholder's sole power of attorney in Minnesota, sold land for him that same year.[49]

As for Chouteau himself, he entered the war years as a very rich man. The census of 1860 valued his holdings in real estate at $400,000, which still included hundreds of lots in Minnesota. His personal estate of $5,000 included the woman and five men he held as enslaved people. In the first year of wartime, his returns from sales by Sibley and Prince totaled $11,909. However, he experienced some losses that he could not use his wealth to replace. He became blind. His wife died. As Chouteau aged and his health worsened, his son Charles handled an increasing amount of the family's business responsibilities.[50]

Chouteau soon lost some of his sources of income, too. After the Emancipation Proclamation, newly emancipated Confederate slaves joined the Union army's effort toward defeating their former captors. As a result, slaveholding Union states began to move away from slavery. In January 1865 Missouri's state government outlawed the practice, and Chouteau's slaves became emancipated. The Confederacy surrendered to the Union weeks later in May, and the reopening of cross-regional travel allowed Chouteau and other southerners to conduct business with Minnesotans once again.

However, Chouteau did not survive a year without the enslaved people who had enriched him. The venerable land baron and entrepreneur died in September as an emperor without an empire. His flagship enterprises—the American Fur Company and Chouteau & Company—were long gone, and everyone except Prince had deserted him in Minnesota. Only the deeds to the properties remained to show that the enslaver had once owned much of the northwestern "free" state.

Minnesota after Slavery

Minnesota did not become a truly free state until months after the end of the Civil War. In December 1865 the Thirteenth Amendment to the Constitution prohibited slavery nationwide and forced all slaveholders to free their slaves.

The amendment also meant that as of December 1865, land in Minnesota was no longer owned by enslavers, and the state stopped benefiting from and financially supporting southern slavery. Several southerners still held real estate in the Northwest, but they no longer paid taxes or purchased additional lots with current income earned from the work of enslaved people. When Pierre Chouteau's survivors sold off his holdings in Minnesota in the late 1860s, some southerners were among the buyers, but none of them held enslaved people. In addition, with the abolition of slavery, mortgage payments from Minnesotans on southerners' lots no longer went to slave plantations in the South. Of course, the fortunes amassed from slave labor continued to support the former slaveholding families that managed to hold on to them.

Although buildings where slaveholders lived and worked in Minnesota did not survive, the state has preserved many of the place-names bestowed by slaveholders. During the war the state changed only names of places whose namesakes lived in the Confederacy. Those named after residents of Union slave states remained untouched. An avenue in St. Paul is still named after Maryland-based slaveholder Harwood Iglehart. And Minnesota still has a town and a lake named for George Clitherall of Alabama.

Places are also still named for Minnesota residents who profited from slaveholders. Several place-names honor employees of slaveholder Pierre

Chouteau Jr., John S. Prince's city of Princeton remains, and Sylvanus B.
Lowry's part of St. Cloud has retained the name Lowry's Addition. St. Paul's
Mackubin Street is named for Iglehart's partner, Charles Mackubin, who
was raised by a slaveholding family. A portion of St. Paul once owned by
Chouteau still bears the name Kittson's Addition, as a salute to his fur
agent Norman Kittson. Minnesota counties are named for Kittson, Henry
Sibley, and Henry Rice.

Some of today's communities once funded by slavery have purged the
slaveholding investors from their collective memory. Several enslavers
bought real estate in Scott County, but the communities of Belle Plaine and
Shakopee have no historical markers for those purchases. Thomas B. Winston invested in multiple counties, but none of them draw attention to his
investments. J. Travis Rosser's portion of West St. Paul and Darius Starbuck's part of Big Lake have no public acknowledgments of their former
owners. The Payne-Phalen neighborhood in St. Paul retains the southern
flowery street names bestowed by William Sprigg Hall, Harwood Iglehart,
and Charles Mackubin—but not the story of their origin.

Many Minnesotans whose professional lives had ties to slavery experienced further successes in the state after the war ended. Having cut
ties to human and real estate property in the South as the war began, they
lost very little of their personal wealth at the war's end. R. J. Mendenhall
headed Minnesota's state bank for decades. Former Buchanan appointee
Samuel L. Hays won the position of probate judge in Benton County, and
William Sprigg Hall became a judge in St. Paul. Former Marylander John
Nicols served in the Minnesota legislature. Former Chouteau employee
John S. Prince won another election as mayor of St. Paul.

Some southerners who had invested in Minnesota lands also rebounded
well. Starbuck became a US attorney. Former US vice president John
Breckinridge, whom Henry Rice recruited to buy real estate, engaged in
insurance and railroad businesses in Kentucky. William B. Stokes, who
bought land in central Minnesota, won election to the US House of Representatives. Beriah Magoffin and James L. Orr became governors of Kentucky and South Carolina, respectively.

Meanwhile, Minnesota played at least a financial role in Reconstruction.
For Confederates who owned real estate in the Northwest, that land held
part of the key to their rebuilding of their lives after the war. By 1865 Union
forces had laid much of the South to waste, and the rental and mortgage

payments and occasional sales of land from Minnesota provided former Confederates owning the property with much-needed income.

A significant part of the legacy of slavery in Minnesota concerned higher education. After having closed for almost a decade, the University of Minnesota finally reopened in 1867. The institute never fully repaid former slaveholder William Aiken's loan; thus, money from his massive plantation remains a part of the university's funds. Two years later the St. Cloud State Normal School opened at the Stearns House. Christopher C. Andrews, the antislavery newspaper publisher who had conducted real estate transactions with slaveholders in St. Cloud and served in the Union army, served on the school's board in the late 1860s; he would later become a pioneering forester. In the following decade, Macalester College used the shuttered Winslow House, where Eliza Winston had stayed with her captors before winning her freedom in court, for its first sessions of classes.

Some businesses and institutions in Minnesota survived the transition from slavery to freedom better than others did. The St. Paul Marine and Fire Insurance Company, which Thomas Winston supported, merged with the Travelers Group and is now part of the Travelers Companies. Lowry's *Minnesota Union* changed its name to *St. Cloud Times* and never ceased publication. Samuel Hays's mill in central Minnesota runs today as Heim Milling. Rosser, Sibley, Ramsey, Iglehart, and Daniel Robertson participated in the early development of the Minnesota Historical Society, and the state's Democratic-Farmer-Labor Party has roots in the Democratic Party that slaveholding migrants and appointees once populated. The southern tourism business never recovered from the Civil War's eruption, and the hotels that had catered to southerners closed their doors.

Similarly, some establishments that Minnesotans supported in the South also lasted through the war. Cumberland University, which had acquired land in St. Cloud, is still in operation in Tennessee, and the Cumberland Presbyterian Church continues to conduct services (but no longer in central Minnesota). The Bank of Cape Fear, whose employees James Bradley and Israel Lash had bought real estate in Minnesota, eventually became Wachovia Bank, which Wells Fargo absorbed in 2009.

Meanwhile, the enslaved people whose labor funded Minnesota's early development rebuilt their lives as free people. Many of them remained farm laborers and worked for their former masters, as Fielding did for Henry S. Dawson in Louisiana. The ex-slaves had more agency than during slavery in receiving wages for their labor and choosing where to work, although the ferocious reaction to Reconstruction would reimpose brutal restrictions. Similarly, domestic slaves became employees of their former enslavers after emancipation. Rosetta Johnson stayed with Harwood Iglehart's father in Maryland, just as she had done when Iglehart moved to Minnesota. Rosina Burnett returned to Anna Forstall's parents in New Orleans after leaving Minnesota with Anna, her husband, her mother, and her children. Burnett stayed with Anna's parents until her father's death, at which point the eighty-year-old former slave moved in with Anna and her husband and children. In Burnett's final years, she was ill and bedridden, and the Forstalls cared for her until her death in 1882.[1]

Some former slaveholders retained as much of their prewar lifestyles as they could, at the expense of the people they once owned. In Missouri John B. Sarpy's daughter Adele employed at least one of the family's former slaves after the Civil War ended. The freedman was, in Adele's words, "a sneaky old fellow we had," and he often scared her by "appearing when I least expected him." The ex-slave remained with Adele's household after the children reached adulthood, but she did not reward his loyalty with more humane treatment. She noted that "even when quite an old man, he narrowly escaped a flogging from my present son-in-law, who was courting my daughter, for indulging in his stealthy instincts." In South Carolina, William Aiken—who had opposed secession—remained wealthy and retained both his plantation Jehosee and his mansion in Charleston after the war ended, and some of his former slaves continued to work for him as free people.[2]

For many freedpeople, rebuilding their lives meant reconstituting their families on their own terms. The former slaves of Thomas Calhoun, whose sales allowed him to buy land in St. Cloud, lived together in Wilson County, Tennessee, after slavery. Matriarch Cherry married a man close to her age, and they lived next door to her daughter Lucinda, who herself had a new husband and child, in 1870. Both of Samuel Hays's former slaves Chloe and Ellen married and started families in Albert Lea, and years later Chloe's granddaughter Cora Ray married the pioneering African American baseball player Walter Ball. Back in West Virginia, Chloe's son Napoleon adopted the surname Ratliff and fathered eighteen children with his two wives. Another son, Albert Ratliff, married in West Virginia before moving to Albert Lea to live near his mother. Chloe and Stephen, the father of Ellen, never reunited.[3]

Most of the enslaved people brought to Minnesota did not permanently stay there, and most of the slaves belonging to investing masters never saw the state their labor helped to build. This meant that these families were not present to pass down their traditions and histories to their fellow Minnesotans over the years. The neighborhoods and institutions they made possible in Minnesota continued to evolve but forsook their identities as slavery-fueled entities. As a result, few locations in Minnesota honor slaves who played local but unseen historic roles. For example, a historical marker in St. Cloud notes the former existence of the Stearns House, but it fails to mention that the hotel welcomed slaveholders and slaves.

Minnesota's ignorance of its history with enslavers may be changing. Recent greater public attention to the slaves' stories and histories has led to more public recognition of the state's seen and unseen unfree. St. Cloud officially dedicated a new park in May 2017 and christened it Butler Park in honor of Thomas Calhoun's slaves Mary and John Butler, who had lived in the city. The park sits alongside the Mississippi River at a location where steamboats likely docked to allow slaveholders to disembark with their human property, and the park's sign tells the name of the park and the story of its namesakes. The park ushered in a new era, in which the story of slavery and the story of Minnesota become permanently intertwined, and slavery's reach is visible to all.

Acknowledgments

I owe a debt of thanks to many people for the publication of *Slavery's Reach*. Ann Regan and Laura Weber of the Minnesota Historical Society exhibited great faith in my research on Minnesota's relationships with southern slaveholders. I thank them for their encouragement, feedback, and wisdom as I wrote and edited. I am also grateful to MNHS for publishing my book.

Several government facilities were crucial to my research. I thank the recorder's offices of Benton, McLeod, Ramsey, Sherburne, Stearns, Washington, and Wright Counties in Minnesota. I thank the recorder's office in Wilson County, Tennessee, for sending information to me. I am also thankful for historical societies in Benton, Hennepin, Ramsey, Sherburne, and Stearns County, Minnesota. I thank Mayor Dave Kleis of St. Cloud for his assistance in locating records. Outside of Minnesota, the historical society in Anne Arundel County, Maryland, offered support.

Descendants and estates of some of the figures in my book also gave me invaluable assistance. I am grateful for the help that the Aiken-Rhett House staff gave me. I thank descendants of Thomas Calhoun and of slaves Chloe Butler and Cherry Calhoun for corresponding with me about their family histories.

I appreciate the help I received from several academic institutions. I thank Yuichiro Onishi, Catherine Squires, Mark Pedelty, and Ezekiel Joubert of the University of Minnesota for their work with me researching their institution's ties to slavery; thanks also to the institution's Institute for Advanced Study for its scholarship funding this work. I am grateful to Oklahoma State University, the University of Massachusetts Amherst, and Harvard University for my institutional training and to St. Cloud State University for employing me during my research.

I thank my family for their support during my many years of research on this topic. Most of all, I thank my wife, Sampada.

Appendix

Timeline of Slavery in Minnesota

1787: The Northwest Ordinance became law in the United States. The law established Northwest Territory, which included part of what later became Minnesota Territory, and prohibited the practice of slavery there.

1820: The Missouri Compromise became law in the United States. The law established a boundary line for future slave states and future free states in the nation's new territory Louisiana. The part of Louisiana that later became Minnesota Territory lay in the area reserved for free states, thus prohibiting slavery.

1825: The United States finished construction of Fort Snelling in what later became Minnesota Territory. Although the fort lay in free land and federal law prohibited slavery there, slaveholding military officers brought slaves there and received stipends for them.

1842: Chouteau & Company was created by Missouri-based enslavers and managed posts for the fur trade throughout the future Minnesota Territory.

1849: The United States organized Minnesota Territory, whose government affirmed the prohibitions of slavery as stipulated in the Northwest Ordinance and the Missouri Compromise.

1850: The Fugitive Slave Act became law in the United States, requiring residents of all states and territories—including Minnesota Territory—to return fugitive slaves to their enslavers. The law imposed stiff penalties on violators.

1853: President Franklin Pierce appointed enslaver Joseph Travis Rosser to a federal office in Minnesota Territory. Rosser served as territorial secretary—the territory's second-highest executive office.

Henry Rice, a former fur agent for Chouteau & Company, began his first term in the US Congress as a delegate for Minnesota in the House of Representatives. While there, he cultivated business relationships with slaveholding southern colleagues.

1854: The Kansas-Nebraska Act became law in the United States, allowing for two free territories to decide for themselves whether to enter the Union as free or slave states. This notion of popular sovereignty disregarded the Missouri Compromise, and some Minnesotans considered the new law applicable to them.

1856: Enslaver William Aiken of South Carolina loaned thousands of dollars to the University of Minnesota. He was never fully repaid.

Sylvanus Lowry, a former fur agent for Chouteau & Company, became president of the town council of St. Cloud, Minnesota—a position akin to mayor. That same year he sold land to enslavers.

John S. Prince, an employee of Chouteau & Company, cofounded Princeton, Minnesota.

1857: The US Supreme Court's *Dred Scott* decision legalized slavery in all federal territories—including Minnesota.

President James Buchanan appointed enslavers George Clitherall, Samuel Hays, and Charles Wagner to federal offices in Minnesota. Meanwhile, Rosser left the position of territorial secretary.

Thomas Calhoun brought enslaved woman Mary Butler from the slave state Tennessee to Minnesota for full-time residency. While in Minnesota she gave birth to her son John, who was born a slave because of *Dred Scott*.

1858: Minnesota became a free state. The new state's prohibition of slavery did not include any procedure for emancipating any enslaved people within Minnesota's borders at the time.

Henry Sibley, an employee of Chouteau & Company, became governor of Minnesota.

Thomas Calhoun returned Mary Butler and her Minnesota-born son John to Tennessee as enslaved people. Under the Fugitive Slave Act, he could legally do so.

Norman Kittson, a former fur agent for Chouteau & Company, became the mayor of St. Paul, Minnesota.

1860: Two separate bills legalizing slavery during tourism seasons—one in the house and the other in the senate—failed in the Minnesota legislature. The rejections showed the state government's unwillingness to pass laws to appease enslavers. All Republicans and most Democrats voted against the bills, but among the proponents were sellers of land to enslavers.

A district court in Minnesota declared enslaved woman Eliza Winston free. No court in Minnesota had previously decided on slavery, and the decision reinforced Minnesota's status as a free state.

1861: The Civil War began, cutting off enslavers in Confederate slave states from access to Minnesota. However, enslavers holding real estate in Minnesota at the war's outbreak retained ownership of their lots for the four-year duration of the war.

1862: The Rebellion Act became law, prohibiting Confederate residents from suing in Minnesota's courts. As a result, Aiken lost legal access to retrieving the money he had loaned to the University of Minnesota. The law was overturned the following year.

1865: The Thirteenth Amendment to the US Constitution became law, prohibiting slavery nationwide.

Notes

Notes to Introduction

1. *Minnesota Pioneer* quoted in Bruce M. White, "The Power of Whiteness, or The Life and Times of Joseph Rolette, Jr.," *Minnesota History* 56, no. 4 (1998–99): 186.

2. J. Fletcher Williams, *A History of the City of St. Paul to 1875* (1876; repr., St. Paul: Minnesota Historical Society Press, 1983), 358.

Notes to Chapter One

1. Walt Bachman, *Northern Slave, Black Dakota: The Life and Times of Joseph Godfrey* (Bloomington, MN: Pond Dakota Press, 2013), 6–12; Mary Lethert Wingerd, *North Country: The Making of Minnesota* (Minneapolis: University of Minnesota Press, 2010), 387.

2. *Rachael, a woman of color v. Walker, William*, November 1834, case no. 82, St. Louis Circuit Court; *Courtney, a woman of color v. Rayburn, Samuel*, March 1836, case no. 10, St. Louis Circuit Court; Lea VanderVelde, *Mrs. Dred Scott* (New York: Oxford University Press, 2009), 203; Edlie L. Wong, *Neither Fugitive nor Free: Atlantic Slavery, Freedom Suits, and the Legal Culture of Travel* (New York: New York University Press, 2009), 137; Bachman, *Northern Slave, Black Dakota*, 29–30.

3. Rhoda R. Gilman, *Henry Hastings Sibley: Divided Heart* (St. Paul: Minnesota Historical Society Press, 2004), 73–74, 79, 82, 84, 92; Rhoda R. Gilman, Carolyn Gilman, and Deborah L. Miller, *The Red River Trails: Oxcart Routes between St. Paul and the Selkirk Settlement, 1820–1878* (St. Paul: Minnesota Historical Society Press, 1979), 12.

4. US Census 1830, St. Louis Upper Ward, MO, 364; Stan Hoig, *The Chouteaus: First Family of the Fur Trade* (Albuquerque: University of New Mexico Press, 2008), 202; Lea VanderVelde, *Redemption Songs: Suing for Freedom before Dred Scott* (Oxford: Oxford University Press, 2014), 180.

5. *Francois La Grange v. Pierre Chouteau, Jr.*, 1827, Circuit Court of St. Louis County, MO; *Theotiste v. Pierre Chouteau, Jr.*, 1827, Circuit Court of St. Louis County, MO.

6. Rudolf Friederich Kurz, et al., *On the Upper Missouri: The Journal of Rudolf Friederich Kurz, 1851–1852* (Norman: University of Oklahoma Press, 2005), 168.

7. US Census 1840, St. Louis, MO, 38; US Slave Schedule 1850, Ward 3, St. Louis, MO, 2; US Slave Schedule 1850, Ward 4, St. Louis, MO, 3; US Slave Schedule 1860, Ward 4, St. Louis, MO, 1; Paul Finkelman, *Dred Scott v. Sandford: A Brief History with Documents* (Boston: Bedford, 1997), 23–24.

8. Richard Edwards and M. Hopewell, *Edwards's Great West and Her Commercial Metropolis* (St. Louis: Edwards's Monthly, 1860), 535–36; Walter Barlow Stevens, *St. Louis: The Fourth City, 1764–1911*, vol. 2 (St. Louis: S. J. Clarke, 1911), 669; Paul Edmond Beckwith, *Creoles of St. Louis* (St. Louis: Nixon-Jones, 1893), 121–22; J. Thomas Scharf, *History of St. Louis City and County: From the Earliest Periods to the Present Day*, vol. 1 (Philadelphia: Louis H. Everts, 1883), 581; Albert Watkins, *Publications of the Nebraska State Historical Society* 20 (1922): 34; *American State Papers: Public Lands*, vol. 6, ed. Asbury Dickins and John W. Forney (Washington: Gales & Seaton, 1860), 792; US Census 1850, St. Louis Ward 4, MO, 123. For estimating currently value: Historical Currency Conversions, https://futureboy.us/fsp/dollar.fsp; Inflation Calculator, https://www.officialdata.org/.

9. Document no. 43, Records of the Circuit Court, Civil Courts Building, St. Louis, MO.

10. Adele Sarpy Morrison, *Memoirs of Adele Sarpy Morrison* (St. Louis: Adele Sarpy Morrison, 1911), 1–3.

11. Morrison, *Memoirs*, 1, 8.

12. Morrison, *Memoirs*, 9.

13. Morrison, *Memoirs*, 2–3, 8–10.

14. Frederick L. Billon, *Annals of St. Louis in Its Territorial Days, from 1804 to 1821* (St. Louis: Nixon-Jones, 1888), 180.

15. Jane Spector Davis, *Guide to a Microfilm Edition of the Henry Hastings Sibley Papers* (St. Paul: Minnesota Historical Society, 1968), 11; Rhoda R. Gilman, "The Last Days of the Mississippi Fur Trade," *Minnesota History* 42, no. 4 (1970): 136–37; "Hon. H. H. Sibley," *St. Paul Daily Pioneer and Democrat*, October 11, 1857, 2; Erling Jorstad, "Personal Politics in the Origins of Minnesota's Democratic Party," *Minnesota History* 36, no. 7 (1959): 260, 264.

16. Gilman, *Henry Hastings Sibley*, 82, 110–11; Jorstad, "Personal Politics," 262; Ernst D. Kargau, *The German Element in St. Louis* (Baltimore: Clearfield, 2000), 118.

17. Gilman, *Henry Hastings Sibley*, 110–11; James Terry White, *The National Cyclopaedia of American Biography*, vol. 12 (New York: James T. White, 1904), 213; US Slave Schedule 1850, Henrico County, VA, 15; Martha B. Katz-Hyman and Kym S. Rice, *World of a Slave: Encyclopedia of the Material Life of Slaves in the United States*, vol. 1, *A–I* (Santa Barbara, CA: Greenwood, 2011), 313, 457, 510.

18. "Address of Henry H. Sibley, of Minnesota, to the People of Minnesota Territory," June 1849, Henry H. Sibley Papers, in *Collections of the Minnesota Historical Society* 1 (1852; repr., 1901): 42–43.

19. Bachman, *Northern Slave, Black Dakota*, 49–50.

20. John F. A. Sanford to H. H. Sibley, July 28, 1849, Henry H. Sibley Papers, Minnesota Historical Society, St. Paul (hereafter, MNHS), reel 6, frames 46–48.

21. Matti Kaups, "North Shore Commercial Fishing, 1849–1870," *Minnesota History* 46, no. 2 (1978): 46; Jorstad, "Personal Politics," 263; Wingerd, *North Country*, 197–98; George Hage, *Newspapers on the Minnesota Frontier* (St. Paul: Minnesota Historical Society, 1967), 26; Gilman, *Henry Hastings Sibley*, 113; Henry M. Rice to William A. Aitkin, October 13, 1849, Letterpress, vol. 1, Henry M. Rice and Family Papers, MNHS; advertisement, *Prairie du Chien Patriot*, August 7, 1850.

22. Davis, *Guide to Sibley Papers*, 11; Norman W. Kittson to H. H. Sibley, December 8, 1850, Henry H. Sibley Papers, reel 8, frames 102–4.

23. H. H. Sibley to Senator Henry S. Foote, February 15, 1850, in "Beautiful Picture of Minnesota," *Alexandria (VA) Gazette*, February 21, 1850, 2; Debby Applegate, *The Most Famous Man in America: The Biography of Henry Ward Beecher* (New York: Doubleday, 2006), 224; Melba Porter Hay, *The Papers of Henry Clay*, vol. 10 (Lexington: University Press of Kentucky, 1991), 681, 687.

24. *Vicksburg (MS) Whig*, October 2, 1850, 3; Wingerd, *North Country*, 238–39.

25. Gilman, *Henry Hastings Sibley*, 126–27, 252n8.

26. William E. Lass, *Minnesota: A History*, 2nd ed. (New York: W. W. Norton, 1998), 116.

27. Merlin Stonehouse, *John Wesley North and the Reform Frontier* (Minneapolis: University of Minnesota Press, 1965), 57; "The Third Annual Report of the Board of Regents of the University of Minnesota, 1854," University of Minnesota Archives, Annual and Biennial Reports of the University, Elmer L. Andersen Library, Minneapolis, 2–3, 7–8; "The First Annual Report of the Board of Regents of the University of Minnesota to the Council and House of Representatives, 1852," University of Minnesota Archives, 2; "The Second Annual Report of the Board of Regents of the University of Minnesota to the Council and House of Representatives, 1853," University of Minnesota Archives, 2; US Slave Schedule 1850, Ward 3, District of Columbia, 1; William Watts Folwell, *A History of Minnesota*, vol. 1 (St. Paul: Minnesota Historical Society, 1921), 378.

28. "P. Chouteau, Jr. & Co. Accounts," Henry H. Sibley Papers, reel 10, frame 27; *Pierre Chouteau, Jr. Day Book, 1852–1859*, Pierre Chouteau Jr. and Family Papers, MNHS, reel 15, 255–56.

29. Gilman, *Henry Hastings Sibley*, 140; Pierre Chouteau Jr. to H. H. Sibley, March 1855, Henry H. Sibley Papers, reel 10, frames 314–15; Pierre Chouteau Jr. to H. H. Sibley, June 16, 1855, Henry H. Sibley Papers, reel 10, frame 341; real estate inventory, Henry H. Sibley Papers, reel 10, frames 691–99.

30. *Journal of the Council of Minnesota during the Fourth Session of the Legislative Assembly* (St. Paul: Joseph R. Brown, 1853), 189; Herbert A. Kellar, "The Minnesota

State Archives: Their Character, Condition, and Historical Value," *Minnesota History Bulletin* (May 1915): 37–38; *Compendium of History and Biography of Central and Northern Minnesota* (Chicago: Geo. A. Ogle, 1904), 59.

31. Norman W. Kittson to H. H. Sibley, February 9, 1854, Henry H. Sibley Papers, reel 10, frames 74–75; Clarence W. Rife, "Norman W. Kittson, a Fur-Trader at Pembina," *Minnesota History* 6, no. 3 (1925): 227, 234, 251; Gilman, Gilman, and Miller, *Red River Trails*, 12; Gilman, *Henry Hastings Sibley*, 142; Thomas McLean Newson, *Pen Pictures of St. Paul Minnesota* (St. Paul: Thomas McLean Newson, 1886), 431.

32. Henry B. Wenzell, *Minnesota Reports*, vol. 61 (St. Paul: West, 1896), 5–6; William Jay Whipple, *The History of Winona County, Minnesota*, vol. 1 (Chicago: H. H. Hill and Company, 1883), 205; J. Fletcher Williams, et al., *History of the Upper Mississippi Valley* (Minneapolis: Minnesota Historical Company, 1881), 343; Stephen George, *Enterprising Minnesota: 150 Years of Business Pioneers* (Minneapolis: University of Minnesota Press, 2003), 12.

33. *Glasgow (MO) Weekly Times*, December 8, 1853, 1; *St. Paul Daily Pioneer*, February 6, 1855, 3.

34. *St. Paul Daily Pioneer*, February 8, 1855, 4; Gilman, *Henry Hastings Sibley*, 139; Robert Desty, *Supreme Court Reporter*, vol. 3 (St. Paul: West, 1884), 626; *Minnesota Reports*, vol. 61 (St. Paul: West, 1896), 8; advertisement, *St. Paul Daily Times*, September 10, 1855, 4.

35. *St. Paul Daily Pioneer*, September 10, 1855, 3; George E. Warner and Charles M. Foote, *History of Ramsey County and the City of St. Paul* (Minneapolis: North Star Publishing, 1881), 591; Henry A. Castle, *History of St. Paul and Vicinity*, vol. 3 (Chicago: Lewis, 1912), 1005; *St. Paul Daily Pioneer*, April 26, 1857, 3; John Fletcher Williams, *A History of the City of St. Paul* (St. Paul: Minnesota Historical Society, 1876), 386; advertisement, *Belle Plaine Enquirer*, November 17, 1859, 2.

36. Lass, *Minnesota*, 121; Mille Lacs County Historical Society, *Mille Lacs County* (Princeton, MN: Arnold's, 1989), 8; *Minneapolis Daily Tribune*, January 7, 1868, 2; Finkelman, *Dred Scott v. Sandford*, 23, 25, 27.

37. *Pierre Chouteau Jr. & Co. Land Book*, Pierre Chouteau Jr. and Family Papers, 1–26; US Slave Schedule 1860, St. Louis Ward 4, MO, 1; Wingerd, *North Country*, 161.

Notes to Chapter Two

1. US Census 1830, Petersburg, Dinwiddie County, VA, 365; *Petersburg (VA) Progress-Index*, November 10, 1968, 3; *Ohio Statesman*, November 29, 1843; US Confederate Officers Card Index, 1861–65, Roa–Ros, image 2684, Military Order of the Stars and Bars, via FamilySearch, www.familysearch.org; *Baltimore American Republican and Daily Clipper*, May 14, 1845, 1; US Census 1850, Petersburg, Dinwiddie County, VA, 430; *Proceedings of the Democratic National Convention Held at Baltimore, June 1–5, 1852* (Washington, DC: Robert Armstrong, 1852), 20, 64.

2. "Married," *New World* (New York), June 24, 1843, 760; US Census 1850, Petersburg, Dinwiddie County, VA, 430; US Slave Schedule 1850, Petersburg, Dinwiddie County, VA, 330; Virginia Armistead Garber, *The Armistead Family, 1635–1910* (Richmond, VA: Whippet & Shepperson, 1910), 66; US Census 1830, Fauquier County, VA, 33; US Census 1830, Petersburg, Dinwiddie County, VA, 25.

3. *Journal of the Executive Proceedings of the Senate of the United States of America from December 6, 1852 to March 3, 1855, Inclusive,* vol. 9 (Washington, DC: Government Printing Office, 1887), 131, 142; US Congress, "Fort Snelling Investigation," report no. 351, House of Representatives, 35th Cong., 1st sess., 211; *St. Paul Daily Globe,* May 25, 1882, 3; *Richmond (VA) Daily Dispatch,* July 13, 1853; Thomas McLean Newson, *Pen Pictures of St. Paul Minnesota* (St. Paul: Thomas McLean Newson, 1886), 384.

4. I. Van Etten, "Building Commissioners' Report," February 10, 1853, *Journal of the House of Representatives during the Fourth Session of the Legislative Assembly of the Territory of Minnesota* (St. Paul: Joseph R. Brown, 1853), 131.

5. Chas. E. Flandrau, "Rosser's Daughter," *St. Paul Globe,* July 19, 1895, 8; "J. Travis Rosser Probably Killed," *St. Paul Daily Press,* May 2, 1863, 1.

6. Neil B. Thompson, "A Half Century of Capital Conflict: How St. Paul Kept the Seat of Government," *Minnesota History* 43, no. 7 (1973): 241; *Christine Siebert v. J. Travis Rosser and Others, Minnesota Reports: Cases Argued and Determined in the Supreme Court of Minnesota July, 1877–April, 1878,* vol. 24 (St. Paul: West, 1879), 155; advertisement, *St. Paul Daily Minnesotian,* June 27, 1854, 1.

7. "Pen Pictures of St. Paul, Minnesota," *St. Paul Sunday Globe,* November 30, 1884, 10; Newson, *Pen Pictures of St. Paul Minnesota,* 384.

8. "CGW Forerunner Chartered in 1854," *Oelwein (IA) Daily Register,* July 21, 1948; Hiram Fairchild Stevens, *History of the Bench and Bar of Minnesota,* vol. 1 (Minneapolis: Legal, 1904), 37, 42; "Message from the President of the United States," executive document no. 35, January 16, 1855, 33rd Cong., 2nd sess., 10; Rasmus S. Saby, "Railroad Legislation in Minnesota, 1849 to 1875," in *Collections of the Minnesota Historical Society* 15 (1915): 17.

9. Return I. Holcombe, *Minnesota in Three Centuries,* vol. 2 (n.p.: Publishing Society of Minnesota, 1908), 472; John James Lafferty, *Sketches and Portraits of the Virginia Conference, Methodist Episcopal Church, South* (Richmond, VA: Christian Advocate Office, 1890), 6–7; *Richmond Daily Dispatch,* March 28, 1865; "Estimates—Sioux Annuities," executive document no. 34, January 15, 1855, 33rd Cong., 2nd sess., 6, 8; *Evening Star* (Washington, DC), April 18, 1854, 2.

10. *St. Paul Daily Minnesotian,* June 4, 1855, 2.

11. *St. Paul Daily Times,* October 12, 1855, 2; *Weekly Minnesotian* (St. Paul), September 29, 1855, 3.

12. Council of Minnesota proceedings, February 4, 1856, *Journal of the Council of Minnesota during the Seventh Session of the Legislative Assembly* (St. Paul: Joseph R. Brown, 1856), 112–13; J. T. Rosser to President of the Council John B. Brisbin, February 5, 1856, *Journal of the Council of Minnesota,* 120.

13. Rosser to Brisbin, February 5, 1856, 120–21.

14. Council of Minnesota proceedings, February 12, 1856, *Journal of the Council of Minnesota*, 133–35; "J. Travis Rosser Probably Killed."

15. *Journal of the House of Representatives during the Seventh Session of the Legislative Assembly of the Territory of Minnesota* (St. Paul: Owens & Moore, 1856), 327.

16. David W. Parker, *Calendar of Papers in Washington Archives relating to the Territories of the United States (to 1873)* (Washington, DC: Carnegie Institution, 1911), 211; John H. Stevens, *Personal Recollections of Minnesota and Its People, and Early History of Minneapolis* (Minneapolis: n.p., 1890), 288; "Outrage in the United States Senate," *Bedford (PA) Inquirer and Chronicle*, May 30, 1856, 1; "Washington News and Gossip," *Evening Star*, June 5, 1856, 2.

17. "J. Travis Rosser Probably Killed"; *Evening Star*, July 15, 1856; J. Travis Rosser to H. H. Sibley, January 2, 1857, Henry H. Sibley Papers, MNHS, reel 10, frame 700; "Minnesota Items," *Chicago Tribune*, February 14, 1857, 2.

18. Minnesota Census 1857, St. Paul, Ramsey County, 66; US Census 1860, Upperville, Fauquier County, VA, 5; US Slave Schedule 1860, Upperville, Fauquier County, VA, 2.

19. J. Travis Rosser to H. H. Sibley, January 2, 1857, Henry H. Sibley Papers, reel 10, frame 700; *Session Laws of the Territory of Minnesota Passed by the Legislative Assembly at the Eighth Session, Commencing January 7, 1857* (St. Paul: Earle S. Goodrich, 1857), 206.

20. Minnesota Census 1857, St. Paul, Ramsey County, 66; *Richmond Daily Dispatch*, June 1, 1857.

21. "Democratic State Convention," *Weekly Minnesotian*, September 19, 1857, 2.

22. "Queer Playing Cards," *Quad-City Times* (Davenport, IA), January 1891, 3; US Census 1830, New Bern, Craven County, NC, 5; Nelson F. Smith, *History of Pickens County, Ala.* (Carrollton, AL: Pickens Republican, 1856), 70; US Census 1840, Greene County, AL, 14; *Independent Monitor* (Tuscaloosa, AL), November 3, 1841, 3; advertisement, *New Orleans Picayune*, April 12, 1851, 4; "Point Clear," *New Orleans Picayune*, April 24, 1851, 1; *Monroe (MS) Democrat*, May 14, 1851, 4; US Slave Schedule 1850, Mobile, Mobile County, AL, 6; advertisement, *New Orleans Picayune*, November 2, 1855, 1.

23. Smith, *History of Pickens County*, 73; *Montgomery Weekly Advertiser*, June 18, 1856, 4; "The Barbecue at Dorah's Mill, in Pickens Co.," *Montgomery Weekly Advertiser*, September 24, 1856, 4; *Tuskegee (AL) Republican*, January 15, 1857, 2.

24. US Census 1840, Greene County, AL, 10.

25. US Census 1850, Mobile, Mobile County, AL, 72; US Slave Schedule 1850, Mobile, Mobile County, AL, 20.

26. *Evening Star*, November 3, 1856, 1; *Journal of the Executive Proceedings of the Senate of the United States of America from December 3, 1855 to June 16, 1858, Inclusive*, vol. 10 (Washington, DC: Government Printing Office, 1887), 356; US Slave Schedule 1850, America, Barnwell County, SC, 115; US Slave Schedule 1850, District 17, Gilmer County, VA, 1; John W. Mason, *History of Otter Tail County,*

Minnesota: Its People, Industries and Institutions (Indianapolis: B. F. Bowen, 1916), 86.

27. *Evening Star*, April 6, 1857, 2; *Journal of the Executive Proceedings of the Senate of the United States of America from December 3, 1855 to June 16, 1858, Inclusive*, vol. 10, 356.

28. US Census 1860, Otter Tail County, MN, 1; Mason, *History of Otter Tail County*, 86; Richard L. Hahn, *George Bush Burgwin Clitherall* (Forest Lake, MN: Richard L. Hahn, 1994), 39, 50, 60; "How Towns Grow in the Northwest," *Duluth Minnesotian*, January 21, 1871, 3.

29. "Visitors to the V. A. Military Institute," *Richmond Daily Dispatch*, June 8, 1854; "Political Matters," *Richmond Daily Dispatch*, July 7, 1854; "Electoral College of Virginia," *Richmond Daily Dispatch*, December 4, 1856; US Census 1830, Lewis County, VA, 240; US Slave Schedule 1850, Seventeenth District, Gilmer County, VA, 1.

30. *Northwestern Bank of Virginia v. Hays et al.*, Supreme Court of Appeals of West Virginia, December 22, 1892, in *Southeastern Reporter*, vol. 16, 561; *Sauk Rapids (MN) Frontiersman*, September 24, 1857; Letter from St. Cloud, June 26, 1857, *St. Paul Daily Pioneer*, July 7, 1857.

31. *Sauk Rapids Frontiersman*, October 15, 1857, 3; *Sauk Rapids Frontiersman*, April 1, 1858, 2; US Slave Schedule 1850, Seventeenth District, Gilmer County, VA, 1; US Slave Schedule 1860, Calhoun County, VA, 1; US Census 1860, Stearns County, MN, 18–19; US Census 1870, Sherman, Calhoun County, WV, 12; Bone Ratliff, Civil War pension application, National Archives, Washington, DC; "Bone Ratliff," *West Virginia Marriages Index, 1853–1970*, FamilySearch, Salt Lake City, UT; US Census 1860, Stearns County, MN, 18.

32. *Sauk Rapids Frontiersman*, March 18, 1858, 2; *Sauk Rapids Frontiersman*, April 1, 1858, 2.

33. Mortgage Book A, Stearns County Recorder's Office, 318.

34. "Palmetto Club," *Washington (DC) Union*, August 28, 1856, 3; US Slave Schedule 1850, America, Barnwell County, SC, 115; US Slave Schedule 1850, Christ Church, Charleston County, SC, 11; Lucy B. Wayne, "'Burning Brick and Making a Large Fortune at It Too': Landscape Archaeology and Lowcountry Brickmaking," in *Carolina's Historical Landscapes: Archaeological Perspectives*, ed. Linda France Stine (Knoxville: University of Tennessee Press, 1997), 101; advertisement, *Stillwater Messenger*, June 7, 1859, 2; Henry Carrison, "A Businessman in Crisis: Col. Daniel Jordan and the Civil War," *South Carolina Historical Magazine* (October 2001): 340.

35. *St. Cloud Democrat*, February 24, 1859, 2.

36. *Stearns County Grantee Index, 1858–1860*, Stearns County Recorder's Office, 26; *Sauk Rapids Frontiersman*, June 24, 1858, 2; *Sauk Rapids Frontiersman*, September 29, 1859, 3; *Sauk Rapids Frontiersman*, November 3, 1859, 2; *Sauk Rapids Frontiersman*, November 10, 1859, 2.

37. *St. Cloud Democrat,* July 14, 1859.

38. *Pierre Chouteau, Jr. Ledger, 1853–1857,* Pierre Chouteau Jr. and Family Papers, MNHS, reel 19, 70.

39. Henry H. Sibley, address, June 3, 1858, in *Inaugural Address of the Hon. Henry H. Sibley, Governor of Minnesota* (St. Paul: Earle S. Goodrich, 1858), 15.

Notes to Chapter Three

1. "Minnesota," *Nashville Union and American,* May 21, 1853; Rhoda R. Gilman, *Henry Hastings Sibley: Divided Heart* (St. Paul: Minnesota Historical Society Press, 2004), 128.

2. "Correspondence of the Baltimore Patriot," *Tuskegee (AL) Republican,* October 7, 1852, 2.

3. "Minnesota Matters," *Nashville Tennessean,* December 15, 1852, 2; J. W. Patterson, "The Post Office in Early Minnesota," *Minnesota History* 40, no. 2 (1966): 85–86.

4. *Tuskegee Republican,* June 17, 1852, 2; *Tuskegee Republican,* August 19, 1852, 4; US Slave Schedule 1850, District 21, Macon County, AL, 108; US Census 1850, District 21, Macon County, AL, 145; Minnesota Census 1857, Township 117, Range 21, Hennepin County, 78; US Census 1860, Richfield, Hennepin County, MN, 151.

5. Willis Gorman, speech, March 2, 1875, quoted in William A. Spencer, "In Memoriam," *Reports of Cases Argued and Determined in the Supreme Court of Minnesota,* vol. 20 (Chicago: Callaghan, 1878), xii; Lucius F. Hubbard and Return I. Holcombe, *Minnesota in Three Centuries,* vol. 3 (n.p.: Publishing Society of Minnesota, 1908), 61; Thomas McLean Newson, *Pen Pictures of St. Paul Minnesota* (St. Paul: Thomas McLean Newson, 1886), 461.

6. Willis Gorman speech; Hubbard and Holcombe, *Minnesota in Three Centuries,* vol. 3, 61; Newson, *Pen Pictures of St. Paul Minnesota,* 461; Ramsey County Book of Deeds 1849–1858, MNHS, 156; Index to Deed Records, Ramsey County Register of Deeds, E8.

7. US 1850 Census; David Vassar Taylor, *African Americans in Minnesota* (St. Paul: Minnesota Historical Society Press, 2002), 3–4.

8. US Census 1850, Annapolis, Anne Arundel County, MD, 537; Joshua Dorsey Warfield, *The Founders of Anne Arundel and Howard Counties, Maryland* (Baltimore: Kohn & Pollock, 1905), 317; William Hall, petition, July 13, 1852, Orphans Court of Anne Arundel County, Maryland, *Register of Wills, 1851–1874,* Maryland State Archives, Annapolis, MD, 519–21.

9. US Census 1850, Annapolis, Anne Arundel County, MD, 531–32; US Slave Schedule 1850, Annapolis, Anne Arundel County, MD, 240; *Quinquennial Catalogue of the Officers and Graduates of Harvard University, 1636–1900* (Cambridge, MA: Harvard University Press, 1900), 427, 686; US Slave Schedule 1860, Annapolis, Anne Arundel County, MD, 4; *Anne Arundel County Manumission Record: 1844–1866,* vol. 832, Maryland State Archives, Annapolis, 198.

10. US Census 1840, Annapolis, Anne Arundel County, MD; US Census 1850, Annapolis, Anne Arundel County, MD, 531–32; US Slave Schedule 1850, Annapolis, Anne Arundel County, MD, 240; Newson, *Pen Pictures of St. Paul Minnesota*, 486–87.

11. "Third Street," *St. Paul Globe*, September 7, 1884, 9; Edward D. Neill, *History of Ramsey County and the City of St. Paul: Including the Explorers and Pioneers of Minnesota* (Minneapolis: North Star Publishing, 1881), 442; Newson, *Pen Pictures of St. Paul Minnesota*, 487.

12. Elizabeth Mackubin, will, *Wills of Anne Arundel, Maryland: 1841–1868*, FamilySearch, Salt Lake City, UT, 364–65; *Baltimore Sun*, January 13, 1853, 4; George Mackubin, will, *Wills of Anne Arundel, Maryland: 1841–1868*, 187.

13. Warren Upham, *Minnesota Geographic Names: Their Origin and Historical Significance* (St. Paul: Minnesota Historical Society Press, 1920), 624; George E. Warner and Charles M. Foote, *History of Ramsey County and the City of St. Paul* (Minneapolis: North Star Publishing, 1881); Donald Empson, *The Street Where You Live: A Guide to the Place Names of St. Paul* (Minneapolis: University of Minnesota Press, 2006), 13, 135, 176; *St. Paul Pioneer*, May 2, 1857, 2.

14. Willis Gorman speech; John Fletcher Williams, *A History of the City of St. Paul* (St. Paul: Minnesota Historical Society, 1876), 428; *Baltimore Sun*, May 8, 1856, 1; *First, Second, and Third Annual Reports of the St. Paul Public Library for the Years Ending February 28, 1883–4–5* (St. Paul: H. M. Smyth, 1887), 32.

15. Henry A. Castle, "General James Shields: Soldier, Orator, Statesman," in *Collections of the Minnesota Historical Society* 15 (1915): 721.

16. US Census 1840, District 5, Frederick County, MD, 5, 9; US Census 1850, District 30, Lewis County, VA, 17.

17. US Slave Schedule 1850, District 30, Lewis County, VA, 1.

18. Christopher P. Lehman, *Slavery in the Upper Mississippi Valley: A History of Human Bondage in Illinois, Iowa, Minnesota and Wisconsin* (Jefferson, NC: McFarland, 2011), 133–34.

19. Minnesota Census 1857, Little Falls, Morrison County, 4; *St. Cloud Democrat*, August 11, 1859, 5; Minnesota Census 1857, St. Anthony, Hennepin County, 73.

20. Minnesota Census 1857, St. Anthony, Hennepin County, 73.

21. James E. Homans, ed., *The Cyclopaedia of American Biography*, vol. 8 (New York: Press Association Compilers, 1918), 457–58; Henry A. Castle, *History of St. Paul and Vicinity*, vol. 3 (Chicago: Lewis, 1912), 1040.

22. Homans, *Cyclopaedia of American Biography*, 458; US Census 1830, District 2, Caroline County, MD, 23.

23. "Minnesota Historical Society," *St. Paul Daily Pioneer*, January 16, 1856, 2; *Minnesota Democrat*, May 23, 1855, 3; *Weekly Minnesotian* (St. Paul), May 31, 1856, 4; Homans, *Cyclopedia of American Biography*, 458.

24. Caroline County, Maryland Circuit Court, Certificates of Freedom, 1857–64, vol. 835, 5; US Census 1870, Ward 2, Baltimore, MD, 156.

25. Caroline County, Maryland Circuit Court, Certificates of Freedom, 1827–57, vol. 834, 294–95; Caroline County, Maryland Circuit Court, Certificates of Freedom, 1806–27, vol. 836, 185; Caroline County, Maryland Circuit Court, Certificates of Freedom, 1857–64, vol. 835, 82–83; US Census 1870, District 2, Caroline County, MD, 3.

26. Tamara J. Eastman, *The Great Fire of Petersburg, Virginia* (Charleston, SC: History Press, 2016), 27; Diane Barnes, *Artisan Workers in the Upper South: Petersburg, Virginia, 1820–1865* (Baton Rouge: Louisiana State University Press, 2008), 6–8.

27. US Slave Schedule 1850, 98th Regiment, Mecklenburg County, VA, 455; Minnesota Census 1857, Belle Plaine Precinct, Scott County, 73; *St. Paul Daily Pioneer*, March 14, 1857, 2; US Census 1850, Petersburg, Dinwiddie County, VA, 178.

28. *Daily Express* (VA), July 25, 1855, 3.

29. *Daily Express*, November 9, 1855, 3; "Tobacco and Sweet Potatoes," *Belle Plaine Enquirer*, July 29, 1858, 2.

30. US Census 1840, Petersburg South Ward, Dinwiddie County, VA, 16; *Richmond (VA) Enquirer*, March 24, 1848, 2; US Slave Schedule 1850, Petersburg, Dinwiddie County, VA, 291; Deed Book D, Scott County Recorder, 103–4, 474; Deed Book F, Scott County Recorder, 145; *Belle Plaine Enquirer*, September 23, 1858, 2.

31. US Census 1850, Petersburg, Dinwiddie County, VA, 178; Deed Book F, Scott County Recorder, 589; Hargrove Family Papers, series 3, Slave Papers, 1824–66, folder 7, Southern Historical Collection, University of North Carolina at Chapel Hill; US Slave Schedule 1850, Petersburg, Dinwiddie County, VA, 291.

32. Harold Albrecht, *This Is Our Town* (Belle Plaine, MN: Belle Plaine Historical Society, 1977), 10; US Census 1860, Belle Plaine, Scott County, MN, 4; Edward Duffield Neill, *History of the Minnesota Valley: Including the Explorers and Pioneers of Minnesota* (Minneapolis: North Star Publishing, 1882), 329.

33. US Census 1860, Belle Plaine, Scott County, MN, 4; Neill, *History of the Minnesota Valley*, 329; Deed Book F, Scott County Recorder, 146, 294, 390, 570, 573, 585–89.

34. Minnesota Census 1857, St. Paul, Ramsey County, 131; US Slave Schedule 1850, Petersburg, Dinwiddie County, VA, 291; *Belle Plaine Enquirer*, May 12, 1860, 3; US Census 1860, Belle Plaine, Scott County, MN, 4.

35. Sale of Armand Duplantier's male slave to George Garig, July 6, 1806, in Louisiana, Slave Records, 1719–1820, https://www.ancestry.com/search/collections/afrolaslave ("original data: Gwendolyn Midlo Hall, comp., *Afro-Louisiana History and Genealogy, 1719–1820*").

36. US Slave Schedule 1850, Ward 10, East Baton Rouge Parish, LA, 6–7; US Census 1860, Ward 10, East Baton Rouge Parish, LA, 4; Bonnie Martin, "Neighbor-to-Neighbor Capitalism: Local Credit Networks and the Mortgaging of Slaves," in *Slavery's Capitalism: A New History of American Economic Development*, ed. Sven Beckert and Seth Rockman (Philadelphia: University of Pennsylvania Press, 2016), 119.

37. *Baton Rouge Weekly Gazette and Comet*, January 26, 1857, 2.

38. Minnesota Census 1857, Shakopee City, Scott County, 23; US Slave Schedule 1850, Ward 10, East Baton Rouge Parish, LA, 6–7; US Census 1860, Shakopee, Scott County, MN, 12.

39. US Census 1830, Spencer County, KY, 29; Upham, *Minnesota Geographic Names*, 509; Neill, *History of the Minnesota Valley*, 298, 318; Deed Book A, Scott County Recorder, 182.

40. Deed Book B, Scott County Recorder, 135; Deed Book E, Scott County Recorder, 551, 554; Deed Book G, Scott County Recorder, 99, 101, 517; Minnesota Census 1857, Shakopee City, Scott County, 26; US Census 1860, Shakopee, Scott County, MN, 28.

41. Deed Book D, Scott County Recorder, 224, 229; Neill, *History of the Minnesota Valley*, 318; Minnesota Census 1857, Louisville Precinct, Scott County, 42; US Census 1860, Louisville, Scott County, MN, 4.

42. John G. Rice, "The Old Stock Americans," in *They Chose Minnesota: A Survey of the State's Ethnic Groups*, ed. June Drenning Holmquist (St. Paul: Minnesota Historical Society Press, 1981), 58.

Notes to Chapter Four

1. "Progressive," *New Orleans Daily Delta*, July 9, 1852, 2; "From the Great West," *Louisville Daily Courier*, October 2, 1854, 2.

2. "Minnesota," *Nashville Union and American*, May 21, 1853, 2; "Minnesota Matters," *Nashville Tennessean*, December 15, 1852, 2.

3. "Scraps by a Traveler," *St. Louis Republican*, May 30, 1852, 2.

4. US Slave Schedule 1850, St. Louis Ward 2, MO, 2; Donald Empson, *The West Half of the Churchill, Nelson, & Slaughter Addition Residential Area* (Stillwater, MN: Empson Archives, 2002), 10–11; advertisement, *Minnesota Chronicle and Register*, October 27, 1849, 3; advertisement, *Minnesota Democrat*, May 12, 1852, 2.

5. Empson, *West Half of the Churchill, Nelson, & Slaughter Addition*, 10–11; W. H. C. Folsom, *Fifty Years in the Northwest, with an Introduction and Appendix Containing Reminiscences, Incidents, and Notes* (St. Paul: Pioneer Press, 1888), 359; "New Saw Mills on the St. Croix," *Minnesota Democrat*, April 28, 1852, 4; Agnes Mathilda Larson, *The White Pine Industry in Minnesota: A History* (Minneapolis: University of Minnesota Press, 1949), 54; Agnes M. Larson, "When Logs and Lumber Ruled Stillwater," *Minnesota History* 18, no. 2 (1937): 176.

6. *Journal of the House of Representatives during the Fourth Session of the Legislative Assembly of the Territory of Minnesota* (St. Paul: Joseph R. Brown, 1853), 109.

7. Robert V. Kennedy, *Kennedy's St. Louis City Directory for the Year 1857* (St. Louis: R. V. Kennedy, 1857), 25, 81, 188, 220; US Census 1860, St. Louis Ward 2, MO, 271; US Census 1860, St. Louis Ward 5, MO, 42; US Slave Schedule 1850, St. Louis Ward 2, MO, 1; US Slave Schedule 1850, St. Louis Ward 3, MO, 7; US Slave Schedule 1860, St. Louis Ward 2, MO, 1; US Slave Schedule 1860, St. Louis Ward 4, MO, 3; US Slave Schedule 1860, St. Louis Ward 5, MO,

1; John M. Kingsbury and James Josiah Webb, *Trading in Santa Fe: John M. Kingsbury's Correspondence with James Josiah Webb, 1853–1861* (Dallas, TX: Southern Methodist University Press, 1996), 69; Mary Rozier Sharp and Louis James Sharp, *Between the Gabouri: A History of Ferdinand Rozier and "Nearly" All His Descendants* (Ste. Genevieve, MO: Histoire de Rozier, 1981), 66.

8. Deed Book 1, Washington County (MN) Recorder, 165, 279, 421; US Census 1860, Town District, Morgan County, GA, 7; US Slave Schedule 1860, Town District, Morgan County, GA, 5; US Census 1860, Red Lion Hundred, New Castle County, DE, 17; US Slave Schedule 1860, New Castle Hundred, New Castle County, DE, 1; US Slave Schedule 1860, Bolivar, Hardeman County, TN, 3, 8; US Census 1860, Bolivar, Hardeman County, TN, 6, 7.

9. Deed Book 1, Washington County (MN) Recorder, 97; US Slave Schedule 1860, Richmond Ward 2, Henrico County, VA, 20; US Census 1860, Richmond Ward 2, Henrico County, VA, 91; advertisement, *Richmond Daily Dispatch*, October 13, 1857, 4.

10. Don Papson and Tom Calarco, *Secret Lives of the Underground Railroad in New York City: Sydney Howard Gay, Louis Napoleon and the Record of Fugitives* (Jefferson, NC: McFarland, 2015), 165; *Richmond Daily Dispatch*, March 31, 1856, 1; advertisement, *Richmond Daily Dispatch*, March 27, 1856, 4; Eric Foner, *Gateway to Freedom: The Hidden History of the Underground Railroad* (New York: W. W. Norton, 2015), 195, 206.

11. US Census 1860, Richmond Ward 2, Henrico County, VA, 91; US Census 1860, St. Louis Ward 2, MO, 271.

12. Thomas C. Buchanan, *Black Life on the Mississippi: Slaves, Free Blacks, and the Western Steamboat World* (Chapel Hill: University of North Carolina Press, 2004), 22, 40, 92; *St. Paul Times*, June 23, 1857, in "Slavery in Minnesota," *Chicago Tribune*, June 27, 1857, 2; George Byron Merrick, *Old Times on the Upper Mississippi: The Recollections of a Steamboat Pilot from 1854 to 1863* (1909; repr., St. Paul: Minnesota Historical Society Press, 1987), 64.

13. John Hebron Moore, "Simon Gray, Riverman: A Slave Who Was Almost Free," *Mississippi Valley Historical Review* 49, no. 3 (1962): 473.

14. US 1850 Census; Walt Bachman, *Northern Slave, Black Dakota: The Life and Times of Joseph Godfrey* (Bloomington, MN: Pond Dakota Press, 2013), 50; David Vassar Taylor, *African Americans in Minnesota* (St. Paul: Minnesota Historical Society Press, 2002), 4.

15. Laurence Oliphant, "Minnesota and the Far West" (Edinburgh: Blackwood and Sons, 1855), quoted in Randolph Edgar, "The Path of Hennepin: II," *Bellman* 20 (1917): 67. Edgar theorized in 1917 that the proslavery sentiment Oliphant found was "due to the connection between St. Paul and the South by river, and . . . was almost purely local to St. Paul—possibly confined to its transient population." The memory of slaveholder investments in Minnesota had clearly faded by 1917.

16. *Natchez (MS) Daily Courier*, May 18, 1854, 2.

17. "McKenty," *St. Paul Daily Times*, May 26, 1854, 2; advertisement, *Natchez Daily Courier*, May 16, 1854, 2; "Minnesota Land Agency," *New Orleans Picayune*, October 25, 1854, 1; *Richmond Enquirer*, November 17, 1854, 3; *Baltimore Sun*, October 5, 1854, 3; *Weekly Raleigh (NC) Register*, December 20, 1854, 3.

18. "The South Is Coming North," *Weekly Minnesotian* (St. Paul), November 4, 1854, 4; "The Minnesota Fever Abroad," *St. Paul Daily Minnesotian*, December 16, 1854, 2; Scott P. Marler, *The Merchants' Capital: New Orleans and the Political Economy of the Nineteenth-Century South* (Cambridge: Cambridge University Press, 2013), 131; advertisement, *St. Paul Daily Minnesotian*, April 30, 1855, 3.

19. "River Items," *St. Paul Daily Minnesotian*, April 28, 1855, 2; US Slave Schedule 1860, Clarke County, MS, 15; Gayle Graham Yates, *Life and Death in a Small, Southern Town: Memories of Shubuta, Mississippi* (Baton Rouge: Lousiana State University Press, 2004), 93; "The Weather," *St. Paul Daily Minnesotian*, December 14, 1854, 2; "More Coming," *St. Paul Daily Times*, November 8, 1854, 1; "Real Estate," *St. Paul Daily Minnesotian*, May 26, 1855, 2.

20. "South Is Coming North," 4; advertisement, *Natchez Democrat*, March 22, 1828, 6; "Notice," *Vicksburg (MS) Whig*, December 6, 1837, 3.

21. "City Tax Collector Sales," *Vicksburg Whig*, October 17, 1840, 1; advertisement, *Vicksburg Whig*, January 15, 1834, 4; advertisement, *Weekly Mississippian* (Jackson), January 30, 1835, 3; "Bank Commissioners' Report," *Mississippi Free Trader* (Natchez), February 12, 1840, 1; advertisement, *Vicksburg Whig*, March 27, 1838, 3; advertisement, *Vicksburg Whig*, December 29, 1840, 4; advertisement, *Vicksburg Whig*, November 23, 1842, 4; "Important Legal Decision," *Vicksburg Whig*, May 30, 1838, 3.

22. US Slave Schedule 1860, Madison Parish, LA, 127; Linda Banickel, *Milliken's Bend: A Civil War Battle in History and Memory* (Baton Rouge: Louisiana State University Press, 2013), 26.

23. *Boyd and others v. Boyd and others*, in *Federal Reporter*, vol. 2 (St. Paul: West, 1880), 138, 140, 142; William Kauffman Scarborough, *Master of the Big House: Elite Slaveholders of the Mid-Nineteenth Century South* (Baton Rouge: Louisiana State University Press, 2003), 133, 213–15.

24. Edward E. Baptist, *The Half Has Never Been Told: Slavery and the Making of American Capitalism* (New York: Basic Books, 2014), 358; C. Rutherford to Col. Ballard, December 14, 1853, Rice Ballard Papers, Southern Historical Collection, University of North Carolina at Chapel Hill; S. S. Boyd to Rice Ballard, December 14, 1853, Rice Ballard Papers; C. M. Rutherford to Col. Ballard, January 14, 1854, Rice Ballard Papers.

25. Leonard Bond Chapman, *Monograph on the Southgate Family of Scarborough, Maine: Their Ancestors and Descendants* (Portland, ME: Hubbard W. Bryant, 1907), 11–12, 28.

26. "Married," *Natchez (MS) Courier*, November 23, 1838, 4; *Boyd and others v. Boyd and others*, 139; US Slave Schedule 1850, Adams County, MS, 127; Michael

Wayne, *The Reshaping of Plantation Society: The Natchez District, 1860–80* (Urbana: University of Illinois Press, 1983), 12.

27. Joyce L. Broussard, "Stepping Lively in Place: The Free Black Women of Antebellum Natchez," *Mississippi Women: Their Histories, Their Lives,* vol. 2, ed. Elizabeth Anne Payne, Martha H. Swain, and Marjorie Julian Spruill (Athens: University of Georgia Press, 2010), 31; Scarborough, *Master of the Big House,* 213–15; Baptist, *Half Has Never Been Told,* 358–63.

28. Florence Ridlon, *A Black Physician's Struggle for Civil Rights: Edward C. Mazique, M.D.* (Albuquerque: University of New Mexico Press, 2005), 33–34.

29. "Runaways in Jail: Mississippi," *Vicksburg Daily Whig,* October 29, 1856, 3.

30. *Boyd and others v. Boyd and others,* 138, 140, 142; Minnesota Census 1857, Ramsey County, 290; C. C. Andrews, *Minnesota and Dacotah* (Washington, DC: Robert Farnham, 1857), 193; "Walter B. Boyd Dies at Advanced Age of 92," *St. Paul Globe,* June 5, 1903, 10; D. D. T. Leech, *Post Office Directory, or Business Man's Guide to the Post Offices in the United States* (New York: J. H. Colton, 1856), 199.

31. *Boyd and others v. Boyd and others,* 142.

32. Allen Jay, *Autobiography of Allen Jay: Born 1831, Died 1910* (Philadelphia: John C. Winston, 1910), 233.

33. US Census 1840, Guilford County, NC, 228; Richard Mendenhall, petition, North Carolina General Assembly, November 14, 1824, North Carolina Department of Archives and History, Raleigh; Richard Mendenhall, petition, North Carolina General Assembly, November 30, 1825; Jay, *Autobiography of Allen Jay,* 233; Carol Moore, *Guilford County and the Civil War* (Charleston, SC: History Press, 2015), 18.

34. Jay, *Autobiography of Allen Jay,* 233; Moore, *Guilford County and the Civil War,* 18; William T. Auman, *Civil War in the North Carolina Quaker Belt: The Confederate Campaign against Peace Agitators, Deserters and Draft Dodgers* (Jefferson, NC: McFarland, 2014), 31; Georgena Duncan, "'One Negro, Sarah . . . One Horse Named Collier, One Cow and Calf Named Pink': Slave Records from the Arkansas River Valley," *Arkansas Historical Quarterly* 69, no. 4 (2010): 338.

35. Moore, *Guilford County and the Civil War,* 18; US Slave Schedule 1850, Southern Division, Guilford County, NC, 1; "An Asylum for the Oppressed," *National Era* (Washington, DC), July 2, 1857, 107; "Liberation of Slaves," *Raleigh (NC) Christian Advocate,* July 2, 1857, 2; *Columbia (SC) Times,* in *Charlotte Democrat,* July 7, 1857, 2.

36. Sallie W. Stockard, *The History of Guilford County, North Carolina* (Knoxville, TN: Gaut-Ogden, 1902), 60; Levi M. Scott, "The Bench and Bar of Guilford County, Part II," in *Publications of the Guilford County Literary and Historical Association,* vol. 1 (Greensboro, NC: Jos. J. Stone, 1908), 66; *Proceeding and Report of the Annual Meetings of the Minnesota Territorial Pioneers, May 11, 1899 and 1900,* vol. 2 (St. Paul: Pioneer Press, 1901), 134.

37. Deed Book A, Wright County Recorder's Office, 152; Deed Book B, Stearns County Recorder's Office, 442.

38. Slave Schedule 1850, Forsyth County, NC, 17; Sherburne History Center, "First Landowners of Big Lake Township," Sherburne History Center, http://www.sherburnehistorycenter.org/landbl.html.

39. Will of Thomas Adams, Stokes County, North Carolina Probate Court, 1, 10; Frank V. Tursi, *Winston-Salem: A History* (Winston-Salem, NC: John F. Blair, 1994), 93.

40. Michael Shirley, *From Congregation Town to Industrial City: Culture and Social Change in a Southern Community* (New York: New York University Press, 1994), 35; Sarah Bahnson Chapman, introduction to Charles Frederick Bahnson, *Bright and Gloomy Days: The Civil War Correspondence of Captain Charles Frederich Bahnson, a Moravian Confederate* (Knoxville: University of Tennessee Press, 2003), xvi.

41. Advertisement, *Fayetteville (NC) Weekly Observer*, May 20, 1851, 1; William S. Powell, *North Carolina through Four Centuries* (Chapel Hill: University of North Carolina Press, 1989), 305; Alan D. Watson, *Wilmington, North Carolina, to 1861* (Jefferson, NC: McFarland, 2003), 209; Robert B. Starling, "The Plank Road Movement in North Carolina, Part I," *North Carolina Historical Review* 16, no. 2 (1939): 2, 5, 15, 17–19; Wilma A. Dunaway, *Slavery in the American Mountain South* (Cambridge: Cambridge University Press, 2003), 97; Wilma A. Dunaway, *Women, Work and Family in the Antebellum Mountain South* (Cambridge: Cambridge University Press, 2008), 183.

42. "American Meeting in Winston," *Lexington and Yadkin Flag* (Lexington, DC), March 28, 1856, 2.

43. C. Daniel Crews and Lisa Bailey, *Records of the Moravians in North Carolina*, vol. 12 (Raleigh: North Carolina Department of Cultural Resources, 2000), 6234, 6693; advertisement, *Greensboro Patriot*, January 8, 1858, 4; Forsyth County, North Carolina, Probate Court Inventories, 1849–53, vol. 1, 531; "Married," *Fayetteville (NC) Observer*, January 21, 1856, 3.

44. "Proceedings of the Opposition State Convention," *Raleigh Register*, February 25, 1860, 3.

45. *New Orleans Picayune*, May 17, 1857, 7.

Notes to Chapter Five

1. Advertisement, *New Orleans Picayune*, April 3, 1854, 1; "Appraisement and Distribution of Property of Bennett Dyson," 1856, Charles County Probate Court, MD; advertisement, *Port Tobacco (MD) Times and Charles County Advertiser*, May 6, 1858, 3; Harriet A. Washington, *Medical Apartheid: The Dark History of Medical Experimentation on Black Americans from Colonial Times to the Present* (New York: Doubleday, 2006), 43–45.

2. US Census 1840, New Orleans Ward 1, Orleans Parish, LA, 195.

3. US Census 1850, Third Representative District, Orleans Parish, LA, 165; US Slave Schedule 1850, Third Representative District, Orleans Parish, LA, 19; John Hope Franklin and Loren Schweninger, *Runaway Slaves: Rebels on the Plantation*

(New York: Oxford University Press, 1999), 59; Judith Keller Schafer, *Slavery, the Civil Law, and the Supreme Court of Louisiana* (Baton Rouge: Louisiana State University Press, 1994), 108–9.

4. *New Orleans Picayune*, January 4, 1852, 5; *New Orleans Crescent*, December 23, 1852, 1; *New Orleans Picayune*, August 13, 1853, 3; Index of Records of Theodore O. Stark: January–April 1854, May–December 1854, January–March 1855, Orleans Parish Civil District Court; *New Orleans Crescent*, April 3, 1854, 1.

5. *New Orleans Picayune*, June 18, 1855, 3; *St. Paul Pioneer*, November 3, 1855, 3.

6. Mary Lethert Wingerd, *North Country: The Making of Minnesota* (Minneapolis: University of Minnesota Press, 2010), 247–48; "T. B. Winston Inventory," 3, 7, in Probate Records, Ramsey County Probate Court, MN, reel 4, frames 42, 44.

7. *New Orleans Picayune*, December 29, 1855, 5.

8. Thomas Winston to Alexander Ramsey, December 12, 1855, Alexander Ramsey Papers, MNHS, reel 9, frame 602; Helen McCann White, *Guide to a Microfilm Edition of the Alexander Ramsey Papers and Records* (St. Paul: Minnesota Historical Society, 1974), 23; *Session Laws of the Territory of Minnesota Passed by the Legislative Assembly at the Seventh Session, Commencing Wednesday, January 2, 1856* (St. Paul: Joseph R. Brown, 1856), 73–75; Edward Duffield Neill, *History of the Minnesota Valley: Including the Explorers and Pioneers of Minnesota* (Minneapolis: North Star Publishing, 1882), 650–51.

9. *New Orleans Crescent*, May 14, 1856, 4.

10. *St. Paul Daily Pioneer*, April 1, 1857, 2; *New Orleans Crescent*, August 28, 1857, 5; William D. Green, *A Peculiar Imbalance: The Fall and Rise of Racial Equality in Early Minnesota* (St. Paul: Minnesota Historical Society Press, 2007), 89–91.

11. Deed Book E, April 2, 1857, Scott County Recorder's Office, MN; Wingerd, *North Country*, 250–51; *St. Paul Daily Pioneer*, July 17, 1857, 3; "Ignatius Donnelly and His Faded Metropolis," speech at the Minnesota Historical Society, June 27, 1936, *Minnesota History* 17, no. 3 (1936): 274–75; Dudley S. Brainard, "Nininger: A Boom Town of the Fifties," *Minnesota History* 13, no. 2 (1932): 139.

12. *New Orleans Picayune*, June 18, 1859, 2; Deeds, May 3, 1859, Anoka County Recorder's Office, MN; *New Orleans Picayune*, December 25, 1859, 4; *Orleans Parish Will Book*, vol. 12, 1860–1863, FamilySearch, Salt Lake City, UT, 177; Ramsey County Probate Records, March 22, 1861; White, *Guide to Ramsey Papers*, 23, 75; Petition for Succession of Thomas P. Winston, January 26, 1861, Ramsey County Probate Court, MN, 4.

13. Advertisement, *New Orleans Picayune*, April 28, 1857, 3; "Married," *New Orleans Picyaune*, June 2, 1853, 2; "Negras a Vendre," *Louisiana State Gazette*, October 26, 1825, 3.

14. Augustus B. Eason, *History of the St. Croix Valley* (Chicago: H. C. Cooper Jr., 1909), 83; US Census 1840, New Orleans Ward 1, Orleans Parish, LA, 136; Minnesota Census 1857, Washington County, 154; advertisement, *Stillwater Messenger*, September 22, 1857, 4.

15. "Died," *New Orleans Picayune*, December 6, 1857, 4; advertisement, *Stillwater Messenger*, October 19, 1858, 3; "Eureka!," *Stillwater Messenger*, July 1, 1862, 2; *Stillwater Messenger*, December 1, 1883, 4; US Census 1860, Stillwater, Washington County, MN, 86.

16. *Stillwater Messenger*, December 1, 1883, 4.

17. "The Territorial Terror," *Stillwater Messenger*, February 21, 1885, 4; "Appointments by the Governor," *Weekly Minnesotian* (St. Paul), August 21, 1858, 4; "Eureka!," *Stillwater Messenger*, July 1, 1862, 2.

18. "Annual Statement," *Stillwater Messenger*, February 5, 1861, 3; advertisement, *New Orleans Picayune*, January 26, 1861, 8.

19. Advertisement, *Port Tobacco Times and Charles County Advertiser*, April 3, 1850, 3; "District Whig Meetings," *Port Tobacco Times and Charles County Advertiser*, July 17, 1850, 2; "Married," *Port Tobacco Times and Charles County Advertiser*, October 29, 1850, 2.

20. US Census 1830, Durham, Charles County, MD, 112; US Census 1840, District 1, Charles County, MD, 7–8; US Slave Schedule 1850, Hill Top, Charles County, MD, 17, 19; Marie de Mare, *G. P. A. Healy: American Artist* (New York: David McKay, 1954), 173–74.

21. "Executor's Notice," *Port Tobacco Times and Charles County Advertiser*, November 8, 1855, 3; "Appraisement and Distribution of Property of Bennett Dyson," 1856, Charles County Probate Court, MD.

22. *Session Laws 1856*, vol. 623, Maryland State Archives, Annapolis, 499; "Public Sale," *Port Tobacco Times and Charles County Advertiser*, December 11, 1856, 3.

23. "Public Sale," 3; "Notice," *Port Tobacco Times and Charles County Advertiser*, March 5, 1857, 3.

24. "Public Meeting in Nanjemoy District—Free Negroes," *Port Tobacco Times and Charles County Advertiser*, June 25, 1857, 2.

25. Advertisement, *Port Tobacco Times and Charles County Advertiser*, May 6, 1858, 3; Minnesota Census 1857, Minneapolis, Hennepin County, 168.

26. "Letter from Minnesota," *New Orleans Picayune*, May 27, 1857, 8; advertisement, *New Orleans Picayune*, October 11, 1857, 6; advertisement, *Port Tobacco Times and Charles County Advertiser*, May 6, 1858, 3.

27. Advertisement, *Stillwater Messenger*, October 26, 1858, 1; advertisement, *Stillwater Messenger*, November 29, 1859, 1; John S. Haller Jr., *The History of American Homeopathy: The Academic Years, 1820–1935* (New York: Pharmaceutical Products, 2005), 47–48.

28. William Kauffman Scarborough, *Master of the Big House: Elite Slaveholders of the Mid-Nineteenth Century South* (Baton Rouge: Louisiana State University Press, 2003), 185.

29. "Democratic State Convention," *Red Wing (MN) Sentinel*, August 20, 1859, 2.

30. US Census 1860, Hill Top, Charles County, MD, 59; US Slave Schedule 1860, Hill Top, Charles County, MD, 50; advertisement, *Port Tobacco Times and Charles County Advertiser*, November 29, 1860, 2.

31. Minnesota Census 1857, St. Paul, Ramsey County, 66; "Arrivals at the Hotels," *Evening Star* (Washington, DC), November 6, 1857; "Fort Snelling Investigation," report 351, House of Representatives, 35th Cong., 1st sess., April 27, 1858, 82, 211; Thomas Hughes, *History of Blue Earth County and Biographies of Its Leading Citizens* (Chicago: Middle West, 1902), 102.

32. Article from June 12, 1858, *St. Paul Daily Minnesotian*, cited in *Alexandria (VA) Gazette*, July 20, 1858.

33. "J. Travis Rosser," *Belle Plaine Enquirer*, April 21, 1859, 2.

34. *Stillwater Messenger*, May 3, 1859; Chas. E. Flandrau, "Rosser's Daughter," *St. Paul Globe*, July 19, 1895, 8; Ignatius Donnelly, *Donnelliana* (Chicago: F. J. Schulte, 1892), 32; Hughes, *History of Blue Earth County*, 102.

35. *Wabasha County Herald*, June 25, 1859.

36. Donnelly, *Donnelliana*, 32.

37. "Democratic State Convention," *Wabasha County Herald*, January 19, 1860; "Douglas Convention," *Weekly Standard* (Raleigh, NC), September 5, 1860, 1; Erling Jorstad, "Minnesota's Role in the Democratic Rift of 1860," *Minnesota History* 37, no. 2 (1960): 48; "The Democratic Convention," *Red Wing Sentinel*, January 21, 1860, 3; "Mass Meeting of the Democracy of St. Paul," *Red Wing Sentinel*, May 16, 1860, 2.

38. Sean Wilentz, *The Rise of American Democracy: Jefferson to Lincoln* (New York: W. W. Norton, 2006), 757; Shearer Davis Bowman, *At the Precipice: Americans North and South During the Secession Crisis* (Chapel Hill: University of North Carolina Press, 2010), 142.

39. *Weekly Standard* (Raleigh, NC), September 5, 1860, 1; *Raleigh Register*, September 2, 1860, 3.

40. "J. Travis Rosser Probably Killed," *St. Paul Daily Press*, May 2, 1863, 1; Flandrau, "Rosser's Daughter," 8.

Notes to Chapter Six

1. Mary W. Berthel, *Horns of Thunder: The Life and Times of James M. Goodhue* (St. Paul: Minnesota Historical Society, 1948), 144; Frank George O'Brien, *Minnesota Pioneer Sketches: From the Personal Recollections and Observations of a Pioneer Resident* (Minneapolis: Housekeeper Press, 1904), 210.

2. "Hotel Arrivals," *St. Paul Daily Minnesotian*, November 14, 1854, 2; advertisement, *Natchez (MS) Daily Courier*, April 5, 1853, 1; advertisement, *Natchez Free Trader*, July 4, 1855, 3; advertisement, *Natchez Daily Courier*, April 25, 1855, 3.

3. Advertisement, *Mississippian* (Jackson), December 21, 1855, 3; advertisement, *Mississippian*, February 29, 1856, 1; US Census 1840, New Orleans Ward 2, Orleans Parish, LA, 25; US Slave Schedule 1850, Hinds County, MS, 76, 93; US Slave Schedule 1850, Natchez, Adams County, MS, 5; advertisement, *Natchez*

Courier, March 18, 1854, 4; US Slave Schedule 1850, Adams County, MS, 137–38; US Slave Schedule 1850, Warren County, MS, 91–93.

4. Rachel N. Whitall to her brother Caleb Newbold, September 18, November 1, and December 10, 1849, folder "Papers 1848–1858," Henry M. Rice and Family Papers, MNHS; US Slave Schedule, 1850, Henrico County, VA, 15.

5. William Watts Folwell, *A History of Minnesota,* vol. 1 (St. Paul: Minnesota Historical Society, 1921), 373.

6. Paul Finkelman, "Slavery in the Shadow of Liberty: The Problem of Slavery in Congress and the Nation's Capital," in *In the Shadow of Freedom: The Politics of Slavery in the National Capital,* ed. Paul Finkelman and Donald R. Kennon (Athens: Ohio University Press, 2011), 4; Paul Finkelman, preface to *In the Shadow of Freedom,* vii.

7. Finkelman, "Slavery in the Shadow of Liberty," 4; Finkelman, preface to *In the Shadow of Freedom,* vii.

8. US Census 1830, Anderson County, SC, 32; Ulysses Robert Brooks, *South Carolina Bench and Bar,* vol. 1 (Columbia, SC: State, 1908), 184; US Slave Schedule 1850, Western Division, Anderson County, SC, 20; US Slave Schedule 1860, Regiment Village 4, Anderson County, SC, 4; Rice to W. Holcombe, December 9, 1856, Letterpress, vol. 2, Henry M. Rice and Family Papers.

9. "The South Is Coming North," *St. Paul Democrat,* October 28, 1854, 2.

10. Matilda Whitall Rice to her father Gilbert Whitall, July 29, 1853, folder "Papers 1848–1858," Henry M. Rice and Family Papers; US Slave Schedule 1850, Georgetown North West Ward, Washington, DC, 2.

11. Sabine N. Meyer, *We Are What We Drink: The Temperance Battle in Minnesota* (Urbana: University of Illinois Press, 2005), 41.

12. Mary Lethert Wingerd, *North Country: The Making of Minnesota* (Minneapolis: University of Minnesota Press, 2010), 198, 230, 383n36; Stephen George, *Enterprising Minnesota: 150 Years of Business Pioneers* (Minneapolis: University of Minnesota Press, 2003), 12.

13. "Thomas Jefferson," *St. Paul Daily Times,* October 9, 1855, 2; "Minnesota," *Washington (DC) Union,* August 12, 1855, 2; Wingerd, *North Country,* 243–44.

14. US Census 1830, Cedar, Boone County, MS, 9; Merlin Stonehouse, *John Wesley North and the Reform Frontier* (Minneapolis: University of Minnesota Press, 1965), 25; "The Third Annual Report of the Board of Regents of the University of Minnesota to the Council and House of Representatives, 1854," University of Minnesota Archives, Elmer L. Andersen Library, Minneapolis, 5.

15. *House of Representatives Executive Documents, 3rd Session of the 34th Congress, 1856–1857* (Washington, DC: Cornelius Wendell, 1857), 344; I. Atwater, "Supplementary Report Called for by the State Legislature of 1860," in *The Ninth Annual Report of the Board of Regents of the University of Minnesota to the Legislature of the State of Minnesota, 1860,* Annual and Biennial Reports of the University, University of Minnesota, 6; *The Third Annual Report of the Board of Regents of the State*

University to the Legislature of Minnesota, Session of 1863, Annual and Biennial Reports of the University, University of Minnesota, 7.

16. E. B. Johnson, *Dictionary of the University of Minnesota* (Minneapolis: [University of Minnesota?], 1908), 9–12, 159; Christopher P. Lehman, "Brought to Light: The University of Minnesota's Heritage of Slavery," *Hennepin History Magazine* 75, no. 2 (2016): 5–6.

17. Nathaniel Holmes Bishop, *Voyage of the Paper Canoe: A Geographical Journey of 2500 Miles, from Quebec to the Gulf of Mexico* (Bedford, MA: Applewood Books, 1878), 265; Antoinette T. Jackson, *Speaking for the Enslaved: Heritage Interpretation at Antebellum Plantation Sites* (London: Routledge, 2012), 89.

18. Thomas L. Scott, "Nine of the Biggest Slave Owners in American History," *Atlanta Black Star,* December 23, 2014; US Slave Schedule 1850, St. John's Parish, Charleston, SC, 8–18; Bishop, *Voyage of the Paper Canoe,* 261, 266; Henry James, *Notes of a Son and Brother: A Critical Edition* (Charlottesville: University of Virginia, 2011), 312; Maurie D. McInnis, *The Politics of Taste in Antebellum Charleston* (Chapel Hill: University of North Carolina Press, 2005), 208–29.

19. McInnis, *Politics of Taste in Antebellum Charleston,* 211; "A Fugitive," *Camden (SC) Weekly Journal,* September 6, 1859, 1.

20. Robert R. Weyeneth, *Historic Preservation for a Living City: Historic Charleston Foundation, 1947–1997* (Columbia: University of South Carolina Press, 2000), 175; Susan L. Buck, "Paint Discoveries in the Aiken-Rhett House Kitchen and Slave Quarters," *Perspectives in Vernacular Architecture* 10 (2005): 188–89.

21. *Mantorville (MN) Express,* September 10, 1857, 3; Willis M. West, "The University of Minnesota," in *The History of Education in Minnesota,* ed. John N. Greer (Washington: Government Printing Office, 1902), 96; "Our Minnesota Correspondence," *New York Herald,* July 16, 1857, 2.

22. "What Does It Mean," *New Orleans Daily Crescent,* July 27, 1857, 5; "Where They Invest," *Freeman's Champion* (Prairie City, KS), August 13, 1857, 2.

23. "Growth of St. Paul and Bayfield," *Evening Star* (Washington, DC), November 3, 1856, 1.

24. "A Glance All Round," *United States Magazine* 4, no. 2 (February 1857): 216.

25. H. M. Rice to Hon. J. L. Orr, January 31, 1857, Orr and Patterson Family Papers, Southern Historical Collection, Louis Round Wilson Special Collections Library, University of North Carolina, Chapel Hill.

26. "Reports Submitted by the Select Committee Approved to Characterize Certain Alleged Corrupt Combination of Members of Congress," in *House of Representatives Report no. 243,* 34th Cong., 3rd sess., 19, 26, 36, 38.

27. Dudley S. Brainard, "Nininger: A Boom Town of the Fifties," *Minnesota History* 13, no. 2 (1932): 136.

28. *Stillwater Messenger,* September 29, 1857, 2.

29. *St. Paul Daily Pioneer,* April 28, 1856, 3; *St. Paul Daily Pioneer,* May 9, 1857, 3.

30. *Memphis Daily Eagle and Enquirer,* April 10, 1857, 2; R. I. Holcombe and William Bingham, *Compendium of History and Biography of Polk County, Minnesota*

(Minneapolis: W. H. Bingham, 1916), 61; Charles E. Flandrau, *Encyclopedia of Biography of Minnesota* (Chicago: Century, 1900), 366; Calvin L. Brown, "Some Changes in Local Boundaries and Names in Minnesota," *Minnesota History* 4, no. 5–6 (1922): 242; "Minnesota Counties and Historical Facts," Random Acts of Genealogical Kindness, http://www.raogk.org/counties/minnesota. On slave-holding parents, see US Census 1830, Fayette County, KY, 23; US Census 1830, District 165, Wilkes County, GA, 2; US Census 1820, Wilkinson County, MS, 12.

31. Frank H. Heck, *Proud Kentuckian: John C. Breckinridge, 1821–1875* (Lexington: University Press of Kentucky, 1976), 69; James C. Klotter, *The Breckinridges of Kentucky* (Lexington: University Press of Kentucky, 1986), 113. Rice's house on Minnesota Row was at 205 I Street, near New Jersey Avenue and between Second and Third, next to Douglas. *Daily Confederation* (Montgomery, AL), November 23, 1859, 2; *Washington Union*, March 27, 1858, 4; Maury Klein, *Days of Defiance: Sumter, Secession, and the Coming of the Civil War* (New York: Vintage, 1997), 124; Hal H. Smith, "Historic Washington Homes," in *Records of the Columbia Historical Society, Washington, D.C.*, vol. 2 (Washington, DC: Columbia Historical Society, 1908), 263.

32. "Our Minnesota Correspondence," *New York Herald*, July 4, 1857, 8; William D. Green, *A Peculiar Imbalance: The Fall and Rise of Racial Equality in Early Minnesota* (St. Paul: Minnesota Historical Society Press, 2007), 91; "Col. Orr," *Keowee (SC) Courier*, July 25, 1857, 2.

33. Deed Book B, Stearns County Recorder's Office, 92–93; Deed Book B, Benton County Recorder's Office, 505–6.

34. US Census 1840, Abbeville County, SC, 96; US Slave Schedule 1850, Abbeville County, SC, 19–20; "Death of Joel Smith, Esq.," *Abbeville (SC) Press and Banner*, February 23, 1855, 2; "Death of Joel Smith, Esq.," *Greenville (SC) Enterprise*, February 23, 1855, 2; advertisement, *Abbeville Press and Banner*, November 30, 1855, 3.

35. US Slave Schedule 1860, Abbeville County, SC, 57–59; Cheryll Ann Cody, "Kin and Community among the Good Hope People after Emancipation," *Ethnohistory* 41, no. 1 (1993): 28, 69; US Slave Schedule 1860, Bolivar, Jefferson County, AR, 4–5; "Estate of Mrs. Isabella Smith," box 148, roll 4200, Abbeville County Probate Court, SC; will of Augustus M. Smith, *Abbeville County, South Carolina Wills Record, No. 4, 1855–68*, 334; Ruthe Winegarten, *Black Texas Women: A Sourcebook* (Austin: University of Texas Press, 1996), 50.

36. Donald P. McNeilly, *Old South Frontier: Cotton Plantations and the Formation of Arkansas Society, 1819–1861* (Fayetteville: University of Arkansas Press, 2000), 69.

37. Edward E. Baptist, *The Half Has Never Been Told: Slavery and the Making of American Capitalism* (New York: Basic Books, 2014), 22, 25.

38. Herbert G. Gutman, *The Black Family in Slavery and Freedom, 1750–1925* (New York: Vintage, 1976), 46–47, 50–51.

39. US Census 1860, Abbeville County, SC, 71; Carl H. Moneyhon, *The Impact of the Civil War and Reconstruction on Arkansas: Persistence in the Midst of Ruin* (Fayetteville: University of Arkansas Press, 2002), 59–60.

40. Author's perusal of real estate deeds in McLeod, Scott, and Stearns Counties, Minnesota.

41. Victor J. Danilov, *Women and Museums: A Comprehensive Guide* (Lanham, MD: Altamira, 2005), 160; *Mantorville (MN) Express*, September 10, 1857, 3.

42. Johnson, *Dictionary of the University of Minnesota*, 13; West, "University of Minnesota," 96; John B. Gilfillan, *An Historical Sketch of the University of Minnesota* (St. Paul: State Historical Society of Minnesota, 1905), 21–22; James L. Huston, *The Panic of 1857 and the Coming of the Civil War* (Baton Rouge: Louisiana State University Press, 1987), 262; Charles W. Calominis and Larry Schweikart, "The Panic of 1857: Origins, Transmission, and Containment," *Journal of Economic History* 5, no. 4 (December 1991): 808–10.

43. *Baltimore Daily Exchange*, March 30, 1859, 1; *Evansville Daily Journal*, April 11, 1859, 3; *Charleston (SC) Mercury*, May 4, 1859, 2.

44. *Journal of the House of Representatives of the Fourth Session of the Legislature of the State of Minnesota*, 72; US Census 1850, Georgetown North West Ward, Washington, DC, 13; US Slave Schedule 1850, Georgetown North West Ward, Washington, DC, 2.

45. John C. Rives, *Congressional Globe* (Washington, DC: John C. Rives, 1858), 2075–78; *Collections of the Minnesota Historical Society* 8 (1898): 180.

46. Ruth Ketring Nuermberger, *The Clays of Alabama: A Planter-Lawyer-Politician Family* (Lexington: University of Kentucky Press, 1958), 298; "Historical Society Notes," *Minnesota History* 19, no. 2 (1938): 212; C. C. Clay to Henry M. Rice, February 19, 1861, "Papers 1860–1863," Henry M. Rice Papers; US Census 1830, Huntsville, Madison County, AL, 4.

47. US Slave Schedule 1850, Huntsville, Madison County, AL, 7; Nuermberger, *Clays of Alabama*, 13; Daniel S. Dupre, *Transforming the Cotton Frontier: Madison County, Alabama, 1800–1840* (Baton Rouge: Louisiana State University Press, 1997), 2.

Notes to Chapter Seven

1. US Census 1830, Caldwell County, KY, 39; Walt Bachman, *Northern Slave, Black Dakota* (Bloomington, MN: Pond Dakota, 2013), 12–13, 17; Christopher P. Lehman, *Slavery in the Upper Mississippi Valley: A History of Human Bondage in Illinois, Iowa, Minnesota and Wisconsin* (Jefferson, NC: McFarland, 2011), 72–73, 94.

2. William Bell Mitchell, *History of Stearns County, Minnesota*, 2 vols. (Chicago: Cooper, 1915), 2:1442.

3. Deed Book A, Stearns County Recorder's Office, 42; Thomas Calhoun, will, July 31, 1855, in *Wilson County, Tennessee Inventories, Wills, 1853–1858*, 211.

4. Benjamin Wilburn McDonnold, *History of the Cumberland Presbyterian Church* (Nashville: Cumberland Presbyterian Church, 1893), 72–73, 313, 410;

"General Assembly of the Cumberland Presbyterian Church," *Nashville Union and American*, May 22, 1855, 3.

5. Deed Book A, Stearns County Recorder's Office, 277.

6. US Slave Schedule 1850, Lebanon District 5, Wilson County, TN, 4; US Slave Schedule 1860, Lebanon District 10, Wilson County, TN, 35; Deed Book A, Stearns County Recorder's Office, 229, 232.

7. Thomas D. Morris, *Southern Slavery and the Law, 1619–1860* (Chapel Hill: University of North Carolina Press, 1996), 207, 383; Deed Book A, Stearns County Recorder's Office, 257, 258; US Census 1850, Lebanon District 10, Wilson County, TN, 11; US Census 1860, District 10, Wilson County, TN, 184; US Slave Schedule 1850, Lebanon District 5, Wilson County, TN, 4; US Slave Schedule 1860, Lebanon District 10, Wilson County, TN, 38; Deed Book A, Stearns County Recorder's Office, 257–58, 301.

8. Randall M. Miller, "The Fabric of Control: Slavery in Antebellum Southern Textile Mills," *Business History Review* 55, no. 4 (1981): 487; US Slave Schedule 1860, Yazoo, MS, 152–53; will of James W. Hoggatt, *Yazoo County, Mississippi Will Record*, vol. A, August 14, 1863, 311–22; US Census 1860, Yazoo County, MS, 89; US Census 1870, District 3, Yazoo County, MS, 138.

9. James C. Cobb, *The Most Southern Place on Earth: The Mississippi Delta and the Roots of Regional Identity* (New York: Oxford University, 1992), 29–30; William K. Scarborough, "Slavery in Mississippi," in *Dictionary of Afro-American Slavery*, ed. Randall M. Miller and John David Smith (Westport, CT: Praeger, 1997), 485.

10. US Slave Schedule 1850, District 1, De Kalb County, TN, 1; US Slave Schedule 1860, District 9, De Kalb County, TN, 10; *Nashville Christian Advocate*, August 27, 1870; *St. Cloud Democrat*, June 14, 1866, 3; Deed Book A, Stearns County Recorder's Office, 231, 236–37; US Slave Schedule 1850, Districts 3, 8, and 12, De Kalb County, TN, 833; US Slave Schedule 1860, District 1, De Kalb County, TN, 2; *Nashville Tennessean*, July 16, 1852, 2; Paul Wallace Gates, "Southern Investments in Northern Lands before the Civil War," *Journal of Southern History* 5, no. 2 (1939): 170.

11. Minnesota Census 1857, Stearns County; *Nashville Daily Patriot*, July 31, 1856, 2; Mitchell, *History of Stearns County*, 2:1407, 1442, 1462.

12. Deed Book A, Stearns County Recorder's Office, 277.

13. *Nashville Union and American*, March 18, 1857; Deed Book B, Stearns County Recorder's Office, 33, 54; *Sauk Rapids (MN) Frontiersman*, August 27, 1857; Mitchell, *History of Stearns County*, 1:182–83.

14. *Nashville Union and American*, March 18, 1857.

15. Mitchell, *History of Stearns County*, 2:767.

16. Advertisement, *St. Paul Pioneer*, August 12, 1857, 1; advertisement, *St. Cloud Visiter*, December 10, 1857, 1.

17. Minnesota Census 1857, Stearns County; *St. Cloud Democrat*, September 30, 1858, 2.

18. Wilson County [TN] Trust Deed Book EE, 96; Thomas Calhoun, will, July 31, 1855, in *Wilson County, Tennessee Inventories, Wills, 1853–1858*, 211.

19. Minnesota Census 1857, Stearns County.

20. US Slave Schedule 1860, District 9, Wilson County, TN, 27; US Census 1870, District 7, Wilson County, TN, 7.

21. Robert Tracy McKenzie, *One South or Many? Plantation Belt and Upcountry in Civil War–Era Tennessee* (Cambridge: Cambridge University Press, 1994), 5; Stephen V. Ash, *Middle Tennessee Society Transformed, 1860–1870: War and Peace in the Upper South* (Knoxville: University of Tennessee Press, 2006), 44.

22. McDonnold, *History of the Cumberland Presbyterian Church*, 340–41; *Athens (TN) Post*, June 12, 1857, 2.

23. Deed to William M. Provine, June 14, 1858, Wilson County, TN, Deeds; deed to S. L. Calhoun, June 27, 1857, Wilson County, TN, Deeds.

24. *Trustees, Faculty, and Students of Cumberland University* (Lebanon, TN: J. T. Figures, 1846), 6; *1851–1852 Cumberland University Officers and Students Catalogue* (Nashville: McKennie & Brown, 1852), 3; *1855–1856 Catalogue of Cumberland University Officers and Students* (Nashville: Southern Methodist Publishing House, 1856), 4; *Nashville Tennessean*, December 13, 1838, 3; *Nashville Tennessean*, May 28, 1847, 2; Deed Book A, Stearns County Recorder's Office, 613, 626; Deed Book B, Stearns County Recorder's Office, 88; US Slave Schedule 1860, Nashville, Davidson County, TN, 28; US Slave Schedule 1860, District 2, Smith County, TN, 6; US Slave Schedule 1850, Civil District 3, Wilson County, TN, 3.

25. Deed Book B, Stearns County Recorder's Office, 92–94; Mortgage Book B, Benton County Recorder's Office, 505–7; Mitchell, *History of Stearns County*, 2:1493.

26. *St. Paul Times*, in *Chicago Tribune*, June 10, 1857, 2; Lehman, *Slavery in the Upper Mississippi Valley*, 145–46, 161.

27. *St. Paul Times*, in *Chicago Tribune*, July 10, 1857, 2; "A Minnesota Slave Case," *Liberator* (Boston), July 17, 1857, 3.

28. "Meeting in Stearns County," *St. Paul Daily Pioneer*, October 27, 1857, 2; Mitchell, *History of Stearns County*, 1:180, 2:1442.

29. Deed to P. B. Calhoun, January 10, 1858, Wilson County, TN, Deeds.

30. Sylvia D. Hoffert, *Jane Grey Swisshelm: An Unconventional Life, 1815–1884* (Chapel Hill: University of North Carolina Press, 2004), 111.

31. "Our Position," *St. Anthony (MN) Express*, November 1, 1851, 2.

32. Hoffert, *Jane Grey Swisshelm*, 114–16, 118–19.

33. Advertisement, *St. Cloud Democrat*, August 5, 1858, 3; advertisement, *St. Cloud Democrat*, August 5, 1858, 4.

34. Deed Book B, Stearns County Recorder's Office, 376; Mortgage Book B, Benton County Deeds, 742.

35. Judy Fuson and Ria Baker, *DeKalb County* (Charleston, SC: Arcadia, 2012), 114; US Slave Schedule 1850, District 12, Wilson County, TN, 1; US Slave Schedule 1860, District 1, DeKalb County, TN, 1; Deed Book B, Stearns County Recorder's Office, 474.

36. *Winslow House Hotel Register, 1858–1882*, Hennepin History Museum, Minneapolis, 15, 17; Lien Book A, Stearns County Recorder's Office, 5.

37. Deed to William M. Provine; *St. Cloud Democrat*, September 30, 1858, 2; *St. Cloud Democrat*, November 11, 1858, 2.

38. Hoffert, *Jane Grey Swisshelm*, 139–40; *St. Cloud Democrat*, September 30, 1858, 2.

39. *St. Cloud Democrat*, November 11, 1858, 2.

40. "Change of Firm," *Clarksville (TN) Chronicle*, June 18, 1858, 3; *Nashville Tennessean*, June 12, 1858, 3; *St. Cloud Democrat*, September 16, 1858, 2; *St. Cloud Democrat*, October 14, 1858, 2; Hoffert, *Jane Grey Swisshelm*, 121.

41. *St. Paul Pioneer-Democrat*, February 27, 1859.

42. *St. Cloud Democrat*, April 7, 1859; *St. Cloud Democrat*, May 5, 1859.

43. Hoffert, *Jane Grey Swisshelm*, 119.

44. Mitchell, *History of Stearns County*, 2:1311; *Red Wing (MN) Sentinel*, August 20, 1859, 5; Sylvanus B. Lowry to wife, April 7, 1859, Sylvanus B. Lowry and Family Papers, MNHS.

Notes to Chapter Eight

1. Edward E. Baptist, *The Half Has Never Been Told: Slavery and the Making of American Capitalism* (New York: Basic Books, 2014), 353; Harriet A. Washington, *Medical Apartheid: The Dark History of Medical Experimentation on Black Americans from Colonial Times to the Present* (New York: Doubleday, 2006), 44.

2. Daina Ramey Berry, *The Price for Their Pound of Flesh: The Value of the Enslaved, from Womb to Grave, in the Building of a Nation* (Boston: Beacon Press, 2017), 55.

3. Baptist, *Half Has Never Been Told*, 256, 312; Eric Foner, *Gateway to Freedom: The Hidden History of the Underground Railroad* (New York: W. W. Norton, 2015), 44–45, 219.

4. Advertisement, *Republican Advocate* (Shakopee, MN), July 18, 1857, 1; advertisement, *Belle Plaine Enquirer*, November 17, 1859, 2; Virginia Groark, "Slave Policies," *New York Times*, May 5, 2002; Peter Slevin, "In Aetna's Past: Slave Owner Policies," *Washington Post*, March 9, 2000.

5. James L. Huston, *The Panic of 1857 and the Coming of the Civil War* (Baton Rouge: Louisiana State University Press, 1987), 13, 262; James Stuart Olson, *Encyclopedia of the Industrial Revolution in America* (Westport, CT: Greenwood, 2002), 191.

6. *Acts Passed by the General Assembly of the State of North Carolina at the Session of 1833–1834* (Raleigh: Lawrence & Lemay, 1834), 3; William Gouge, *History of Paper Money and Banking* (Philadelphia: T. W. Ustick, 1834), 132; Alan D. Watson, *General Benjamin Smith: A Biography of the North Carolina Governor* (Jefferson, NC: McFarland, 2011), 184; Amanda Cook Gilbert, *Descendants of William Cromartie and Ruhamah Doane and Related Families*, vol. 1 (Bloomington, IN: Westbow, 2013), 63; James Iredell, *Reports of Cases in Equity Argued and Determined in the Supreme*

Court of North Carolina from December Term, 1847, to December Term, 1848, vol. 5 (Raleigh: Seaton Gales, 1849), 269–71; Sylviane A. Diouf, *Slavery's Exiles: The Story of the American Maroons* (New York: New York University Press, 2014), 272–74; J. Christy Judah, *The Two Faces of Dixie: Politicians, Plantations, and Slaves* (n.p.: Coastal Books, 2009), 102; Todd L. Savitt, "Slave Life Insurance and Virginia and North Carolina," *Journal of Southern History* 43, no. 4 (1977): 593, 595, 597–600. In the Bank of Cape Fear's first year, Benjamin Smith, governor of North Carolina in 1810–11, became a stockholder in order to offset his large debt and keep his slaves at his multiple rice plantations. Years later a slaveholding stockholder willed his bank stock and a slave girl to his mother. Also, a man named John Kelly, who owned 117 shares of bank stock, willed both shares and slaves to people. His widow inherited fifty shares and four slaves, and another person acquired twelve shares and one slave.

7. US Census 1820, New Hanover, New Hanover County, NC, 2; US Census 1830, New Hanover County, NC, 37; Mortgage Book A1, McLeod County Recorder, 212–13; US Slave Schedule 1850, Wilmington, New Hanover County, NC, 27; advertisement, *Daily Journal* (Wilmington, NC), September 26, 1851, 4; advertisement, *State Journal* (Raleigh, NC), August 21, 1861, 4; advertisement, *Wilmington (NC) Daily Herald,* May 12, 1856, 3; *St. Paul Daily Pioneer,* November 21, 1857, 3.

8. US Census 1820, Stokes County, NC, 25; US Census 1840, Bethania, Stokes County, NC, 6; William H. Barnes, *The Fortieth Congress of the United States,* vol. 2 (New York: George E. Perine, 1870), 229–30; Heather Fearnbach, *The Bethania Freedman's Community: An Architectural and Historical Context of the Bethania–Rural Hall Road Study Area* (Winston-Salem, NC: Fearnbach History Services, 2012), 17; George W. Hansbrough, *Reports of Cases Decided in the Supreme Court of Appeals of Virginia,* vol. 77 (Richmond, VA: Rush U. Derr, 1884), 603, 606; US Slave Schedule 1850, Forsyth County, NC, 7.

9. Sherburne County Deed Book A, Sherburne County Recorder's Office, 108; Christopher P. Lehman, "Brought to Light: The University of Minnesota's Heritage of Slavery," *Hennepin History Magazine* 75, no. 2 (2016): 5; Rick Rothacker, *Banktown: The Rise and Fall of Charlotte's Big Banks* (Winston-Salem, NC: John F. Blair, 2010), 8.

10. David J. McCord, *The Statutes at Large of South Carolina,* vol. 8 (Columbia, SC: A. S. Johnston, 1840), 85, 90; Charles G. Cordle, "The Bank of Hamburg, South Carolina," *Georgia Historical Quarterly* 23, no. 2 (1939): 148; Lacy K. Ford Jr., "The Tale of Two Entrepreneurs in the Old South: John Springs III and Hiram Hutchison of the South Carolina Upcountry," *South Carolina Historical Magazine* 95, no. 3 (1994): 218–19.

11. McCord, *Statutes at Large of South Carolina,* vol. 8, 85, 90; Mortgage Book B, Benton County Recorder, 507; Deed Book B, Stearns County Recorder's Office, 92–94; US Census 1830, Washington County, VA, 5; Judy Bainbridge, "Historic Beattie House Looking for Someone to Call It Home," *Greenville (SC) News,* June 4, 2014.

12. Deed Book A, Stearns County Recorder's Office, 613; *Nashville Union and American*, March 6, 1856, 3; *Nashville Tennessean*, March 9, 1854, 3; *Public Acts Passed at the First Session of the Twentieth General Assembly of the State of Tennessee* (Nashville: Republican and Gazette, 1833), 70, 75; *Nashville Daily Patriot*, June 9, 1857, 4.

13. *Public Acts of the State of Tennessee in the First Session of the Thirty-Third General Assembly for the Years 1859–60* (Nashville: E. G. Eastman, 1860), 591–92; Terrell Dempsey, *Searching for Jim: Slavery in Sam Clemens's World* (Columbia: University of Missouri Press, 2003), 229; Deed Book I, Washington County (VA) Recorder's Office, 165.

14. "Tennesseans I Wish I'd Known: Thomas Robinson Smith," *Tennessee Genealogical Magazine* (Winter 1996): 171–73; US Slave Schedule 1850, Bolivar, Hardeman County, TN, 1–2; US Slave Schedule 1860, Bolivar, Hardeman County, TN, 3, 8.

15. Walter B. Stevens, *St. Louis: The Fourth City, 1764–1909* (St. Louis: S. J. Clarke, 1909), 307; James Neal Primm, "Getting Ahead: Business, Science, Learning: The Economy of Nineteenth-Century St. Louis," in *St. Louis in the Century of Henry Shaw: A View Beyond the Garden Wall*, ed. Eric Sandweiss (Columbia: University of Missouri Press, 2003), 123.

16. Robert V. Kennedy, *Kennedy's St. Louis City Directory for the Year 1857* (St. Louis: R. V. Kennedy, 1857), 293; Stevens, *St. Louis*, 894, 896; H. A. Trexler, "Slavery in Missouri, 1804–1865," *Johns Hopkins University Studies in Historical and Political Science*, vol. 32 (Baltimore: Johns Hopkins University Press, 1914), 285–86.

17. US Census 1860, Ward 5, St. Louis, MO, 292; US Slave Schedule 1860, Ward 5, St. Louis, MO, 4; Lea VanderVelde, *Mrs. Dred Scott* (New York: Oxford University Press, 2009), 415, 418.

18. Paul Finkelman, *Dred Scott v. Sandford: A Brief History with Documents* (Boston: Bedford, 1997), 19, 22–23; VanderVelde, *Mrs. Dred Scott*, 228, 378, 415, 419.

19. *Richmond (VA) Enquirer*, December 9, 1856, 3.

20. US Census 1850, St. Stephens Parish, King and Queen County, VA, 46; US Slave Schedule 1850, St. Stephens Parish, King and Queen County, VA, 29; US Census 1860, St. Paul, Second Ward, Ramsey County, MN, 146; *St. Paul Globe*, August 9, 1881, 7; Minnesota Census 1857, St. Paul, Ramsey County, 69.

21. US Slave Schedule 1850, Alexandria, Alexandria County, VA, 4; US Slave Schedule 1850, Lexington, Rockbridge County, VA, 4; *Alexandria (VA) Gazette*, January 8, 1858, 1; *Alexandria Gazette*, April 17, 1858, 4.

22. *Weekly Standard* (Raleigh, NC), April 15, 1857, 3; US Slave Schedule 1850, Richmond, Henrico County, VA, 32; US Slave Schedule 1850, Southern Division, Guilford County, NC, 6–7; US Slave Schedule 1850, First District, Orange County, NC, 99–101; US Slave Schedule 1850, Eastern District, Rockingham County, NC, 102–3; US Slave Schedule 1850, Northampton County, NC, 15.

23. Deed Book B, Stearns County Recorder's Office, 145–46, 148; US Slave Schedule 1860, North Division, Guilford County, NC, 27; US Slave Schedule 1860, Salisbury, Rowan County, NC, 1; Thomas J. Ward Jr., *Black Physicians in the Jim Crow South* (Fayetteville: University of Arkansas Press, 2003), 3; R. J. Mendenhall's Diary, April 27 and 29, 1856, and September 4, 1857, Richard Junius and Abby Mendenhall Papers, MNHS; US Slave Schedule 1850, Southern Division, Guilford County, NC, 4; US Slave Schedule 1860, South Division, Guilford County, NC, 13–14; "Worthless Bank Notes," *Wilmington (NC) Commercial,* July 31, 1856, 2; advertisement, *Wilmington (NC) Daily Herald,* December 6, 1854, 4.

24. US Slave Schedule 1850, Georgetown North West Ward, Washington, DC, 2; US Slave Schedule 1850, Ward 2, Washington, DC, 4; Matilda Whitall Rice to her father Gilbert Whitall, July 29, 1853, folder "Papers 1848–1858," Henry M. Rice and Family Papers, MNHS.

25. Advertisement, *Washington (DC) Republic,* April 20, 1850, 7; advertisement, *Washington Republic,* March 2, 1853, 8; Sharon Ann Murphy, *Investing in Life: Insurance in Antebellum America* (Baltimore: Johns Hopkins University Press, 2010), 186, 308; Tim Armstrong, *The Logic of Slavery: Debt, Technology, and Pain in American Literature* (Cambridge: Cambridge University Press, 2012), 43.

26. African Colonization Society, *The African Repository,* vol. 30 (Washington, DC: C. Alexander, 1854), 95; African Colonization Society, *The African Repository,* vol. 31 (Washington, DC: C. Alexander, 1855), 127.

27. *Baltimore Sun,* September 15, 1857, 4.

28. Advertisement, *Evening Star* (Washington, DC), November 10, 1857, 3.

29. Harvey Officer, *Reports of Cases Argued and Defended in the Supreme Court of the State of Minnesota,* vol. 2 (St. Paul: Earle S. Goodrich, 1859), 265; "Local Intelligence," *Evening Star,* September 28, 1857, 3; advertisement, *Weekly American* (Washington, DC), September 19, 1857, 3; "Local News," *Washington (DC) Union,* October 20, 1857, 3.

30. *Minnesota Reports,* vol. 25 (St. Paul: West, 1880), 9; Mortgage Book A, Sibley County Recorder, 382–83.

31. Christopher P. Lehman, "Slaveholder Investment in Territorial Minnesota," *Minnesota History* 65, no. 7 (2017): 268–69; Emily Grey, "The Black Community in Territorial St. Anthony: A Memoir," *Minnesota History* 49, no. 3 (1984): 52; Eric Foner, *The Fiery Trial: Abraham Lincoln and American Slavery* (New York: W. W. Norton, 2010), 145; R. J. Mendenhall's Diary, October 11, 1858, Richard Junius and Abby Mendenhall Papers; US Census 1860, Minneapolis Third Ward, Hennepin County, MN, 219.

32. R. J. Mendenhall's Diary, April 20, 1858, Richard Junius and Abby Mendenhall Papers; Abby Mendenhall, in R. J. Mendenhall's Diary, June 10, 1859, Richard Junius and Abby Mendenhall Papers; Deed Book D, Wright County Recorder, 430–31, 496–97, 539–40.

33. R. J. Mendenhall's Diary, May 17, 1860, Richard Junius and Abby Mendenhall Papers.

34. "The Farmer's Bank," *Greensboro Patriot*, April 15, 1859, 2; *The Bankers' Magazine and Statistical Register*, vol. 14, ed. J. Smith Homans Jr. (New York: J. Smith Homans Jr., 1860), 990; *The Bankers' Magazine and Statistical Register*, vol. 15, ed. J. Smith Homans Jr. (New York: J. Smith Homans Jr., 1861), 990; Deed Book D, Stearns County Recorder's Office, 118–23; Deed Book D, Wright County Recorder, 430–31, 496–97, 539–40.

35. "An Act to Incorporate a Mutual Insurance Company in the Town of Greensborough, North Carolina," in *Laws of the State of North Carolina Passed by the General Assembly at the Session of 1850–51* (Raleigh, NC: Star Office, 1851), 563; advertisement, *Weekly Standard* (Raleigh, NC), January 3, 1855, 1; advertisement, *Greensboro Patriot*, September 20, 1860, 4; advertisement, *Fayetteville (NC) Weekly Observer*, May 30, 1853, 3; advertisement, *State Journal* (Raleigh, NC), February 27, 1861, 1; Sharon Ann Murphy, "Securing Human Property: Slavery, Life Insurance, and Industrialization in the Upper South," *Journal of the Early Republic* 25, no. 4 (2005): 639.

36. US Census 1840, Patrick County, VA, 20; US Slave Schedule 1860, South Division, Guilford County, NC, 13–14.

37. Advertisement, *Wilmington (NC) Daily Herald*, May 23, 1859, 4; US Slave Schedule 1850, Southern Division, Guilford County, NC, 2; "Election Returns," *Weekly Standard* (Raleigh, NC), August 8, 1860, 3.

Notes to Chapter Nine

1. Joseph Farr, "Joseph Farr Remembers the Underground Railroad in St. Paul," ed. Deborah Swanson, *Minnesota History* 57, no. 3 (2000): 125–27.

2. Author's perusal of 1857 Territorial Census and 1860 Federal Census.

3. George Byron Merrick, *Old Times on the Upper Mississippi: The Recollections of a Steamboat Pilot from 1854 to 1863* (1909; repr., St. Paul: Minnesota Historical Society Press, 1987), 64, 128.

4. Frank George O'Brien, *Minnesota Pioneer Sketches: From the Personal Recollections and Observations of a Pioneer Resident* (Minneapolis: Housekeeper Press, 1904), 59; *Winslow House Hotel Register, 1858–1882*, Hennepin History Museum, Minneapolis, 3, 15, 17; Theodore C. Blegen, "The 'Fashionable Tour' on the Upper Mississippi," *Minnesota History* 20, no. 4 (1939): 377–96; "Notes and Documents: St. Paul in 1849," *Minnesota History* 22, no. 1 (1941): 57.

5. Mary McLean Hardy, *A Brief History of the Ancestry and Posterity of Allen MacLean, 1715–1786* (Berkeley, CA: Marquand, 1905), 31; Louis Mitchell, *The Woodbridge Record: Being an Account of the Descendants of the Rev. John Woodbridge of Newbury, Mass.* (New Haven, CT: Private, 1883), 176.

6. O'Brien, *Minnesota Pioneer Sketches*, 59; advertisement, *New Orleans Picayune*, June 10, 1859; Lien Book A, Stearns County Recorder's Office, 5; *Winslow House Hotel Register, 1858–1882*, 13, 17; *New Era* (Sauk Rapids, MN), May 17, 1860.

7. "Fragments of Travel," *Memphis Daily Appeal*, September 17, 1859, 1; US Slave Schedule 1850, District 9, Madison County, TN, 9; US Slave Schedule 1850,

District 15, Madison County, TN, 4, 8; US Slave Schedule 1850, Lafayette County, MS, 66; US Slave Schedule 1850, Western District, Madison Parish, LA, 16–17; "Arrivals at the Stearns House," *St. Cloud Democrat*, September 22, 1859, 3.

8. *Winslow House Hotel Register, 1858–1882*, 38, 49, 77; US Slave Schedule 1860, Frankfort District 1, Franklin County, KY, 20.

9. *Pierre Chouteau, Jr. Ledger, 1855–1862*, Pierre Chouteau Jr. and Family Papers, MNHS, reel 19, 236.

10. "Minnesota," letter, March 10, 1860, *New Orleans Picayune*, March 25, 1860.

11. *Pierre Chouteau, Jr. Ledger, 1853–1857*, Pierre Chouteau Jr. and Family Papers, reel 19, 70.

12. *Inaugural Message of Governor Ramsey to the Senate and House of Representatives of the State of Minnesota* (St. Paul: Minnesotian and Times, 1860), 23.

13. "Official," *Constitution* (Washington, DC), February 18, 1860, 3; US Census 1860, Fourth Ward, Washington, DC, 12.

14. John B. Sanborn, "The Work of the Second State Legislature, 1859–60," *Collections of the Minnesota Historical Society* 10, no. 2 (1905): 624.

15. "Slavery in Minnesota," *Stillwater Messenger*, March 20, 1860, 2; "From St. Paul," *Freeborn County Eagle* (Albert Lea), March 24, 1860, 2; Mary Lethert Wingerd, *North Country: The Making of Minnesota* (Minneapolis: University of Minnesota Press, 2010), 256; William D. Green, *A Peculiar Imbalance: The Fall and Rise of Racial Equality in Early Minnesota* (St. Paul: Minnesota Historical Society Press, 2007), 94.

16. "Slavery in Minnesota," *Stillwater Messenger*, March 20, 1860, 2; "From St. Paul," *Freeborn County Eagle*, March 24, 1860, 2; Wingerd, *North Country*, 256–57; Green, *Peculiar Imbalance*, 95–98.

17. *Annual Report of the Board of Regents of the State University to the Legislature of Minnesota*, 1861, 22, 23; US Slave Schedule 1860, Vicksburg, Warren County, MS, 15; *Winslow House Hotel Register, 1858–1882*, 98, 103, 110.

18. US Slave Schedule 1860, Issaquena County, MS, 2–4; William D. Green, "Eliza Winston and the Politics of Freedom in Minnesota, 1854–60," *Minnesota History* 57, no. 3 (2000): 106; *Winslow House Hotel Register, 1858–1882*, 103; Edward E. Baptist, *The Half Has Never Been Told: Slavery and the Making of American Capitalism* (New York: Basic Books, 2014), 360.

19. Stovall was reported later as with "2 servants" at the Stearns House, presumably without having left the Winslow House to return to the South and bring a slave up to Minnesota for the Stearns House. *St. Cloud Democrat*, September 22, 1859, 3. Similarly, Dawson was listed with "servant" at the Stearns House on page 3 of the September 6, 1860, *St. Cloud Democrat*.

20. *St. Anthony (MN) Express*, June 30, 1860; *Falls Evening News* (St. Anthony, MN), July 19, 1860; *Minnesotian and Times* (St. Paul), February 29, 1860; *New Era*, August 26, 1860; *Chatfield (MN) Republican*, August 7, 1860, 2.

21. "Is Minnesota a Free State?" *State Atlas* (Minneapolis), in *Liberator* (Boston), August 10, 1860, 125.

22. Irene S. Gillis and Norman E. Gillis, *Biographical and Historical Memoirs of Mississippi* (Baton Rouge, LA: Irene S. and Norman E. Gillis), 624; Muriel Tillinghast Ireys, *Memoirs of Muriel Tillinghast Ireys: Papers of the Washington County Historical Society*, ed. William D. McCain and Charlotte Capers (Jackson: Mississippi Department of Archives and History, 1954), 292, 302, 306–7.

23. Letter from St. Anthony, Minnesota, August 21, 1860, *Nashville Union and American*, September 19, 1860; *Claiborne County Wills*, Claiborne County Register of Deeds, Claiborne County, TN, 307, 407.

24. Letter from St. Anthony, Minnesota, August 21, 1860, *Nashville Union and American*, September 19, 1860.

25. Anthony E. Kaye, *Joining Places: Slave Neighborhoods in the Old South* (Chapel Hill: University of North Carolina Press, 2007), 85, 90.

26. Letter from St. Anthony, Minnesota, August 21, 1860, in "Abolition Outrage in Minnesota," *New Orleans Delta*, reprinted in *Nashville Union and American*, September 19, 1860; Green, *Peculiar Imbalance*, 95–97.

27. Green, *Peculiar Imbalance*, 93; *Falls Evening News*, July 24, 1860; *Falls Evening News*, July 26, 1860.

28. *Winslow House Hotel Register, 1858–1882*, 110; "Negro Excitement at St. Paul, Minnesota," *Vicksburg (MS) Whig*, September 5, 1860, 3.

29. "Negro Excitement at St. Paul, Minnesota," *Vicksburg Whig*, September 5, 1860, 3.

30. "The Minneapolis 'Slave' Case," *St. Cloud Democrat*, September 6, 1860, 1.

31. "Editorial Correspondence," letter, August 19, 1860, *New Orleans Picayune*, August 26, 1860, 1.

32. Green, "Eliza Winston and the Politics of Freedom," 107–10; "The Minneapolis 'Slave' Case," *St. Cloud Democrat*, September 6, 1860, 1.

33. "Slave Case in Minneapolis," *State Atlas*, in *Mantorville (MN) Express*, September 1, 1860, 1; "Southerners in the Northwest," *Charleston (SC) Courier*, September 14, 1860, 1; Green, *Peculiar Imbalance*, 112; *Winslow House Hotel Register, 1858–1882*, 111, 114–17, 123.

34. *Daily Delta* (New Orleans), September 15, 1860, 1; letter from St. Anthony, Minnesota, August 21, 1860, reprinted in *Nashville Union and American*, September 19, 1860; *St. Anthony Express*, September 1, 1860; *St. Anthony Express*, October 6, 1860.

35. Letter from St. Anthony, Minnesota, August 21, 1860, reprinted in *Nashville Union and American*, September 19, 1860.

36. *Louisville Daily Courier*, December 17, 1860, 2; *Daily Delta*, September 15, 1860, 1.

37. *Winslow House Hotel Register, 1858–1882*, 143; "Minnesota Items," *Stillwater Messenger*, December 25, 1860, 2; Joseph W. Zalusky, "Winslow House Register," *Hennepin County History* 24 (1967): 6.

38. Deed Book D, Stearns County Recorder's Office, 118–23; Deed Book D, Wright County Recorder's Office, 430–31; US Slave Schedule 1860, South Division, Guilford County, NC, 13–14.

39. *Winslow House Hotel Register, 1858–1882,* 106; "Hunting Party," *St. Cloud Democrat,* October 11, 1860, 3; *Weekly Mississippian* (Jackson), September 26, 1860, 2; *Vicksburg Whig,* October 17, 1860, 1; W. C. Smedes to Rice Ballard, December 26, 1853, Rice Ballard Papers, Southern Historical Collection, University of North Carolina at Chapel Hill; "List of Arrivals at the Stearns House for the Past Week," *St. Cloud Democrat,* September 6, 1860, 3; *Winslow House Hotel Register, 1858–1882,* 140.

40. "Hunting Party," *St. Cloud Democrat,* October 11, 1860, 3; US Census 1870, Fifth Ward, Madison Parish, LA, 3–5.

41. C. C. Clay to Rice, February 19, 1861, folder "Papers 1860–1863," Henry M. Rice and Family Papers, MNHS; Virginia Clay-Clopton, *A Belle of the Fifties: Memoirs of Mrs. Clay, of Alabama,* ed. Ada Sterling (New York: Doubleday, Page, 1905), 153–54.

42. US Slave Schedule 1860, Huntsville, Madison County, AL, 13; Clay-Clopton, *Belle of the Fifties,* 153–54; *Chatfield (MN) Democrat,* March 23, 1861, 3; John Hope Franklin, *A Southern Odyssey: Travelers in the Antebellum North* (Baton Rouge: Louisiana State University Press, 1976), 19.

43. Clay-Clopton, *Belle of the Fifties,* 155.

Notes to Chapter Ten

1. Victor B. Howard, "John Brown's Raid at Harper's Ferry and the Sectional Crisis in North Carolina," *North Carolina Historical Review* 55, no. 4 (1978): 412.

2. Ann Simpson to Alexander Ramsey, November 24, 1860, Alexander Ramsey Papers, MNHS, reel 11, frames 518–19; Ann Simpson to Alexander Ramsey, December 11, 1860, Alexander Ramsey Papers, reel 9, frames 558–59; "Petition for Succession of Thomas P. Winston," January 26, 1861, Ramsey County Probate Court, MN, 1–2.

3. Sylvanus B. Lowry to wife, January 16, 1861, Sylvanus B. Lowry and Family Papers, MNHS.

4. Advertisement, *Vicksburg (MS) Whig,* April 3, 1861, 2; advertisement, *Vicksburg Whig,* April 10, 1861, 2; advertisement, *Vicksburg Whig,* April 17, 1861, 4.

5. US Census 1870, New Bern Sixth Ward, Craven County, NC, 37; US Slave Schedule 1850, New Bern, Craven County, NC, 8; US Census 1850, New Bern, Craven County, NC, 293.

6. Obituary, *Daily True Delta* (New Orleans), November 18, 1860, 6; obituary, *New Orleans Picayune,* November 6, 1860, 8; obituary, *New Orleans Picayune,* November 12, 1860, 8; Nathaniel Cheairs Hughes Jr., *The Pride of the Confederate Artillery: The Washington Artillery in the Army of Tennessee* (Baton Rouge: Louisiana State University Press, 1997), 350; Heritage Auction Gallery, *Heritage Auction Galleries Inaugural Auction of Civil War History, December 2006, Nashville,*

Tennessee, Session Two (Dallas: Heritage Auctions, 2006), 150; Carol Moore, *Guilford County and the Civil War* (Charleston, SC: History Press, 2015), 38.

7. American Gas Light Association, *Report of Proceedings*, vol. 9 (Providence, RI: E. L. Freeman, 1892), 660; "Barbarism of Slavery," *Stillwater Messenger*, August 27, 1861, 2.

8. "Barbarism of Slavery," *Stillwater Messenger*, August 27, 1861, 2; "A Stirring Appeal," *Stillwater Messenger*, April 1, 1862, 2.

9. Deed Book D, Stearns County Recorder's Office, 187, 217.

10. "Local Matters," *Richmond (VA) Daily Dispatch*, April 30, 1861, 1; Geo. Deas, letter, August 13, 1861, in *The War of the Rebellion: A Compilation of the Official Records of the Union and Confederate Armies*, House of Representatives, 55th Cong., 1st sess. (Washington, DC: Government Printing Office, 1897), 230; Robert J. Driver, *10th Virginia Cavalry* (Lynchburg, VA: H. E. Howard), 3; US Confederate Officers Card Index, 1861–65, Roa-Ros, image 2683, Military Order of the Stars and Bars, via FamilySearch, www.familysearch.org.

11. Edward G. Longacre, *The Early Morning of War: Bull Run, 1861* (Norman: University of Oklahoma Press, 2014), 473; "Auch Er," *Minnesota Staats-Zeitung* (St. Paul), August 31, 1861; *Princeton (MN) Union*, September 15, 1910, 4.

12. "J. Travis Rosser Probably Killed," *St. Paul Daily Press*, May 2, 1863, 1.

13. "Sound Words," *Wabasha County Herald*, June 4, 1863; Christopher P. Lehman, *Slavery in the Upper Mississippi Valley: A History of Human Bondage in Illinois, Iowa, Minnesota and Wisconsin* (Jefferson, NC: McFarland, 2011), 180–81; Joseph W. McKinney, *Brandy Station, Virginia, June 9, 1863: The Largest Cavalry Battle of the Civil War* (Jefferson, NC: McFarland, 2006), 189.

14. Catherine Ann Devereux Edmondston, *Journal of a Secesh Lady: The Diary of Catherine Ann Devereux Edmondston, 1860–1866*, ed. Beth G. Crabtree and James W. Patton (Raleigh: North Carolina Division of Archives and History, 1979); US Confederate Officers Card Index, 1861–65, Roa-Ros, image 2683.

15. *Richmond Daily Dispatch*, March 28, 1865, 4.

16. US Census 1860, Mobile Sixth Ward, Mobile County, AL, 163; US Slave Schedule 1860, Mobile Sixth Ward, Mobile County, AL, 21.

17. John Wintermute Mason, *History of Otter Tail County, Minnesota: Its People, Industries, and Institutions* (Indianapolis: B. F. Bowen, 1916), 84, 468; "The Coming of the Latter Day Saints to Otter Tail County," *Minnesota History* 13, no. 4 (1932): 385; Richard Cecil Todd, *Confederate Finance* (Athens: University of Georgia Press, 1954), 91; Richard L. Hahn, *George Bush Burgwin Clitherall* (Forest Lake, MN: Richard L. Hahn, 1994), 60.

18. "Declining to Hold Office," *Alexandria (VA) Gazette*, November 23, 1860, 2; *Stillwater Messenger*, December 24, 1861, 3.

19. US Slave Schedule 1860, 98th Regiment, Mecklenburg County, VA, 4; US Census 1860, Belle Plaine, Scott County, MN, 28.

20. US Slave Schedule 1850, Lenoir County, NC, 29; Bond Book A, Wright County Recorder, 118–20; Deed Book D, Wright County Recorder, 715–19; Deed

Book E, Wright County Recorder, 6–7; Thomas E. Drake, "Quakers in Minnesota," *Minnesota History* 18, no. 3 (1937): 252; Moore, *Guilford County and the Civil War*, 19.

21. US Slave Schedule 1860, North Division, Guilford County, NC, 15, 23; Gordon L. Jones, *Confederate Odyssey: The George W. Wray, Jr. Civil War Collection at the Atlanta History Center* (Athens: University of Georgia Press, 2014), 164; Moore, *Guilford County and the Civil War*, 38.

22. Deed Book D, Stearns County Recorder's Office, 577, 579, 582.

23. Deed Book H, Stearns County Recorder's Office, 483–84; Power of Attorney Records Book A, Stearns County Recorder's Office, 87. Charles Vanderburgh was the same judge who had declared Eliza Winston free in 1860.

24. *Chatfield (MN) Democrat*, November 24, 1860, 2.

25. Walter N. Trenery, "The Minnesota Rebellion Act of 1862: A Legal Dilemma of the Civil War," *Minnesota History* 35, no. 1 (1956): 2.

26. Trenery, "The Minnesota Rebellion Act of 1862," 2–3.

27. Trenery, "The Minnesota Rebellion Act of 1862," 4–5.

28. Trenery, "The Minnesota Rebellion Act of 1862," 7–9.

29. *Wabashaw County Herald* (Read's Landing, MN), January 18, 1862, 2; *St. Cloud Democrat*, February 20, 1862, 1.

30. Trenery, "Minnesota Rebellion Act of 1862," 3–4; *Crisis* (Columbus, OH), April 9, 1862, 84; *The Third Annual Report of the Board of Regents of the State University to the Legislature of Minnesota, Session of 1863*, 7.

31. *Journal of the House of Representatives of the Fourth Session of the Legislature of the State of Minnesota* (St. Paul: Wm. R. Marshall, 1862), 72; Uriah Thomas to regents, November 29, 1862, in *The Third Annual Report of the Board of Regents, Session of 1863*, 7.

32. Uriah Thomas to regents, November 29, 1862, in *The Third Annual Report of the Board of Regents, Session of 1863*, 7.

33. University of Minnesota Board of Regents, minutes, July 13, 1864, *Minutes of the University of Minnesota Board of Regents, April 5, 1860 to February 29, 1868*, 55; University of Minnesota Board of Regents, minutes, September 6, 1864, *Minutes of the University of Minnesota Board of Regents, April 5, 1860 to February 29, 1868*, 57; University of Minnesota Treasurer Report, December 31, 1864, *Minutes of the University of Minnesota Board of Regents, April 5, 1860 to February 29, 1868*, 69.

34. "St. Paul Streets Named After Pioneers," *St. Paul Globe*, August 17, 1902, 17; Thomas McLean Newson, *Pen Pictures of St. Paul Minnesota* (St. Paul: Thomas McLean Newson, 1886), 487; J. Fletcher Williams, *A History of the City of St. Paul to 1875* (1876; repr., St. Paul: Minnesota Historical Society Press, 1983), 413; *Anne Arundel County Manumission Record: 1844–1866*, vol. 832, 198; William D. Green, *A Peculiar Imbalance: The Fall and Rise of Racial Equality in Early Minnesota* (St. Paul: Minnesota Historical Society Press, 2007), 174.

35. Lehman, *Slavery in the Upper Mississippi Valley*, 176–77; Christopher P. Lehman, "The Longest Emancipation: A St. Cloud Slave's Four-Year Journey to

Emancipation," *Crossings: A Publication of the Stearns History Museum* (June/July 2016): 9; William Fletcher, "A Few Reminiscences," *Sauk Rapids (MN) Sentinel,* August 18, 1927; William Butler and Chloe Topsail, marriage certificate, August 25, 1861, Stearns County License Center; US Census 1860, Stearns County, MN, 18; US Census 1850, Seventh Ward, Washington, DC, 111.

36. Lehman, "Longest Emancipation," 9; Lehman, *Slavery in the Upper Mississippi Valley,* 176–77; Fletcher, "Few Reminiscences"; obituary for W. H. Butler, *Albert Lea Enterprise,* October 18, 1899, 5.

37. *Minnesota Union* (St. Cloud), June 13, 1861, 1; Power of Attorney Book A, Stearns County Recorder's Office, 46; Deed Book D, Stearns County Recorder's Office, 245; Deed Record F, Stearns County Recorder's Office, 63.

38. "Introductory," *Minnesota Union,* June 13, 1861, 2.

39. "The Real Question—the Revolt," *Minnesota Union,* June 13, 1861, 2; "Were the Disunionists Afraid?" *Minnesota Union,* June 13, 1861, 2.

40. Sylvia D. Hoffert, "Jane Grey Swisshelm and the Negotiation of Gender Roles on the Minnesota Frontier," *Frontiers: A Journal of Women's Studies* 18, no. 3 (1997): 34; US Census 1870, Girard, Clayton County, IA, 16; Lehman, *Slavery in the Upper Mississippi Valley,* 189. In 1864 Sylvanus Lowry, suffering from mental illness, attempted to kill his sister, and she, her children, and Sylvanus's parents left Minnesota for Iowa before the end of the year.

41. John G. Nicolay and John Hay, *Abraham Lincoln: A History,* vol. 2 (New York: Century, 1909), 414; Mark J. Stegmaier, *Henry Adams in the Secession Crisis: Dispatches to the Boston Daily Advertiser, December 1860–March 1861* (Baton Rouge: Louisiana State University Press, 2012), 62; Daniel W. Crofts, *Reluctant Confederates: Upper South Unionists in the Secession Crisis* (Chapel Hill: University of North Carolina Press, 1989), 423.

42. Richard B. McCaslin, *Portraits of Conflict: A Photographic History of South Carolina in the Civil War* (Fayetteville: University of Arkansas Press, 1994), 87.

43. Calvin L. Brown, "Some Changes in Locale Boundaries and Names in Minnesota," *Minnesota History* 20 (1922): 242; "Minnesota Counties and Historical Facts," Random Acts of Genealogical Kindness, http://www.raogk.org/counties/minnesota.

44. *Baltimore Sun,* November 6, 1861, 4; *Nashville Daily Patriot,* November 12, 1861, 2.

45. Mary Chesnut, *A Diary from Dixie* (Chapel Hill: University of North Carolina Press, 1997), 205.

46. Green, *Peculiar Imbalance,* 128.

47. Louis S. Gerteis, *The Civil War in Missouri: A Military History* (Columbia: University of Missouri Press, 2012), 4–6; *Pierre Chouteau, Jr. Ledger, 1855–1862,* Pierre Chouteau Jr. and Family Papers, MNHS, reel 19, 244, 246.

48. Green, *Peculiar Imbalance,* 131–32; Rhoda R. Gilman, *Henry Hastings Sibley: Divided Heart* (St. Paul: Minnesota Historical Society Press, 2004), 195.

49. *Pierre Chouteau, Jr. Ledger, 1855–1862,* Pierre Chouteau Jr. and Family Papers, reel 19, 248.

50. US Census 1860, St. Louis Ward 4, MO, 141; US Slave Schedule 1860, St. Louis Ward 4, MO, 1; *Pierre Chouteau, Jr. Day Book, 1852–1859,* Pierre Chouteau Jr. and Family Papers, reel 15, 124.

Notes to Conclusion

1. US Census 1870, Fifth Ward, Madison Parish, LA, 3, 5; US Census 1870, Annapolis, Anne Arundel County, MD, 57; US Census 1870, New Orleans Ward 9, Orleans Parish, LA, 35; US Census 1880, New Orleans District 83, Orleans Parish, LA, 12; "Deaths," *New Orleans Picayune,* November 6, 1882, 1; *Stillwater Messenger,* December 1, 1883, 4.

2. Adele Sarpy Morrison, *Memoirs of Adele Sarpy Morrison* (St. Louis: Adele Sarpy Morrison, 1911), 9–10; "Various Items," *Boston Traveler,* March 22, 1865, 1; *Baltimore Sun,* March 23, 1865, 1.

3. US Census 1870, District 7, Wilson County, TN, 7; Christopher P. Lehman, "The Longest Emancipation: A St. Cloud Slave's Four-Year Journey to Freedom," *Crossings: A Publication of the Stearns History Museum* (June/July 2016): 9.

Index

Page numbers in *italic* refer to illustrations.